HELL-HOLE
ROBBEN ISLAND

HELL-HOLE
ROBBEN ISLAND

Prisoner No. 872/63
Moses Dlamini

Reminiscences of a Political Prisoner in South Africa

Africa World Press
of the Africa Research & Publications Project

P.O. Box 1892
Trenton, New Jersey 08608

Though throughout the book reference has been made to PAC and ANC members, these are in actual fact, former members of both organisations, as the PAC and the ANC were both banned in April, 1960.

AFRICA WORLD PRESS
P.O. Box 1892,
Trenton, N.J. 08608

Not for sale in Europe

Copyright © Moses Dlamini

All rights reserved. No part of this publication may be reproduced, stored in a retrieval system or transmitted in any form or by any means electronic, mechanical, photocopying, recording or otherwise without the prior written permission of the publishers.

Typeset by Russell Press

Cover design by Carol Mitchell

Library of Congress Catalog Card Number: 84-072593

ISBN 0-86543-008-X cloth
ISBN 0-86543-009-8 paper

Dedicated to Sobukwe, to all Azanian patriots who are languishing in prison, and to those who died at the hands of the police and in prison in their noble struggle for a free Azania.

Contents

		Page
	Introduction	9

Part 1 — THE BIG FIVES

Chapter		
1	The arrival	15
2	An introduction to Robben Island	22
3	The Quarryspan	28
4	Its an old cry for the land	42
5	Listen, we pity those still coming	50
6	Inspection	64
7	'Faith of our fathers living still'	67
8	Christmas Day	73
9	The prison dispensary	75
10	The Big Six	80
11	Old Man Vakalisa	85
12	Asking for more	101
13	The boulders roll on	103
14	The fall of the Big Six	109
15	Gantsha Khuboni	113
16	Bitter April	119
17	The man from the Red Cross	123
18	Dum-Dum	128
19	Bombed	131
20	The-Horn-of-the-Guinea-Fowl	140
21	We are starving	151
22	The fall of the Big Fives	153
23	Farewell to the wrecks of Apartheid	159

Part 2 — MORAL VICTORY

24	Cultural renaissance	170
25	The forbidden fruit	177
26	The hunger strike	181
27	Farewell to Robben Island Prison	194
	Epilogue	198

Introduction

From amongst the budding crop of talented writers in Azania (South Africa), Moses Dlamini has produced one of the best accounts of the harsh realities of the Black man's life in that tortured country. Encapsulated in an account of his imprisonment on the infamous Robben Island, he has captured in a gripping and enraging account all the violence, brutality, degradation and dehumanisation of a colonialism and racialism that could only be viewed as something absurd, even comic, were it not for the horrendous distortions that it wrought in the lives both of the victims and its perpetrators. His story of the brutalities underlines the central dilemma of the black-white relationship; on the one hand, of a racialism so blind in its fury and hatred that it can only devour itself as his story shows; and on the other of a people driven to the depths of despair and yet spurred to revolutionary struggle by a simple yearning for dignity and compassion.

Prison in the conditions of oppression in a country like South Africa — as indeed in most Third World countries — is a place where you are stripped of every vestige of human dignity — debased, demoralised, dehumanised, so that your spirit is broken to accept the perverted logic of the oppressor. It's like being locked in the same room forever with a torturer whose untrammelled powers of hate and contempt degrade you with every conceivable human atrocity. Such was Robben Island — 11 kilometres in the Atlantic off Cape Town, mostly of a sandy surface.

But the events on the Island duplicated what took place in the ordinary, everyday life in the ramshackle and dilapidated little boxes called houses in shanty towns like Soweto. The flashbacks to his life in the townships with its attendant poverty, misery and ever lurking insecurities and anxieties show the continuum between the daily occurrence and prison conditions. A continuous cycle for even after release from prison, you are banned, hounded, circumscribed to vegetate on some barren veld on the flimsiest manufactured charge.

In the end you are forced into exile.

Written in simple and direct prose, in a uniquely South African style, Moses allows the story to flow out of him. He is after all narrating what happens daily in the lives of millions of people, and a million tongues speak. He does not have to resort to literary imagination or a Dickensian flow of language to describe the stark realities of brutality. Cutting across the spectrum of life in South Africa he in fact has encompassed several books in one. Each facet of life is a tragic story of its own in its suffering, pain and anguish. There is the ordinary life of the Black man and his family trapped in the vicious circle of poverty and struggle; of gang warfare exploding in brutal murders and crimes when the oppressed turn their wrath against one another; or the harsh conditions of Leeuwkop Prison itself from where Moses and others were transferred to the Island; of the inhuman exploitation of farm labourers, often made to dig with their bare hands, often whipped to death. He traverses these various brutal worlds.

In the midst of the encompassing misery and barbarism of these worlds there is always the struggle to salvage something dignified: Moses' father remonstrating with the gangsters to join the ANC Youth League rather than vent their frustrations against one another: the struggle on the Island to resist enforced homosexuality meant to degrade the political prisoners. Somehow evil becomes joined to good and *vice versa* in an ever-increasing spiral, turning one into the other, as when his beloved Nomsa betrays him to the Special Branch and he concludes that she has become one with the Big Five gangsters who terrorised the prisoners on the Island, a symbol of human perversion that haunts the book. But peace was not to be with Nomsa. Over the years remorse would eat her and she would dwindle to a shadow of her once vibrant self. That happens again and again with various characters in the book. A will to evil and betrayal followed by deep regret and repentence. Good and evil stalk one another like taunting pairs.

In this world of arbitrariness the relationship between oppressor and oppressed is distorted and reason and logic made to stand on its head. When a prisoner complains that the dust affects his health he is told: "There's nothing wrong with dust. Dust is healthy and clean. It has no germs. You go and ask the doctor." He might as well have told him that it never existed, that it was all his imagination.

In such a world of absolutes every whim is law. Yes baas, no baas. The frenzied imagination of absolute power can manufacture any excuse as a justification. It is repeated daily in all its starkness in the highest echelons of power, in the all-White Parliament: "we are the upholders of Western civilisation and democracy" (even when they deliberately flout every principle of that supposedly noble pillar of modern society); "the Bantustans are places where the Africans can develop themselves" (even when it is as barren as any desert, *all* the best land stolen by the colonialists); "we brought civilisation to the kaffir" (even when he's never enjoyed the fruits of that supposed civilisation). And so on. There need be no women to rape, no bombs to throw. The whimsical accusation and then the order for senseless beatings on defenceless people.

Yet the beatings, the torture and persecution had a purpose. Like the lectures on the usefulness of the Bantustans they aimed at acquiescence, to get you to accept the brutal laws laid down by the oppressor's unrelenting baton. The book in fact describes a struggle between the temptation to acquiesce or to say NO. The Big Five gangsters and the "Horn-of-the-the-Guinea-Fowl (nickname for Enock Mathibela) acquiesced and ended in disaster, losing their manhood, thrown to the wolves by the very forces they attempted to placate. Was it an ironical twist of fate that the Big Five sealed their doom with the confessions by their own leaders, perhaps the stirring of a buried repentance for the brutalities they inflicted on their fellow prisoners.

Eventually there was triumph against the barbarism and cruelties. Human will and strength triumphed in an almost legendary manner and the prison burst into songs about flowers and blue skies. Oom Dellie, the cruel warder, was sent down, but to join the Watchtower Bible Society, "going about the country preaching about the coming Armageddon and trying to convince his fellow Boers to repent. Ultimately he committed suicide." There was victory too when one of the warders' wives committed adultery with one of the prisoners, and then refused to testify that he had raped her. (In South Africa a white woman could only have sexual intercourse with a Black if she's been raped!). In the end even the contradictions of life caught up with the persecutors.

Reading this harrowing account of cruelty and suffering I felt first a burning rage, even hate, but in the end a sorrow that such cruel madness could exist in human beings. It made me wonder who was really oppressed, those who indulged in such barbarities, or those who in the midst of their sufferings dreamed of freedom and the simple verities of life. In the Hegelian dialectic the slave frees the master whose corruption had led him astray from the simple beauties of human co-operation, fellowship and respect. Moses' story verifies this dialectic, he himself looking forward, despite his bitter experiences, to an eventual free non-racial South Africa. But to one anchored in revolutionary struggle. The last words that ring in his ears as he finally prepares to leave Robben Island are: "You must continue with the work outside from where you left off. There is no holiday in the struggle. A revolutionary never rests." Or, as Subukwe, whose calm dignity and sense of resistance and rebellion inspired the prisoners, said: "We are the tools of history and when we are gone history will find other tools." The ever-increasing spiral in the struggle between good and evil, between the forces of liberation and oppression.

BENNIE BUNSEE
(Editor *Ikwezi/Tlhatsi*)

Part One

The Big Five

1. *The Arrival*

As we went into the boat, we saw looming in the distance, what was to be our home for a very long time. For me, with a six-year sentence, it was to be my home for almost two-and-a-half years. For some of us it was going to be their home for life. With insults and shoving from the prison warders escorting us, there was no time to have a proper look at the island. A single sharp glance at the place assured me that it was full of trees. Manacled on our hands and legs in twos, we were taken to the cabin and there made to lie down — flat on our backs despite the fact that there were seats nearby. We were one hundred in number, all of us dog-tired. My right ankle was still painful, suppurating with pus; the leg-irons had caused a wound. Many other comrades were complaining of the same problem. The ankle wounds of some comrades were already becoming septic.

As soon as we had settled down, the boat began to move. We heard the engine droning. A warder came in holding a pick-handle. He told us in Afrikaans that anyone who opened his mouth would have a taste of the pick-handle on his head. Soon after, three other Boer warders came in with pick-handles in their hands waving them menacingly at us. They called us kaffirs and communists. We all kept our mouths shut, for we had anticipated such provocations. They soon left us alone, after one of them had remarked that we smelled like shit. This was true, because three of our comrades had had bowel movements inside the trucks while we were on our way to Cape Town harbour. They had had running stomachs after we had eaten maize porridge and half-cooked beans the previous day at Bloemfontein Prison on our way from Leeuwkop Maximum Prison near Johannesburg.

As the boat plied the one-and-a-half hours, 11 kilometers distance from Cape Town harbour to Robben Island, I reminisced on the last hectic days we had endured at Leeuwkop Maximum Prison.

* * *

On the morning of 6 December 1963, we had been visited in our cell by a young lieutenant in the company of a Chief Warder called van Staden. When they stood at the door of our cell, we all stood up, following prison discipline. In their eyes lurked hatred and in their mouths were mocking sneers. The Chief Warder asked us in his small voice why we had not jumped up when we saw them. We did not reply. Then he said we thought we were kings and I saw a scowl on the lieutenant's face. The latter then moved to the next four cells which were also occupied by political prisoners. The Chief Warder followed him. We were left stunned, still standing. Later on we sat down and engaged in various topics of discussion, trying to dismiss from our minds what had happened. After about 10 to 15 minutes, they returned, this time in the company of Lieutenant-colonel du Toit, the Commanding Officer. We all stood up at attention — 44 in number, almost simultaneously. The Chief Warder opened the grille and the lieutenant-colonel stepped inside the cell and looked at us individually from our feet up to our faces, from left to right. For a long time silence reigned in the cell as he continued sizing us up. When he had finished, he lifted up his baton and pointed at the left-hand corner of the cell, high up above our heads where there was an old crack in the wall. "So you want to escape, eh?" he said in Afrikaans pointing at the crack. No one among us responded. Actually we were overcome by shock and surprise as we looked at the old crack.

"Who are those responsible for that?" he barked, eyes ferociously looking from one man to another. There was an incoherent mumbling from some of us. "Who are they?" he barked again ferociously.

"Excuse me, sir," began Kanye in English, "when we were transferred from cell six to this cell a month ago, we found the crack already there and we reported . . ."

"Bly Stil!", the young lieutenant (also surnamed van Staden) shrieked, moving towards him and with his baton striking him on the head.

"Who's your 'sir'?" enquired the lieutenant-colonel also moving towards Kanye.

The Chief Warder who was near Kanye, then began pulling out the hair of his moustache with his nails. The lieutenant and the lieutenant-colonel stopped and admired what their junior officer was doing. "You must say 'baas' to a White man when you talk to him," the Chief Warder kept on saying as he kept plucking out the hair. Blood began coming out where the hair had been pulled out.

Satisfied about what had been done to Kanye, the lieutenant-colonel approached one old man named Tolepi, a former farm-hand who no longer seemed normal. "Ou man," he said eyeing Tolepi, "who are responsible for that crack?"

"I don't know baas," replied Tolepi in Afrikaans displaying a humble foolish smile."

"If you don't point them out," added the Chief Warder, "you are going to suffer with them. Speak out and shame the devil."

"No one did it baas," replied Tolepi laughing timidly.

"And you 'kleintjie' (small one)" said the lieutenant-colonel, pointing to 16-year-old Samuel Mokudubete, "who did that?"

"No one did it," said Samuel in English, "we found the place like this when we were transferred to this cell a month ago."

"We found the place like this," I said defiantly.

"We found the place like this," said Paul next to me also drawing himself up.

"We found the place like this," added five others almost simultaneously.

"Bly stil," thundered the young lieutenant, "one more mouth open and you'll shit." There was complete silence. The young lieutenant looked at the lieutenant-colonel.

"Since," began the lieutenant-colonel, assuming a dignified posture, "you are unwilling to point out those responsible for that crack, you are all charged with attempting to escape from prison. Those of you who have lawyers will be given papers to write to them."

'This is it,' I said to myself as my heart began pumping faster and faster, 'now that the Boers have got us, they won't want to see us out of prison again.'

"How many of you have lawyers?" asked the lieutenant-colonel. Four hands went up. In fact, they didn't even have lawyers. They were only hoping to write to the Defence and Aid appointed lawyers who had previously defended some of us in our trials. "Papers are coming for you to write to your lawyers." With that Lieutenant-colonel du Toit stepped proudly out of the cell, followed by his juniors, leaving us confused and exasperated.

Someone said they were joking. Another said the Boers have a very funny sense of humour — enjoying seeing Blacks in trouble. A third comrade called them sadists, capable of commiting any crime in the name of Western civilisation and Christianity.

We were still commenting on their hatred for the Blacks when suddenly they appeared again and the grille was opened. Lieutenant-colonel du Toit had brought along a number of warders, all White. Looking at us with disdain, he instructed us to stand exactly where we were. There should be no slight movement, he said. Any slight movement of the limbs would be taken as an attempt at assault. We stood still like pillars apprehensive of what was going to happen.

"Strip," he shouted, "and be quick."

Quickly, we began removing our convict short pants and shirts. One by one we were searched for 'dangerous weapons' and tobacco, while the warders kept on taunting us and hurling insults, time and again hitting some of the comrades.

After they had finished, the warders stepped out of the cell. We remained with Lieutenant-colonel du Toit, Lieutenant van Staden and Chief Warder van Staden. And we stood at attention along the four corners of the cell — all naked, wondering what was in store for us next. Our convict clothes littered the floor. Except for some small pieces of soap which we had made into dice for playing ludo and some other games on our blankets, the warders had found nothing. After the three officers had feasted their eyes on the various shapes of our physique, we were told to leave our clothes in the cell and taken to the exercise yard in front of the cells, running.

About 30 yards from the cells there was a 30-foot wall which encompassed the whole cell-block. Running in a straight line, we were directed to this wall. On our way to the wall, we saw in a white coat an African 'doctor' with 'Mazawatee' (wire-rim) spectacles, thick brown gloves and a plastic bucket filled with liquid soap called 'soap-soap' in prison parlance. We all guessed what was going to happen when we saw this sinister figure. He was going to repeat the same ritual he had performed the day we were admitted three months back. It was a ritual which every convict, including many of our leaders, had to undergo after being admitted to Leeuwkop Maximum Prison.

In front of the wall we were harshly and with kicks, instructed to bend down and touch our toes. As we were 44 in number, we stood in a long line next to one another, our heads touching the wall — a distance of a yard from each other. Meanwhile, warders were moving up and down carrying pick-handles and truncheons beating down the heads and shoulders of those who had not bent properly. I peeped through my outstretched left arm and saw the 'doctor' putting on his thick brown gloves and guessed that he was about to begin with the ritual. I almost lost my balance as I anticipated the pain I was going to feel as he thrust his middle finger into my rectum. I could imagine wincing in pain as he turned it round and round. I felt a blow on my shoulder and jumped up. "Bend and touch your toes," said my assailant, the Chief Warder, "you must look straight down, neither left nor right."

"Hy's 'n vetgat" (he's big buttocked) said another warder behind me, "the doctor is going to enjoy himself on this one."

I bent down and touched my toes, looking straight at them. I thought of many other African leaders and wondered whether this is what they too had to undergo in prison in the struggle for freedom and independence. I also wondered whether the Nazis ever did this to their victims who were their political opponents.

When I heard a shriek, I guessed that the 'doctor' had begun with the poking of someone's rectum. From a comrade on my right I heard his teeth chattering. I heard the sound of a pick-handle thumping on someone's back. The blows were repeated about five times. I do not

The arrival

know who was the victim as it was some distance from me. I heard somebody muttering 'devils' inbetween his teeth. There was a shout of 'bly stil' from a warder behind us. Meanwhile the 'doctor' continued with his thing. I wondered whether he enjoyed this job of piercing people's rectums daily. It was really a terrible way of earning one's living to support one's family.

I heard someone grunting like a hog and when I peeped, I saw him falling down on his buttocks, flat. There was a rain of blows on him and in no time, he was up, his hands touching his toes again, feet astride. The 'doctor' stepped to his next victim. I heard a prolonged bellowing sound next to me and my knees buckled. I turned to look but a karate chop sent me down, my hands touching my toes again.

Soon the 'doctor' stood behind me. He first patted my buttocks and while I was concentrating on that, he abruptly thrust his thick gloved middle-finger into my rectum and with the finger half-bent, he turned it round and round for almost a minute. Dizzy with pain, I winced and winced to no avail. By the time he proceeded to the next man, my rectum was so painful that I thought it was bleeding internally.

The poking continued. Others bore the excruciating pain stoically, without even emitting a single sound — only a man's contorted face showed the agony he was undergoing. I was one of the people whose stools had trickles of blood after this. The excuse for making us undergo all this humiliation was that they were looking for hidden weapons and tobacco in our rectums.

After we had all been poked, chains were brought. Still naked, we were made to stand in one line. We were each manacled on our hands and leg-irons fastened on our feet. Then we were told to run around the rectangular yard. The warders stood in a long line, at a distance of about 10 yards from each other.

Lieutenant-colonel du Toit told us to start running. After removing his cap, which showed us his semi-bald head, he went to Monty the first man in front and began jogging, telling him to keep pace with him. But the leg-irons were heavy and eating into our ankles. As a result we could only jog at a slow trot. Du Toit became angry and began hitting Monty with his baton. Instead of running, Monty suddenly changed and walked slowly. We all followed suit. He was then removed from us and taken to Block A and handed over to a sergeant warder who was very uncouth and notorious for assaulting convicts, to be 'disciplined'. He was further told that for refusing to run he would be denied his lunch and supper that day. The next man in front, Boxie, also refused to run. He too was taken to Block A to be further 'disciplined'. The following three comrades also refused to run despite the beatings. They too suffered the fate of the first two.

Through the gate leading to our Block, we could see on the other side, in the yard of Block A, the five comrades who had been removed from us defying 'Magalies' the Header Warder, despite beatings. What is more, they were returning his insults.

Lieutenant-colonel du Toit then went to fetch old man Tolepi, who was third from last, and placed him in front. He instructed him to begin trotting. Tolepi began trotting slowly at the same pace we had maintained at first and we followed him round the square. By the time we finished the fifth round, blisters were coming out from our ankles whereas blood could already be seen oozing out from some comrades. After two more rounds, we were taken to the kitchen for our lunch. As we walked slowly towards the gate leading to the kitchen, we saw on the other side in Block A, our comrades still defying Magalies.

Criminal convicts were surprised as we walked, to see a long line of naked chained bodies taking their food. We were then taken to the isolation cells of Block D and locked three in each cell. Eating while naked is really a harrowing experience. It is something which is abnormal. There being no alternative, we sat down to our meals. Later on we were taken to fetch our supper in the same condition. As there were no blankets in the isolation cells, we slept just like that, still manacled and in leg-irons. That night, despite orders by warders not to make noise, we sang freedom songs until about 10 o'clock at night. At one time a warder came with a pail of water and splashed it at each group of three trying to silence us, to no avail.

The following day as soon as our cells were opened, Lieutenant-colonel du Toit told us that he had received many complaints from many warders and their families who lived in the vicinity about the noise we had made by our singing. He told us that he was giving us the last warning not to repeat the noise again. After this we were again taken for exercise in the square at about 10 o'clock and the blisters became worse as we were once again beaten to run faster and we resisted. We were kept in this condition until the 9th of December 1963, when we were awoken at 4am and given prison clothes. As we had been singing again the previous night until late at night, Lieutenant-colonel du Toit told us that because of our defiance, we were now to be taken to Robben Island that same day where we were going to be taught manners. We were later joined by other comrades who were 56 in number, about 15 of them belonging to the African National Congress. At 5am, a hundred in number, travelling on four trucks with two saloon cars and three landrovers as escort, our journey to Robben Island began.

* * *

Mpanza, to whom I had been manacled, pulled the leg-irons and I almost screamed. He had hurt me on the wound in my left ankle. The pain brought my thoughts to the present. I eyed him viciously and he mumbled an apology. "Sorry Moses," he said, "sorry son of the soil."

The boat went up and down as it cut through the waves. After what seemed a long time, it slowed down and ultimately docked. We had arrived at Robben Island. We were taken out of the boat with insults and yells onto two waiting trucks where we were packed like sardines.

The trucks made a U-turn, drove past the gate leading to the docks and took the tarred road leading to the New Prison — a distance of about a quarter kilometer from the docks. The whole area to the New Prison was covered with trees. When we were at the docks we could not see the prison structures, we could only see the shimmering light of the roofs.

When we arrived at the New Prison, the handcuffs and leg-irons were removed. Lieutenant-colonel du Toit formally handed us over to the Robben Island Prison Commandant. Within our hearing, he told the latter that we were hardnuts and needed to be taught manners. Lieutenant-colonel Steyn, the Robben Island Prison Commandant, gave us a wicked smile and nodded knowingly to what his colleague was telling him. He hardly welcomed us or told us what to expect from him. He didn't even tell us what type of prison Robben Island was. We had expected that he was going to give us a short speech as du Toit had done after our arrival in Leeukwop Maximum Prison after our conviction. We were mistaken. He kept on listening to du Toit telling him about how 'cheeky' and 'stubborn' we were. He only nodded without any comment, with the wicked smile on his face and his green eyes flashing at us from time to time. He had two big, ugly incisor teeth with a gap inbetween and made no effort to hide them.

It was already late afternoon and opposite to where we were standing, there was Section B (later changed to Section A) and through the window-bars we saw other prisoners peeping at us. Some of them recognised some of us and waved their hands in silence. We were later divided into two groups of 50 each and taken to Section A (later change to Section B) which was empty. We were put into cells one and two. The cells had recently been completed and smelled of wet paint. We found blankets and sisal mats inside. After dividing them three blankets and one sisal mat for each man, we went to the showers which were adjacent to the toilets to wash (at that time with sea water). Afterwards we rested and reminisced about Leeukwop Maximum Prison and the two-and-a-half days' journey to Robben Island. That night we slept like logs not knowing what the morrow held but anticipating many confrontations with the enemy.

2. An Introduction to Robben Island

Early the following morning at 4am we were woken by a bell which rang so loud that we all sat up. Some rushed to the toilets to relieve themselves, while others went to bathe. Those of us who remained folded our blankets and sisal mats. About an hour later, we were told to stand in twos in readiness to be counted. Later on a Head Warder came with a big book and we were counted as we marched out of the cell.

Outside we found about 20 warders standing in a semi-circle around Section A. We were searched for 'dangerous weapons' after being told to lift our hands up. After the searching, we were allowed to pass through to join other prisoners from Section B who were standing in a slow-moving queue to the kitchen for breakfast. The line moved in silence until we reached the kitchen. When my turn came, I was given an aluminium plate, a quarter filled with 'pap' (soft porridge made out of maize meal). Following others before me, I took a plastic cup and scooped black coffee from a drum nearby. Then I went to join other prisoners who were squatting on their toes on a sandy area next to the kitchen. The warders, all Boers, were standing right around us. The pap had a bad taste and many of us new arrivals could not finish it. When we wanted to throw it away, comrades who had arrived earlier in the island told us to give it to them. We gave them our plates and they shared it among themselves. They told us that because of starvation there, in a week's time we would be bolting everything we could lay our hands on.

Because of having been kept inside cells for three months, some for five, our group looked light complexioned and well-fed compared to the comrades we found in the island who were all sun-burnt and emaciated.

At 6am prisoners began queuing according to their workspans. At about 6.30am they were counted and marched out of the main gate to their work place escorted by their warders. All the warders were White in Robben Island; there was hardly a single Black warder throughout the whole prison.

We, the new arrivals, were assigned two warders and marched off to the Old Prison for registration — a distance of about half a kilometre from the New Prison. On the way we met other prisoners from the Old Prison on their way to work. There were a number of faces I recognised among them. They all looked sun-burnt and worn out. I signalled to those I knew and they signalled back.

The gravel road by which we trudged was lined on both sides with tall trees. It was whitish in colour and appeared as though it had been covered with lime. We followed it until it suddenly turned left and then we saw ahead of us old structures built of corrugated iron and wood. We were taken to the Reception Office and made to stand to attention in four lines of 25 each as though we were in a parade. One of the warders who had come with us went into the office to report our presence.

While we were standing there we saw criminal convicts, about a hundred in number, coming out of the Old Prison cells and being escorted to the boat we had come with the previous day, back to the mainland maximum prisons. Most of us were shocked by the sight of such human beings. At No.4 Prison (The Fort) where I came across hardened criminal convicts and at Leeuwkop Maximum Prison where I had spent three months, I had never come across such a species of prisoners. My whole body trembled at the sight of them. Eyes lurking and blood-red, scars on their heads and faces, tattoos on their chests and arms, grim-faced, they looked at us as though they were going to devour us. We looked at them sympathetically. They were the products of apartheid justice. I wondered whether any of them could ever be rehabilitated to live normal lives again. It was only later that we heard about the havoc that some of them had done to some of our comrades — for many of them belonged to the Big Fives, a prison gang that helped warders in ill-treating other prisoners.

"So these are the new pigs who arrived yesterday," said an African convict who came to stand at the door to look at us.

"They are beautiful, aren't they?" said a warder who came out of the Reception and also came to stand at the door.

"Very much," said the convict admiring us.

"You'll get a good wyfie here," said the warder. The convict laughed aloud.

I wondered what these people were talking about. For a 'wyfie' in the Afrikaans language is the female of an animal. And who amongst us could be a 'wyfie'?

"All of you listen," said the warder, "when your name is called, you must run to the office." We did not respond but looked at him defiantly.

"When the baas calls you, you must run," repeated the convict. We remained silent and looked at him disdainfully.

The warder then moved up and down the lines looking us in our faces. We looked right in front of us pretending that we were ignoring him with our defiant faces. And then he stopped. He had found the weakest link in the chain. It was old man Tolepi. Years of working as a farmhand had tamed him. I'm sure when their eyes met, he smiled and blushed apologetically. He shouldn't have looked at the warder — he should have avoided his eyes. We had told him that repeatedly at Leeuwkop Maximum Prison. Since he was one of us, he had to observe our code of conduct towards the enemy.

"You understand 'ou man'?" said the warder looking at him straight in the eyes and drawing himself up.

"Yes I understand baas," said Tolepi in Afrikaans smiling meekly. Another error again. We were all angry. We had repeatedly told him not to call these warders baas. 'Baas' means master. And these warders are not our masters. There could be no compromise on this. A European could not become our master simply because of his colour.

"You must run when your name is called. If you don't run, you'll get this." And the warder passed the baton next to Tolepi's nose.

"I understand clearly baas," said Tolepi smilingly humbly. The way he smiled we could see from his face that he knew from experience what was conveyed to him. The warder walked back to the office triumphantly.

When I looked at Tolepi with his bow-legs and face full of boils, I thought of my maternal grandfather who was also a farmhand in one of the Boer farms in Eeram in Harrismith district. I imagined that he too, were he with us, would have behaved in a similar manner. I imagined him at that time of the day already at work toiling. Tall and rather stooped, with rough hands, a gruff voice, eyes full of sadness and sorrow, tattered clothing, with rags tied around his feet, he presented a grim picture of man's inhumanity to man. I remembered the last time I saw him when I had visited Harrismith in December 1961 as he came back from the fields tramping slowly, wearily along and the tears had filled my eyes at the mere sight of him — for he was chained like other farm labourers to the farm.

Three warders together with the two men who had earlier escorted us, came to stand between us and the office. The convict came with a list and began calling out our names. As soon as the man responded, the warders shouted at him to run, pushing him from behind. Someone behind our lines whispered, "trot with dignity comrades."

It was as though the warders had heard him. When the next man was called and came up trotting with dignity from the bottom line, the warders charged at him with batons and began beating him on the ribs and shoulders. And that became the trend with the rest of us. There was absolutely no reason why we were made to run because after being beaten, pushed and shoved into the office, you still had to wait for the man before you, who was still being registered.

Now that the warders were five in number, they constituted a mob — a mob armed with batons.

"Moses Dlamini," my name was called.

"Yes," I responded almost defiantly.

The mob did not wait for me to trot with dignity towards the office; they charged at me, beating and shoving me from behind. As with their other victims, they did not touch my face. Inside the office, I found to my exasperation, that the Receptionist had not yet finished with John Mdakane the man before me. Later on I was given my prison ticket on which were inscribed my name and surname, 872/63 the prison identification number, the offence of furthering the aims of a banned organisation and membership of a banned organisation and the sentence of three years on each account. My height was also checked and they wrote five feet nine inches, my complexion brown. They checked for any marks on my body and found my right hand ring finger minus the nail. It was noted down.

When I had finished inside the office, I was beaten back again to the lines by the same mob of warders. Some of us never got the chance of trotting with dignity to and from the office.

By about 10 o'clock we were still standing and the December heat was unbearable. Oupa Mazibuko who was sickly collapsed. The warders stopped us from going to his assistance. He was soon followed by Gabriel Makgomola who had symptoms of tuberculosis. They lay there for a long time. Later on, two convict hospital assistants came and removed them to the prison hospital. It was later discovered that they both suffered from TB.

When we had all been attended to, we were taken to the stores and given prison clothes with Robben Island initials. They consisted of canvas shorts, a canvas jacket and a coarse collarless khaki shirt. Those of Leeuwkop Maximum Prison were packed into bags and taken to the boat. We were also give a pair of old sandals each. You were fortunate if you got the same size for both feet, or sandals of both feet. At 1 o'clock we were given out lunch on rusty plates which consisted of boiled maize mixed with cowpeas. There was also a drink called 'puzamandla', made out of maize flour. At about 4 o'clock we were taken back to the New Prison where we had our supper at 5 o'clock and waited for the workspans to return from work.

We were joined by comrades who were disabled and worked inside the prison doing washing, cleaning cells, dishes, cups and the prison surroundings. Later the workspans returned. There were many old faces we recognised. There were some comrades I had seen in Maseru in January 1963 and in March 1963 before my arrest. They were all emaciated, sunburnt and gloomy; but their faces brightened up when they recognised us. After greetings they briefed us on the current situation in the island. The warders were harsh and beatings at work were frequent. The prison was being run by an evil Chief Warder called Theron who was in charge of the day-to-day administration. They further told us that there was a prison gang known as the Big Fives which was assisting the warders in the ill-treatment of political prisoners at two workspans known as the Quarryspan and the Landbouspan where most of the political prisoners worked. It was also this prison gang which, with the connivance of certain warders, locked up some of our comrades in cells where the criminal convicts of the Big fives were in the majority and where during the night our comrades would be overpowered and assaulted. Thus far about 20 of our comrades had undergone this humiliation and they told us of their names. There had been terrible fights in the Old Prison between some of our comrades and the Big Fives with the Boer warders in the morning taking the side of the Big Fives. At the Landbouspan two of our comrades had been buried alive and urinated into their mouths by the warders in charge of that span. The names of the comrades who had undergone this were Johnson Mlambo and Mninizo Mnyakama.

"Stilte," barked a warder while we were still busy conversing. We all kept quiet. Then I saw coming from the direction of the Zinktronk (a prison wholly built out of corrugated iron just next to the kitchen), a Chief Warder striding proudly towards where we were squatting. "That is Chief Warder Theron," whispered one of the old comrades who was squatting next to me.

Chief Warder Theron carried a baton and was being followed by a criminal convict who had a big head and spindly legs. This criminal convict was called Perdekop by warders (it means horse's head). He was Theron's agter-reier (hanger-on). All the warders stood stiff at attention. Theron came and stood about 10 feet from the front row. Some warders went to him with prisoners' tickets, saluted and mumbled something I could not hear. The tickets were then given to Perdekop who began calling the owners of the tickets by their names. About 70 comrades, bespattered with lime and quarry-stone dust, stood up and went to stand before Theron. He looked at them sneeringly for some seconds. "Two meals off," he said and moved away.

"You don't want to work," said Perdekop, "therefore you deserve to be starved." He too moved away following Theron. The 70 comrades were driven to an empty cell in the Zinktronk to begin their punishment.

After we had been locked up in our cell, we sang freedom songs until the bell rang at 8 o'clock bidding us to sleep. As I slept that night, I wondered how my first day of hard labour was going to be.

What I had seen of the island was frightening. The warders were pugnacious and hostile. Our group from Leeuwkop was very defiant and determined not to undergo any humiliation similar to that experienced by the comrades at the Old Prison. We had to tame the warders and stop the Big Fives from collaborating with them. And why were the political prisoners made to undergo hard labour? When the judges and magistrates sentenced us none of them had pronounced that we were being sentenced to hard labour imprisonment. That is why when we were at Leeuwkop Maximum Prison we were under the impression that political prisoners at Robben Island were just sitting and wiling away time. Now we were faced with reality.

About five minutes after the bell had rung, we were still engaged in conversation. A warder peeped through the window and commanded us to keep quiet. The conversation stopped for some time and continued again after the warder had left. He returned again and told us that since we continued to make noise, we were not going to get our breakfast the following morning. We fell silent. After he had gone, the conversation began again in very low tones. He returned again with a Head Warder. The latter peeped through the window and told us that we were not going to get our breakfast the following day. He told us that after 8 o'clock we were supposed to keep quiet and sleep. With that they left and our conversation stopped for the night.

3. The Quarryspan

The bell rang early at 4 o'clock the following morning and we were up. We prepared our beddings, folded our mats and blankets, washed, dressed and stood ready to be counted. The grille and cell-door were unlocked and Chief Warder Theron stepped in accompanied by the Head Warder. Other warders stood outside. It was our second time to see Chief Warder Theron. He was about five feet five inches tall, had a big head, a large jaw, and a pointed chin. His trousers were oversized and had been tied above his small potbelly with a thick red-polished leather belt. He came in walking like a duck and eyed us viciously with his hands on his hips, a baton in his right hand.

"Who were making noise here last night?" he asked harshly in Afrikaans. Silence.

"I say who was making noise here last night? Are you deaf?" There was no reply.

"One meal off," he said. Still we did not respond; we were sizing him up.

"You are not going to get your breakfast," he repeated as he marched out of the cell. That was our first taste of Theron — the king of Robben Island Prison.

We were counted as we left the cell, searched and marched past the kitchen to squat near other prisoners who were already having their breakfast. At 6.30am prisoners went to stand in lines at their workspans. We stood stupidly not knowing where to go until a corporal called Delport but nicknamed Oom Dellie took us to the Quarryspan — all 98 of us. We joined other prisoners who were standing in lines of four. (Around this time most of the political prisoners in Robben Island belonged to Poqo/PAC. The ANC had about 30 political prisoners).

The Quarryspan was the biggest and numbered about 600, about 60 of them criminal convicts who were too dangerous to be kept in any of the mainland maximum prisons (according to prison officials). The small workspans which consisted of a warder and 5 to 10 prisoners each, were the first to be taken out of the main gate. Chief Warder Theron stood near the gate and watched as the workspans were counted out. There was the tennis court span, the lighthousespan, the

The Quarryspan

woodspan, the GI stores-span, the Menasiespan, the plumbingspan, the carpenters-span, the electricityspan, the mechanics-span, the dockspan, the loosespan and the washingspan. Then came the buildingspan which was followed by the Landbouspan; and lastly came the biggest of them all — the Quarryspan. All these spans went out of the main gate carrying their food for lunch which consisted of boiled maize and puzamandla. Because our span was too big, our food was in three 44-gallon drums which had been cut in half. One drum carried puzamandla and the other two maize. The drums had been fitted with handles on the sides and two comrades for each drum ran in front carrying the heavy drum for a distance of about 200 yards and then others would rush to relieve them for the same distance. It was very tiresome.

After going past the gate, we turned north in the direction of the docks until we reached the main tarred road where we were joined by other prisoners from the Old Prison; then we turned east in the direction of Table Mountain. Walking in front at a distance of about a hundred yards was a warder with an FN rifle, immediately followed by the six prisoners who carried the heavy three half-drums filled with our food. On the sides were warders who kept on screaming and beating us to keep in lines. We were expected to walk in straight lines like soldiers in a parade. "Four-four, four-four," the warders screamed as they kicked and slapped us. The Big Fives were also there helping the warders. To be beaten by someone you despise is annoying and makes one more defiant.

Four other warders with FNs walked off the road inbetween the trees lining the road. Corporal Oom Dellie followed from behind with three other warders carrying .303s.

The whole road is lined with trees on the sides until it reaches the Guest House which is situated on the northern side of the small dorpie of Robben Island. After going past the Guest House, we turned southwards and found ourselves facing the sea. Eleven kilometers away Cape Town city was glaring at us with its tall skyscrapers and shining lights. Looming above it was Table Mountain with a white mist above it and clouds further up.

We marched on along the coastline smelling the sea until we arrived at the quarry. The whole distance from the New Prison to the quarry was about two kilometres — counting the many twists and turns. All along the way warders beat and barked at us assisted by the few criminal convicts who were members of the Big Fives.

When we arrived at the quarry the eight warders carrying FN rifles took up strategic positions right round the workplace. The other warders unearthed sticks and pick-handles from where they had been hidden. The pushing and shoving began. Pushed by the Big Fives and shoved by the warders with the big sticks and pick-handles, we were made to stand on one side while the older prisoners were pushed and shoved and given old rusty, squeaking wheelbarrows. Others were given 14lb hammers. Others were given picks and shovels. The last group was pushed and shoved and given 4lb hammers and wire-mesh for their eyes.

When our turn came, we too were pushed and shoved and given work tools and divided to go and work among the different work groups. The whole area which was dead and quiet when we arrived now buzzed with activity. Some of those who did not have work tools were sent to go and push cocopans and the rest sent to go and clear the dam (near where the rocks were being drilled) of debris. This consisted of going inside the water bare-footed and searching for any small rocks or tools inside.

See the criminal convicts as they run up and down, to and fro, around and about; shoving a political prisoner here, slapping another there, kicking and insulting others; running to the warders to give reports and take instructions and in turn giving new instructions to political prisoners and showing others how to do their work. The older political prisoners are already beginning with their work. We the new arrivals are still fumbling and confused, but angry at all this ill-treatment.

Corporal Oom Dellie is barking out orders like a commander, carrying a big stick, which he uses time and again from one prisoner's head to another. The noise coming from the compressor engine and water pump is unbearable. I'm working with those who are carrying the 14lb hammers. The hammers go up and come down crushing on the chisels. The old rusty wheelbarrows squeak and squeal filled with quarry stones. They move forward all the same.

There is Meintjies one of the Big Fives, running to Oom Dellie with a flask of coffee. See how he curtsies and gives Oom Dellie the flask. Oom Dellie takes the flask and pours out the coffee. Meintjies meanwhile bends down removes a cloth from his back pocket and begins polishing Oom Dellie's shoes. See, how Oom Dellie surveys his realm like a warlord. Look at how his eyes lurk. He has seen something wrong. He hurriedly hands over the flask to Meintjies. And Meintjies runs with it back to the office and is back again running after his master. Oom Dellie has pounced upon his victim. He hits him with a stick on the head. The criminal convict is also kicking at the man. "Bloody Poqo," barks Oom Dellie, "you think there's time to play. Go back and fill this wheelbarrow. This is not a full load. And you must bloody stop resting along the way."

"He's cheeky baas," harps Meintjies pushing the man, "this is not South Africa; this is Robben Island. And this is White man's territory.

C'mon." The man goes back with his load accompanied by Meintjies who keeps yelping at him.

There is Oom Dellie going among the stone crushers. Look at how he swings his stick from head to head. Blood gushes out of Vakalisa's head. He tries to stand up and confront Oom Dellie but falls sideways. There is no time for old men here. He's still tired from the long journey from Leeuwkop Maximum Prison. Another Big Fives convict, Muisbek (a name given to him by warders meaning mouse's mouth), runs to Oom Dellie's assistance. He looks like a bulldog, with his big mouth, ready to be told when to bite. "Does he want to fight you baas?" he asks. Oom Dellie ignores him.

"Sit up man and crush the stones," orders Oom Dellie. Old man Vakalisa sits up, puts a hand on his head and when he looks at it, sees blood. He looks appealingly to Oom Dellie as though to say 'pity me White man I'm old and sick.'

"If you don't work hard," said Oom Dellie loudly, "and fail to fill half-a-drum of crushed stones by the time we knock off, you'll get three meals off tomorrow."

The sun is now getting hot and sweat begins to drip from our faces and bodies. The 4lb hammers crush and crush at the quarry stones making them smaller and smaller into half-inch and quarter-inch particles; and of course, dust comes out as a by-product.

There is Meintjies again. See how he drives another prisoner who's pushing a wheelbarrow. The wheelbarrow stops. It has stuck into sand with an extra load of heavy stones. Look at how the man struggles to take it out of the sand. See his tongue coming out. See the muscles of his arms and legs, how taut they are. He pushes. The weelbarrow does not move. He runs to the front and pulls out the wheel. It moves. See the man again struggling with the load and trying to maintain his balance. The wheelbarrow squeaks, creaks, squeals and is stuck again. The man appeals to Meintjies to remove some of the load. "You have done this deliverately," says Meintjies, "you must push it out. I'm not going to help you this time."

There we go again. Muscles taut, tongue out. The wheelbarrow does not move. More screaming, shrieking and abuse. The man puts some saliva on his palms, rubs them and pushes. The wheelbarrow does not budge. He go to the front and lifts up the wheel a little and pulls it forward. Hurrah!!! It is out.

Oom Dellie is back in his office again. He has three tickets belonging to prisoners who he is going to punish. They work too slowly. He puts them on the table. Meintjies sees him, leaves his victim and runs to serve him with coffee. He curtsies as he gives Oom Dellie the coffee. He removes the cloth from his back pocket and begins polishing Oom Dellie's shoes. Oom Dellie drinks while looking around in his kingdom, to see whether everything was going according to plan. He finishes his coffee, takes his stick and comes to our group of 14lb hammers. We are busy swinging the hammers up and bringing them down to crush onto the chisels. Oom Dellie has seen something wrong. Look at how he walks amongst us like a witch hunter. See how he surveys us individually. See the 14lb hammers go up and listen to the thudding sound as they come crushing onto the chisels. Dust and sparks of fire fly about. We are already wet because of sweat. He listens to the song we are singing.

'Joji, Joji sigebengu	George, George is a rogue
Utshontsh'inkomo zabantu.	He stole people's cattle.
Wadlamaphaphu enkomo zabantu.	He ate the lungs of people's cattle.
Joji sigebengu.	George is a rogue.
Thina sibanjelw'amahhala.	We've been convicted for nothing.
Uthi masenze njani?	You must say what we do?
Wadlamathamb'enkomo zabantu.	He ate the bones of people's cattle.
Joji siegebengu.'	George is a rogue.

Oom Dellie sizes us up. He sees the sweat dripping down our faces. Some of us have their legs tied with old rags to protect them from the sharp splinters of rock flying about. He shows an evil smile and then shouts something. But his voice is drowned by the noise from the water engine, the compressor and the singing. We see his lips moving up and down but continue with our work. The 14lb hammers go up and are swung back with a thud. The chisels sink into the rock. Splinters fly about and the words of the song are drummed repeatedly into our heads. That bloody George was a smart rogue. Imagine a man stealing other people's cattle, killing them one by one and eating, of all things, only the lungs and bones. He left the liver, the T-bone steak, the fillet and the ox-tail. After finishing the lungs, he goes, of all things, for the bones. The bones have no meat. There's only marrow. Hah, clever George, he left the meat for us and we were caught eating it though we did not do the pilfering.

The hammers go up as the song moves from a crescendo to a fortissimo. Look at Fynkyk, another Big Fives 'agter-reier' standing before us and leading the song with nothing in his hands. See how he swerves his body rhythmically. He's now dancing the popular Boer dance — 'Tiekie-draai' (Tickey-turn). Look at how his legs and arms swing. He now moves sideways and turns right round. He takes another quick turn and is now facing us. I marvel at his gracefulness. A blow strikes me on the head. I turn round agitated and come face to face with a grinning Oom Dellie. "Damn you," he barks, "you are no

longer working but looking at Fynkyk. Get on with your work."
I put my hand on my head and feel there's a lump where he has hit me. I turn around and fall in step with the others, jerk my 14lb hammer up and bring it down crushing onto the chisel. I better not look at Fynfyk with his 'Tiekie-draai' but concentrate on singing about George the rogue and hitting at the chisel. The chisel goes in. I wonder where is she now. My Nomsa, my old spark. With her round brown eyes, bushy eyebrows and chocolate brown soft lips which she always pouted at me before giving me a deep kiss. Ah, those delicious kisses, forever warm and tantalising. And those round tender jutting breasts! How I used to pat and squeeze them while she hugged me closer. Awu! Awu! Is she as wretched as I am? Only time will tell.

Suddenly the stone cracks from the main rock. The song stops. We go for crowbars to disconnect it completely. Other prisoners are already waiting with long ropes to pull it away to a waiting truck back to prison where Sections C and D are still under construction. With our hammers and chisels we move forward.

The sun is scorching hot. The faces of the other prisoners look horrible. They are filled with sweat and dust, with lines where sweat is running through. I wonder how I look. My stomach growls. I'm hungry. I wonder when are we going to get our lunch. Oom Dellie comes. He demands my ticket. I give him. He moves away. He takes the tickets of two others who have been pointed out by Fynkyk. Hueey! So this is how life is on this island. I wonder whether some of us will be able to leave this place alive or still sane. I could imagine leaving prison like a vegetable, unable to speak coherently — stuttering or with a slur and fearing any White man I come across. And when someone tells of the struggle for freedom — looking at him in shock and just shaking my head.

Oom Dellie is gone. My eyes follow him. He is now shouting at the prisoners pushing the cocopans. Muisbek is gesticulating. He points at three prisoners. Their tickets are taken. The cocopan moves. Oom Dellie and Muisbek follow from behind. Then the rails go uphill and the cocopan slows down. There is pushing and heaving and panting. Slowly . . . slowly . . . it goes. And then it stops. Oom Dellie's stick finds its targets. One, two, three. Muisbek is also kicking. The cocopan moves. Slowly . . . slowly. It stops again. The stick swings again. The cocopan moves. It goes past the gradient. It now moves downhill. Faster . . . faster. The prisoners run along towards its destination to empty the sand before going back again for another load.

My lips are salty. It is the sweat. My tongue is parched. It is the thirst. The heat is unbearable. The sun's rays are piercing. A convict comes with a four gallon tin of water. It is passed around. I drink a mug full from a rusty jam container. I ask for more. The criminal convict refuses. He passes on to the next man. Fynkyk shouts orders. The song begins. It is taken up. We fall in step. The 14lb hammers go up and come down thudding on the chisels.

Since morning all those who had wanted to go and pass urine or have bowel movements have been refused permission. They had refused to say the password: 'baas'. A few old men had mentioned the password and had been allowed to go and relieve themselves. Oom Dellie and the other warders were uncompromising, "If you don't say 'baas' then you can't go to relieve yourself" Oom Dellie had said, "otherwise you must sweat the urine out." And so we had worked with our bladders loaded to capacity. Some whose resistance was weak messed themselves up. What did it matter? After all, the trousers dried up quickly. It wasn't so easy to say 'baas'.

By the time the bell rang for lunch, our group had cut out five big rocks. I dragged my legs towards the queue which had already formed next to the rest-shelter. We stood in double lines as we were counted and afterwards allowed to take our food which was being dished out by the Big Fives. As there were no cups for the puzamandla, the drink was poured into the dish which contained the maize. After getting my food, I went to a quiet corner and sat down to eat my maize. Three criminal convicts came to where I was sitting and told me to move off to another place as the corner belonged to the Big Fives. I stood up and went to find another place avoiding corners this time.

Later on I asked one of the comrades from the Old Prison to relieve me at the 14lb hammers group. I already had blisters on my hands and could not cope with the work. He willingly agreed and told me I could go and sit at his place and crush the quarry stones with a 4lb hammer.

The bell rings. We are rushed out of the shed. Time to go and crush the stone into powder this time. The comrade from the Old Prison takes me to where he had been sitting and gives me his wire-mesh goggles to put over my eyes. I take the wire-mesh gogles which have one-eighth inch holes and put them over my eyes. With such big holes I wonder how are they going to protect my pupils from the sharp splinters of quarry stones that will shoot out like jets towards my face. Through the wire-mesh goggles I watch the comrade as he moves away to the 14lb hammers group to replace me.

The comrades sitting on my left and right are already pounding the rocks into little pieces. A warder called Fourie (nick-named Sdakwa by prisoners), moves up and down carrying a big stick, supervising, screaming time and again and giving sharp precise orders that we should pound the stones quickly. The order is that the pieces we churn out should be quarter-inch in size.

I take the 4lb hammer, feel its weight and begin pounding. There is

The Quarryspan

no talking, no laughing or whispering. Only the pounding goes on mechanically. There is the sound of thudding and thudding going on simultaneously and continuously from four rows of about 30 each. Fourie keeps on reminding us that if by 5 o'clock any of us have failed to fill half a 44-gallon drum of crushed quarter-inch stones, those people would be punished and given three meals off the following day.

After pounding for about an hour, one comrade called Mike Maimane, who is doing a 20-year stretch had his eye pierced by a sharp splinter of rock which flew through the one-eighth inch holes of wire mesh. In pain, he places a hand over the pierced eye and goes to Fourie to report. The warder examines him, sees the damage and takes him to Oom Dellie. Oom Dellie orders another warder to escort him to the prison hospital.

As I continue pounding and pounding the little rocks, I wonder what the idea is of putting this wire-mesh over our eyes when it can't protect them from the sharp splinters. Some of the splinters fly past my face; but others hit at my nose, forehead and one chips at my mouth.

Comrade Baker Mogale sitting on my right is already in trouble. Nature calls. He stands up and walks heavily towards the warder called Fourie.

"And now?" asks Fourie aggressively in Afrikaans.

"I'm asking for permission to go to the toilet sir," says Baker in English proudly.

"Aha!" exclaims Fourie, "so you're an Englishman and you call me your sir. Who's your sir?"

"Well," says Baker, wire-mesh goggles still over his eyes, arms akimbo, "I didn't know that you do not want to be called sir. May I please go to the toilet 'meneer'?" (mister).

"I'm not your 'sir' and I'm not your 'meneer'. I'm your baas. Understand" Baker is silent.

"You must first say baas to me before I can consider whether to give you permission to go to the toilet or not."

"Going to the toilet is not a privilege," says Baker, "it is an act of nature. Surely you can't deny me that."

"So you're a BA eh? I'll show you what we do to BA's here."

"Being a BA has nothing to do with granting me permission to go and relieve myself."

"Go and sit down and pound those rocks again," commands Fourie pushing Baker roughly away.

"But surely you can't be so brutal," says Baker. Fourie continues to push him. Baker shakes his head, turns round and moves heavily to sit down. He begins pounding at the quarry stones again.

A few minutes later I smell some kind of odour. Steve Lepee on my

left whispers to me: "What has happened?"
"It's Baker," I whisper back, "he had no other option."
"My bladder is also loaded to capacity," whispers Steve.
"I'm also in the same trouble," I say.
Oom Dellie comes with his big stick. Steve stands up and approaches him. "Ja," he grins, showing him a wicked smile.
"I'm asking for permission to go and relieve myself," says Steve.
"There's no time for relieving yourself here, you must sweat the urine out. C'mon sit down and crush these stones."
Steve turns round, sits down and begins pounding the quarry stones into quarter-inch particles again. A few moments later, the front part of my coarse short pants was all wet. My body had failed to sweat the urine out. But at least I'm relieved. I can now pound the stones faster and produce much better quarter-inch particles. Steve coughs. I look at him. His face shows relief. I look at the front part of his trousers and find it all wet. He's now pounding faster chipping out better particles. Two other comrades in the row immediately behind ours messed themselves up also. It was far better to allow nature to takes its course than to submit to the uncouth warders.
The sun is now sinking towards the west and a cold breeze from the sea is blowing and cooling the whole area. The political prisoners pushing wheelbarrows are now tired and just dragging their feet along. The 14lb hammers now go up with an extra effort and those of us who are sitting and crushing the small stones do it as though our hands are numb. Even the compressor engine and the water engine have changed their sound. They drone as though they are protesting that they are tired. The squeaking wheelbarrows now move and stop frequently as though their axles are bent. Even the warders now move lazily about only shouting here and there. But not the Big Fives. They are as active as ever; running from one warder to another, reporting this and whispering that, after running back to prisoners to drive them on and on.
Oom Dellie is now standing outside his office drinking coffee. Meintjies is kneeling before him polishing his shoes. After finishing his shoes, he stands up to polish his buttons and corporal's stripes. When Meintjies finishes, Oom Dellie gives him the remnants of the coffee and some sandwich left-overs. Meintjies goes out with the coffee which had been poured into an old rusty jam tin and eats his rewards for the day. Other Big Fives also go to different warders with their rusty tins to collect coffee and sandwich remnants. Oom Dellie looks at his watch and decides to go to those working with 4lb hammers. He moves from heap to heap looking for those who have failed to fill half a drum of crushed quarry stones. The Big Fives walk before him and point to those who they consider have failed to fill the

The Quarryspan

quota. Many tickets are taken. When Oom Dellie finishes he moved back to the officer and instructs Muisbek to ring the bell. It is time up and the long sought after rest.

The journey back to prison was like the retreat of a defeated army. Lines irregular. Feet dragging. Some collapse through exhaustion. They are pulled up by the Big Fives and shoved back into the mass. The tired warders try to beat us to walk in lines of four but give up. We were returning back by the road which runs along the seashore. When this great mass was near the single quarters for warders, a halt was called. Oom Dellie screamed orders. Warders and the Big Fives moved up and down making us stand in fours by pulling us this way and that way.

"Four-four," the warders screamed.

"Four-four, four-four," the Big Fives screamed not wanting to be outdone by the warders and shoving and pulling us into lines. When order was restored the march began again until we reached Sobukwe's cell and saw him standing outside. He scooped up soil with his right hand and slowly, slowly, left it to fall back to the ground. And when it got finished, he scooped up another handfull again. Simultaneously, we all removed the old rags over our heads which were called caps and saluted; PAC and ANC prisoners alike. When we had passed him we put back our caps (it was an offence to go without a cap). Oom Dellie screamed. The warders and the Big Fives also screamed, running up and down, shoving us this way and that way as though we were cattle going to be dipped. But it was all to no avail, for we had already saluted our leader.

We marched on until we reached the junction leading to the Old and New Prisons. Another halt was called. Dog tired, we stopped; perspiration mixed with particles of dust, flowed freely down our faces. Prisoners from the Old Prison were sorted out. From another smaller road winding inbetween the trees, came the Landbouspan, its prisoners came dragging their legs along; faces, hair, clothes and legs bespattered with lime dust. It was with difficulty that I identified some of the comrades I knew. They came and stopped next to our span. From this span too some sorting was made of those staying in the New and Old Prisons.

A short tiny prisoner who I later learnt was called Teeman — President of the Big Fives, left the Landbouspan and came to converse with Fynkyk, Muisbek and Meintjies. I saw the faces of the latter turn pale. The journey back to prison began with the accompaniment of the howling and the screaming from the warders and the Big Fives.

When we reached the prison gate we were counted and allowed to pass through into the sandy square for 'tauza' just next to the kitchen. We were commanded to strip naked and stand in eight lines. There was absolutely no privacy. In front of each line was a warder who had to do the searching. Jumping on the left leg, while the right floated in mid-air as though to make a side-kick, simultaneously clicking the tongue to the warder and clapping the hands together, afterwards spinning round on the left leg, then turning round, bending and showing the warder your arse — that was the 'tauza'. And we watched, in astonishment, as one by one the criminal convicts indulged in the orgy, some doing it in style to the pleasure of the warders. When the turn of us political prisoners came, we handed the warders the clothes, opened our mouths, lifted up our hands, turned round with naked dignity and refused to do the 'tauza'. The warders screamed, clapped and kicked us, trying to force us to do the 'tauza', to no avail. We were determined not to have ourselves humiliated to that extent. Ultimately the warders relented and picking up our clothes, which littered the sand, we got dressed and went to queue in the long line for food.

Meanwhile Perdekop came while some of us were dressing. Oom Dellie and the other warders who had the tickets of those to be punished, gave them to him to call out our names. After our names had been called, were were told to stand on one side while the other comrades passed on to collect the food. We stood there stupidly not knowing what was going to happen to us. One by one the other prisoners went past the kitchen and were given badly cooked maize porridge with unwashed, unpeeled finger-sized carrots on top. They sat in long rows on their haunches next to the kitchen and ate their supper with wooden spoons. The warders stood encircling them, watched and listened to the noise they made as they ate like hungry pigs.

While we were standing there, I had noticed that all the warders carried pick-handles. Unlike the previous day, there was tension and I did not understand why. Then the man standing next to me whispered, "The Bix Six are here from Bellville Prison." When I looked right at the back, I saw them sitting on their haunches in their new prison clothes. Many of them had bandages around their heads and arms. Others had old scratches on their faces and heads. They were about a hundred in number. They were busy conversing, defying the warders' orders not to talk. We were later to learn that they had turned everything upside down where they came from: stabbing warders and the criminal convicts of the Big Fives. Their salute was the Victory Sign of Churchill (the one of the Big Fives was the Nazi salute of Adolf Hitler) and their main enemies were the warders, the Big Fives and prison conditions. It was then that I understood why Fynkyk, Muisbek and Meintjies had turned pale after meeting Teeman. Their main rivals had arrived and there was going to be war.

From the direction of the Zinktronk, I saw Chief Warder Theron come haughtily, walking slowly. His big shining red belt was fastened above his small potbelly. He kept on patting his oversized right trouser leg with his officer's baton.

Theron, looking triumphant, came and stood about five feet away from our group and surveyed us like his favourite pets. Perdekop, who had finished calling our names, went to stand next to him and also surveyed us. Dog-tired, hungry, bespattered with dust, sand and mud, we stood at attention waiting for a decision. Corporal Oom Dellie and other warders went to him to give reports about how we were refusing to work despite all their sweet entreaties. They told Theron that we had been doing absolutely nothing the whole day except lolling about engaged in endless conversations. We were about 60 in number.

After listening to all this, Theron turned proudly to face us, his hand patting the baton slowly on his trousers. "You don't want to work," he began addressing us.

"The work we were given sir . . ." began one comrade.

"Bly stil", said Perdekop, rushing towards him, "when the baas speaks you must keep quiet." He pricked his forefinger at the comrade's cheek and moved back triumphantly. Oom Dellie stood next to Theron grinning.

"You don't want to work," began Theron again, "this is not a hotel where you can eat, sleep and bathe in a heated swimming pool at your leisure. This is prison. Whatever any warder tells you to do, you must do. Do you understand?" There was silence. None of us responded.

"Two meals off, all of you," said Theron. Perdekop stepped forward.

"Because you do not want to work," he said, "you are going to be punished by not getting your supper now and your breakfast tomorrow. Afterwards you will go to work on empty stomachs."

Chief Warder Theron moved away followed by Perdekop. The 60 of us were straight away taken to our respective cells to carry our mats and blankets to an empty cell in the Zinktronk where we would spend the night.

When we came out of our cell carrying the mats and blankets on our shoulders, we saw the Big Six already standing in lines of two outside, next to some of our comrades who had not been punished. I looked at them closely. They were also scrutinising us. They looked haggard and emaciated. Their hands and arms were full of tattoos, mostly of women (unlike the Big Fives whose tattoos were the Swastika). Many of them were toothless, some had front teeth missing and old scars over their eyes, ears, mouths and noses. There were a few among them who were still young. They all looked like men who had left planet earth for another planet and there became engaged in wars and after many years had now returned to find human society completely changed from what it was. Some of them greeted us sadly.

It had been a hectic day and it was Kenya's Independence Day. We had earlier decided that that evening we were going to hold some commemoration of this important occasion in Africa's history.

Standing in front of the Big Six in the left row was a handsome light complexioned man in his late 20s with a bandage over his head and tattoos of women on his arms. As we were about to pass him, he called us and showed us the Victory Sign. "I'm Georgie," he said smiling (he had two front teeth missing), addressing us, "I'm President of the Big Six. Don't worry, very soon we'll deal with the Big Fives.'

"I'm Dladla," said the dark complexioned man behind him, also showing the Victory Sign, "I'm the Chief Justice of the Big Six. There are some among the Big Fives who have already been sentenced to death."

We left them conversing with some of our comrades and moved on with our loads to the Zinktronk on wobbly legs. Soon we were counted and marched into an empty cell to begin our punishment. Hungry and tired, we unfolded our mats and blankets and stretched our legs to rest. About an hour after we had been counted, while still resting, the warders came again, opened the door and screamed at us to stand up. We stood up on our blankets not knowing what was going to happen. They moved right around the cell counting us again, touching each man as they did so, and trampling on our blankets much to our chagrin. When they had finished they went to congregate at the door and each announced what number he had found. One said we were 60 another said 59 and yet another said we were 61. And so the counting began again. "60", said the warder who held the book. Two others agreed with him and a third merely nodded. They moved out of the cell and locked us in again. We collapsed back on our blankets trying to imagine how it was in Kenya at that time, for soon the Union Jack was going to be lowered and the Kenyan flag hoisted.

About two hours later one comrade called us to order. We all sat up. He asked us to sing a revolutionary song. I began it. It was an old nationalist song which had been sung by our grandfathers during the passive resistance campaigns.

'Thina sizwe esintsundu,   We the black nation,
Sikhalela izwe lethu,   We cry for our land,
Elathathwa ngabamhlophe;   Which was taken by the Whites;
Mabauyeke umhlaba wethu.   Let them leave our land.

Abantwana be-Afrika,	The children of Africa,
Bakhalela izwe labo,	Cry for their land,
Elathathwa ngabamhlope,	Which was taken by the Whites
Mabauyeke umhlaba wethu.'	Let them leave our land.

As we sang it, I could see that the morale of the comrades was going up. When we repeated it again, we seemed to have been rejuvenated. After calling out our motto of 'Service, Suffering and Sacrifice', we saluted and amid shouts of 'Long live the independence of Kenya', 'Long live African unity', 'Forward Ever, Backwards Never', the short ceremony ended.

4. It's an Old Cry for the Land

As I lay down on my bedding with the blankets going as far as my nose, my eyes cast at the concrete ceiling above, this song brought back memories of my youth and the first time I had heard it sung in 1949.

* * *

I was a young boy then of 11 years, full of energy and the zest for living. There was a tall oak tree in front of our house. It stood next to Harrison Street which joins Union Road, the main street in Kliptown.

One day while I was playing with my cousin Abel, swinging from branch to branch on the oak tree, I saw a procession coming up from the Klipspruit river. As they came nearer to go past the oak tree, I heard that they were singing a melancholy song. I told Abel that we should climb down and follow them, but he refused, saying that he had no interest in processions. I climbed down alone and stood at the street side. Two bearded stout men walked in front carrying the ANC flag. Immediately behind them walked an old grey-bearded man with a smaller white flag. After him followed a number of women dressed in sack-cloth uniforms. Other old men followed behind the women. There were no young men and women. It was only the old and middle-aged. People stood by along the street as they sang and passed, walking up slowly up to where I stood under the oak tree. They were about a hundred in number. 'This is something,' I said to myself and decided to follow them, though not knowing their destination. I called on Abel to come down and join me, but once again he refused. I ran up to the prcession as it went past and went to walk next to the grey-bearded old man with the white flag.

The procession went past the railway crossing, past the Union Road main shopping centre, past the petrol station, singing the melancholy song again and again until I knew it by heart by the time we branched and took the road leading to the police station.

As we approached the Kliptown Police Station, we walked slower and the singing stopped. We marched on silently and when we reached the gate of the police station we stopped. The ANC flag was lowered.

The grey-bearded old man went to stand at the gate and held the white flag higher. Some policemen who were milling around the station signalled to us to stop where we were. I wondered what was going to happen. When a tall European with a decorated cap came out of his office carrying a baton, followed by other policemen, I heard someone from behind whispering "the captain". Some of the policemen carried long spears.

I saw the old man's grey beard shaking. When I looked behind, I could only see fear and confusion in the eyes of the people. It seemed to me as though some of them wanted to run away.

When the captain was near, the grey-bearded old man removed his old hat and shrank it into a small piece, put the hand which held it behind his back and let the white flag drop down.

"Madala (old man)", said the captain, "you worry us every time. What is wrong now?"

"Good morning my baas," said the old man meekly.

The captain pretended he had not heard the greeting. Dropping down his shrivelled hat, the old man, with trembling hands, produced a letter and bowing, gave it to the captain. The captain glanced at it and asked "What language is this?"

"It is Zulu my baas," said the old man. The captain called an African sergeant and told him to read it aloud and tell him what it says.

"Great 'mnumzane' (sir)," began the sergeant translating, "we are crying about the police liquor raids in the location of Jabavu. African beer is a staple food since the days of our ancestors. When parents are arrested for liquor, many children become destitute. We also appeal against the pass and permit raids. We cannot get sleep at night. We also appeal for police protection at Nancefield station where many people are pick-pocketed, stabbed and some killed on pay-day on Fridays. We also appeal for police protection at the shops where shopkeepers and buyers alike are robbed by 'tsotsis'. This is not the first time we are making these appeals 'mnumzane' but is merely a humble reminder. Your in peace — the people of Jabavu location."

The black sergeant handed the letter back to the captain.

"You belong to the ANC?" asked the captain.

"Yes my baas."

"You are not recognised by the government," said the captain; "the government recognises the Advisory Boards. They are the bodies which must bring your grievances to the notice of the government. Concerning beer you are only allowed by law to brew one four-gallon tin of kaffir beer on week-ends only. Anyone who brews more than the four-gallon tin, will be breaking the law and once caught, will be arrested and charged. Anyone who brews during the weekdays will also be breaking the law and will be arrested and charged. The question of passes and permits is a matter which must be raised by the four senators who represent blacks with the Minister of Native Affairs. There is nothing I can do about it. It is required by law that every Bantu above the age of 16 years must carry a pass allowing him to reside and work in a particular magisterial district. Anyone found without a pass or a permit entitling him to be in any particular magisterial district during the day or night shall have committed an offence and when found, will be arrested and charged before a court of law. You complain of pick-pocketing, robbery, stabbings and killings at Nancefield station and around the shops in Jabavu. This is caused by the many 'tsotsis' who are roaming about in Jabavu, Moroka and other locations. These people have no passes and permits to be in the magisterial area of Johannesburg. And they don't work. They live on pick-pocketing you people who are protecting them when my police are hunting them out. How do you expect my policemen to assist you when you are thwarting their operations? You must tell all the law-abiding residents of Jabavu to assist the police in hunting out these criminals and vagrants. Then you shall stay in peace and no one will rob you of your hard-earned wages on Fridays. Is it clear 'madala'?"

"It is clear my baas," said the old man, his face a mass of confusion and disappointment.

"Now go and do as I have advised you." With that the captain went back to his office, followed by his entourage.

The old man picked up his shrivelled old hat which lay like a ball near his feet and began slowly stretching it out bit by bit. Then he picked up the white flag and turned slowly to face his followers. He addressed them in Zulu and told them what the captain had said in response to their requests. There was confusion intermingled with exasperation in the faces of his followers as they listened. The old man also seemed confused. One old stout woman commented, after the old man had spoken, that this was the same reply they had got on the two previous occasions they had come here. This was followed by simultaneous mumblings of dissatisfaction from others, especially the women who were more vociferous. An African constable came to tell them that they should not hold a meeting before the premises of the police station, it was an offence against the law and we could all be arrested and charged.

The march back to Jabavu began, but the procession was no longer orderly. They moved in small groups which engaged in discussions and arguments. I followed along moving from one group to another. One group talked about Dr Malan, the then Prime Minister and said he was the worst premier ever to be in power in the Union of South

Africa and that there were worse times ahead for the Blacks. Another group talked of the betrayal by the British who at the time of the Union of the four colonies handed over power to the people of European descent only and ignored the large majority of the Blacks — the rightful owners of the land. Another group talked of Christianity and said prayer was the only salvation for Blacks — that national prayer meetings should be organised and God would have pity and assist us.

When I reached home I went to see my aunt Bellina the eldest sister of my father who, together with her four children stayed with us after her husband had died mysteriously on a Boer farm in Balfour North in 1940 where they were both farmhands. I told her everything that had happened and what I had heard and seen. I asked her about the land question. I asked her about the British and I asked her about Dr Malan — the bad premier and who was this powerful man called 'government'.

"It is a long story my child," she said, "I shall have to tell you all this privately. You parents must not know, otherwise they will reprimand me. Your father is a member of the ANC Youth League and he must not hear me discussing politics with you."

Thus began my daily sessions after school hours with aunt Bellina about the history of our people; how the Black man was dispossessed of the land and how he became a slave afterwards. She also told me about how my parents had escaped from Boer Farms in the Harrismith district where I was born where they were both farmhands. My cousin Abel was not interested in all this. He showed more interest in stories about big crime and big-time gangsters. He also loved going to the Sanscouci Cinema to see Western films.

In 1950 I was doing my standard two and Abel who was a year younger was doing his standard one. We were both students at Lilydale Baptist School (later changed to Lilydale Community School with the introduction of Bantu Education). One evening that year policemen arrived at home led by an informer. They found 10 bottles of brandy hidden in the house after the informer had pointed out where they were hidden. For some time now my father had been selling European liquor at home to augment his weekly wages. Until this incident he had never been apprehended. The informer who exposed him had previously been one of his customers. After the discovery of the 10 bottles, Snyman, the Boer policeman who led the raid, punched my father in the belly and demanded to know where he had hidden others. While my father was half-bent, wincing in pain, his hands holding his belly, my mother screamed from the corner where she had been standing and told Snyman that he had no right to assault my father after they had already found the liquor. Snyman told my mother to keep quiet, otherwise she too would be arrested and charged for obstructing the law. But my mother would not stop shouting at the policeman. As a result, when my father was handcuffed and taken away, she too was told that she was under arrest.

All this happened while Abel and I watched. We had been sitting around the brazier when the police entered and had seen and heard everything. Attracted by the noise aunt Bellina had come in from her room and only saw my father in handcuffs and my mother following behind with the police escort. She called one Black policeman and asked what had happened but was ignored. She came into the room and saw us standing bewildered. She asked me what had happened and I told her everything including the punching of my father and my mother's reaction.

"When I'm a big man," said Abel before aunt Bellina could respond to my story, "I want to kill a policeman."

"When I'm a big man auntie," I also said, "I want to fight White people so that they should stop ill-treating Black people."

"Auk – " exclaimed aunt Bellina, "you just don't know what you are saying. The Whites are invincible. If you do any of these things you'll only end up in prison. Black leaders are now fighting with their mouths because our people have been defeated several times over the last 200 years. Tribalism and disunity and lack of guns have always been our undoing. Sleep my children, it is already late. Tomorrow I'll have to go about looking for money for the fine." With that she went back to her room.

The following day late in the afternoon, my mother returned with aunt Bellina. Somehow, aunt Bellina had managed to scrape the £100 fine from among the family's relatives and friends. Early that morning she had gone to the police station to pay the fine. The case against my mother was dropped; only my father had been charged. Afterwards he had gone to the Kliptown Railway Station to board a train to work in Booysens.

I was overjoyed to see my mother and I told her so. "Where did you sleep mama?" I asked.

"At the police station," she said.

"Is there a bed there?"

"No," she said, "I slept on the cement floor with many other women who had also been arrested in liquor raids. Some are from Jabavu, Moroka, Pimvile and Albertynsville locations.

Later on I heard them discussing the £100 fine that aunt Bellina had borrowed and how life was going to be hard. "I shall have to go and look for work," said my mother, "otherwise it will take ages for Philemon to repay the debt."

"I'll also have to look for work," said aunt Bellina, "even if it means having to do washing and ironing for an Indian family."

"I shall never forget Chain," said my mother.

"Who?" asked aunt Bellina.

"That informer who brought the police here — he's a rascal," said my mother.

A few days after this both my mother and aunt Bellina found work in Braamfontein. Their employers were two poor Indian families. Four times a week they went there to do the washing and ironing. At the end of the month they did not get their pay as the Indian families had no money to pay. Instead they were paid in kind — they were given old clothes which they were told were worth their salaries — £1.10.0 a month. They continued working for two more months for the same families and each month the results were the same. In the end they abandoned their employers and found employment elsewhere with other Indians. Despite the delays in being paid by their new employers, they got their pay this time in cash. Meanwhile my father's debtors were pressing on him to settle his debts. It was then that the family made a decision to move from Kliptown to Jabavu and Moroka where the rent was cheaper at 10 shillings a month, compared to the £3 a month which my father was paying for the two rooms we occupied in Kliptown. What is worse — we were now to be separated. Aunt Belina, her four children (including Abel) and two of my sisters were to move with her to Jabavu while my parents, my two younger sisters and myself, were to move to Moroka. The first to move was Aunt Bellina to Jabavu in 1951. We followed in 1952 to Moroka.

The punching of my father further opened my eyes to the reality of the situation in my environment. I began having an interest in the political discussions of elders and I began to realise that it was only Blacks who were being hunted out and arrested for passes and permits. Coloureds, Indians, Chinese and Europeans were never asked for the dom pass. And I began to realise too that in the social strata in Kliptown, Blacks were the underdogs. They were being looked down upon as inferior even by some Coloureds and Indians. I also observed that some Blacks among those who were light-complexioned took Coloured identity cards, refused to speak their mother tongues, shunned other Blacks, moved among Coloured circles and spoke either English or Afrikaans (the languages used by the Coloured community).

In 1952 I watched many Africans being mobilized for the Defiance of Unjust Laws Campaign (in Kliptown where I was still attending school). I read the placards which had been displayed prominently in many places in Kliptown. I saw the volunteers moving up and down rallying other people to support the campaign and take part in the defiance of the unjust laws. Ultimately it fizzled out. The President of the ANC had betrayed his followers leaving many of them in prisons. Once again gloom pervaded the African political atmosphere. And the question was what next.

From that time I began attending meetings of the ANC which were often held at the Dadoo Square between Moroka West and Jabavu. It was also here that I listened to Moses Kotane and Ruth First addressing a mass rally in 1954 and telling the people there about how life was in the socialist countries after their visit to those countries, including China. By this time my political outlook had been enlarged. And I was quick to notice that in these meetings there were some Blacks who did not favour Europeans patronising the ANC. These were known as the Africanists. As the years went by, their voices would become louder and louder until no ANC meeting could be held without there being scuffles between the two groups.

The same year, 1954, I was doing my standard six and happened to be one of the brightest pupils in class. As a result when the supervisors came to test us on English speech, I was chosen to speak on any topic I preferred. And I spoke on how the Blacks were being harassed in Kliptown by policemen, chased about for not having passes and arrested. The supervisor — Gugushe (later to become a 'Minister' in the Basotho Qwa-qwa bantustan), was dumfounded. He called on our teacher who had been standing outside when I gave my speech and asked him about what I had said. Our teacher, Prince Mabilla, denied all that I had said. He told Gugushe, while I stood embarrassed, that he had never seen any Blacks being chased by policemen for passes. After this I was told to go and sit down. Three other pupils were called and they gave their speeches on animals and vehicles to the great delight of the supervisor. I was later to learn that our teacher had denied that blacks were being chased for passes for fear that he may be accused by Gugushe of teaching us politics in school.

Meanwhile my cousin Abel was also developing in the field he had chosen — gangsterism. He left school in 1954 after passing his standard five and became a fully-fledged gangster, much to the dismay and anguish of my parents and aunt Bellina. It was a career which was to have dire consequences for him and the family.

By now we spoke two different languages. While I saw everything involving the life of a Black man in a political context, he saw himself as one day becoming the boss of Jabavu and the neighbouring locations.

*　　*　　*

And I wondered as I lay there looking at the concrete ceiling above me whether he would not have ended like Meintjies, Muisbek, Fynkyk and Teeman, that is, if he had not died in 1956 after a bitter and atrocious gang warfare in Jabavu. But at least he left me with a girl friend — pretty Nomsa — the woman who was now also having sleepless nights because of my internment in Robben Island.

Soon I was fast asleep.

5. 'Listen, we pity those still coming'

While we were standing at the Quarryspan before being counted out in the morning, I saw another warder from the Old Prison talking to Oom Dellie. On closer scrutiny I found it was Jan Kleynhans, the warder in charge of the Landbouspan. After talking for some time as though engaged in argument they came towards our workspan. A few prisoners were pulled out of the Quarryspan and made to stand in rows of four nearby. Then Jan picked out two Indians. This precipitated a fierce argument between him and Oom Dellie. "No," said Oom Dellie, "you cannot have the Indians, they are mine."

"Just for today, Oom Dellie," pleaded Jan, "just for today only."

"No, not now," said Oom Dellie, "I'm not yet through with them."

"But by the time you give them to me they will be crocks," protested Jan, "I want them now."

"No," said Oom Dellie, "I know you Jan. You want to go and ruin them today. No Jan. I want to take my time with these Indians and to enjoy every minute of it."

"I'll handle them nicely today Oom Dellie," pleaded Jan again.

"I say no," repeated Oom Dellie, looking around proudly at us.

"Then give me just one for today only."

"No," said Oom Dellie emphatically, "for the time being, you'll have to wait for the government to bring some more Indians." Jan looked at the three Indians and I could see that his mouth was watering. He bit his lip.

The three Indians in question were Reggie Vandeyar, Shirish Nanabhai and Indres Naidoo who had been in our group from Leeuwkop Maximum Prison. They had been arrested in April 1963 for attempted sabotage and each had been sentenced to 10 years imprisonment. They had been terribly tortured after arrest and their wounds had not yet healed. Reggie still had one of his arms in a sling.

Jan came to where I was standing and pulled eight of us out to go and join the other group thus making us 32 in number. He then led us towards the gate and stopped us just before Chief Warder Theron. He went to the latter, stood at attention and saluted.

"Ja", said Theron in a proud bullying voice, "what's wrong?"

"Chief," said Jan in a meek voice, "I'm only asking for the three Indians from the Quarryspan, just for today chief."

"Did you ask Oom Dellie?"

"He has refused, that's why I'm appealing to you Chief."

"Leave those to Oom Dellie," ruled Theron, "you'll get yours. There are many Indians coming here. There's a group which has just been sentenced in Durban. They are seven. I'll give them all to you when they arrive."

"Thank you Chief," said Jan in disappointment, saluting.

Since our arrival with the three Indians, there had been great excitement among the warders. They were the first Indian political prisoners in the island. The previous day Oom Dellie had been driving them like mad when they were pushing wheelbarrows carrying quarry stones to the 4lb stone crushers.

Jan led us out of the gate as we were counted out. At the junction, we joined other prisoners from the Old Prison. This was the Landbouspan and Jan was in charge assisted by his brother Piet and other warders. Walking in front at a distance of about 50 yards was a convict called William Dlamini. He was the best clad prisoner in the island. He wore spotless white shorts and a jacket, shiny black shoes and socks which went up to his knees. On his head he wore a well-trimmed hat. On the left-hand side of his jacket he had a sparkling metal label inscribed MONITOR in capital letters. In his right hand he carried a walking stick. He walked upright, nose held high as though he was an English country squire on an early morning walk to get fresh air and exercise. (It was only later when he was about to be released in 1965 that we learned that he had been arrested in 1942 at the young age of 16 and sentenced to two years imprisonment. Once a convict, he joined the prison gangs, got a number of further charges and now had ultimately repented and was a Monitor. When he left prison the government arranged for him to be employed by a Durban magistrate as a garden boy as his relatives could not be traced).

On the way to work we were not beaten by the warders or the Big Fives as had happened in the Quarryspan; neither did we walk at a fast pace. There were no warders with FN rifles on either side of us walking inbetween the trees. There were only five warders who carried them. One of them was in front just behind William and the other four were at the back with Jan and other warders. The Big Fives walked behind us engaged in their own conversations. There were three criminal convicts — members of the Big Six who had been hand-picked from the Quarryspan by Jan. They were among the new arrivals.

We were walking along a small sandy road both sides of which were lined with tall trees. When we had left the junction near the prison we had taken another direction and turned south. We proceeded along the southerly direction for about three-quarters of a kilometre until we left the trees behind and came to an open area. From here we could see the sea some distance away. The road then turned eastwards for about 400 metres and then we saw some heaps of sand. We had arrived at the work site. There was a big donga where lime had already been dug out. There were our friends waiting for us — the same old squeaky, cranking wheelbarrows with steel wheels and unoiled axles. There were also picks, spades and shovels. That was all. We the new arrivals were made to stand on one side while the old hands were given their work tools.

Teeman accompanied by Jan then came to us and told us that all writers, poets, artists, doctors, graduates and teachers should stand on one side. About 15 comrades moved out. They were then given wheelbarrows. Later on three of those who had been given wheelbarrows were brought back and their wheelbarrows were given to the three members of the Big Six. The rest of us were given picks, shovels and spades. I was one of those who were given picks.

The old prisoners had already begun working. They had already started a song. But many had not yet caught up with it. There were 10 old prisoners with picks and the seven of us new ones went to join them. Ten feet behind us were the prisoners working with spades and behind them were those carrying shovels, scooping the top sand into heaps and leaving bare the lime. Other prisoners carted off the heap of sand with wheelbarrows to go and dump it at a ditch about 100 metres away. Behind the prisoners with shovels there was a big donga sloping in a semi-circle for about 80 metres. It was from this donga that the lime was dug out and piled into heaps. There were three big heaps which had been piled up on previous occasions. On two of the heaps were groups of prisoners — 30 in all. The first group of 15 was scooping the lime on to the second heap and the second group of 15 were scooping the lime on to the third heap.

For the first few minutes we worked without supervision. William was serving the warders with coffee. Teeman, Bloed and some of the Big Fives were conversing near the warders. We fell in step with the other prisoners carrying picks, left feet forward and right ones behind to maintain balance. We listened to the words of the song and mumbled them as we lifted up our picks.

I did not see how it began, neither did I see the victim at first. They were on him. One was holding him, hands gripped from behind. Teeman and Bloed were punching him with fast blows that rained over all his body. The Big Fives were assaulting one of the Big Six. In a few minutes he was a gory mess and then he screamed and that scream saved him. Jan and the other warders left their coffee and came running. They asked Teeman what the matter was. He told them that the man was a troublemaker and was refusing to work. The victim wanted to speak, but words failed him. Jan told him to stand up. He was still dizzy but he managed to wiggle himself up. His shirt front was covered with blood, his left eye puffed up, his lips torn and his nose bleeding. He was told by Jan to push his wheelbarrow which was filled with sand. He went on struggling with the wheelbarrow with Piet, Jan's elder brother, at his heels, urging him on.

There was another scream and they were on a second man like a pack of wolves. Fists, kicks, karate blows all land on him in quick succession. He had tried to fight back but that had made matters only worse for him. He fell down swooning, his face bespattered with blood and mucus. Bloed kicked him to stand up and work. His teeth, red with blood, a big lump on his right cheek, he tried to wriggle himself up and collapsed again.

"Another troublemaker baas," said Bloed as the warders came along, "we tried to beg him to work but he started assaulting Teeman."

"Pull him out of the way," said Jan, "and place his wheelbarrow next to him, he will recover. We'll teach him the dignity of labour."

Two members of the Big Six had been flattened and only one remained. He was left in suspense and worked himself like a mule.

By now we had caught up with the song and were singing it with gusto as we lifted the picks up and brought them down sinking into the earth. Teeman came and stood on top of a little mound of sand in front of us, loked at us with his little eyes like a witchdoctor out to sniff a wizard. Then he took up the song with a powerful voice that echoed far away into the sea. He stood there, half-bent, right arm lifted up in the Nazi salute of the Big Fives, and then he cast his eyes far into the southern horizon as though he was waiting for white ghosts to rise out of the sea. As he led the song, we followed in the background opening our mouths as wide as possible, until the sound reverberated in the whole area and far beyond the trees and the seashore.

'Ekuseni, ekuseni madoda,
Sikhuluma ngengqauza ekuseni;
Hawuzwa sikhalel'abezayo.
Umama akazalanga,
Uzali'sigebengu.

Ekuseni, Ekuseni ngo-4,
Sikhuluma ngengqauza ekuseni;
Umama akazi lutho,
Uzali'sigebengu.

'In the morning, in the morning men.
We talk about parole in the morning;
Listen, we pity those still coming.
Mama failed when giving birth,
She gave birth to a rogue.

In the morning, in the morning at 4,
We talk about parole in the morning;
Mama knows nothing,
She gave birth to a rogue.

Ekuseni, ekuseni badakiwe,
Sikhuluma ngengqauza ekuseni;
Hawuzwa sikhalela abezayo.
Kubuhlungu bafowethu,
Kubuhlungo ngo-4;
Hawuzwa sikhalela abezayo.'

In the morning, in the morning,
   they're drunk.
We talk about parole in the morning;
Listen, we pity those still coming.
It's painful my brothers,
Its painful at 4 o'clock.
Listen, we pity those still coming.'

Richmond du Preez was one of the ANC political prisoners from the Eastern Cape. He worked with the other political prisoners who were using spades. He wanted to relieve himself, went to ask for permission and was refused. As the pressure to relieve himself was too much, he sat down not far away from where he was working and helped himself. Unfortunately for him, the sharp eyes of Jan Kleynhans and Teeman had seen him. Teeman dropped his outstretched arm, left the song and left the mound. In a moment he was on him, kicking him in the ribs. While Richmond was struggling to pull up his short pants, Jan Kleynhans was already on him with a stick. Teeman retreated back and in a moment he was back on top of his mound, leading the song: 'In the morning, in the morning when they're drunk, we talk about parole in the morning; listen, we pity those still coming.' He's now stretching his arms parallel forward, preparing to do the Zulu war dance — 'indlamu'. Look at his eyes looking far up. And then his left foot goes up touching his chest and comes down stamping hard on the sandy mound. The right foot follows, and then the left. Look how sand and dust fly about. His voice is now inaudible. Old man Tolepi has taken up the song and is now leading it with his rusty voice.

Jan has thrown Richmond on the ground, is beating him and is urging him to rise up and remove his shit. "With your hands," he shouts, "remove it with your hands and don't remove a single grain of sand." Richmond staggers, goes down on his knees, scoops the shit and a blow hits him on the head. "Why do you leave the rest?" screams Jan, "I said you must remove everything."

Richmond goes down again, scoops the rest mixed with sand, is kicked in the belly and falls down on his back.

"I told you not to touch the sand," says Jan, "not a single grain of it. Return all the sand." Richmond stumbled up, the shit which he had had in his hands got scattered when he fell down. He's dazed and looks at his hands. They're a mess.

Look at Teeman. See how he turns his body and swerves to the left. His sharp small eyes see everyting that is happening to Richmond. He turns back again to face us and his legs go up and down rhythmically. Look at old man Tolepi the former farmhand, with his thin bow legs.

He rushes and stands opposite Teeman and joins him in the 'indlamu' war dance. I'm sure his mind is not here, it is far away in the farm in Nigel where he was born and had worked. His eyes are cast at the red ball of fire far up in the skies. Look at how he stamps his thin bow-legs. It is as though they can break at any time. See how the dust flies about around him.

Richmond is now running away and Jan is at his heels. It is a cat and mouse chase. Jan catches up with him and trips him. Richmond falls, is beaten and pushed down the 12-foot donga. He lands on a sandy mound on his back. Jan jumps down after him. He sits on top of him and throttles him. Richmond is now crying and in choking sobs is asking for help. Jan joins him too in the crying while his left hand is pinching Richmond's throat and the right one is punching him at random.

Look at the other warders, Piet, Fourie and the Big Fives. See how they drive those pushing the wheelbarrows. Bloed kicks Steve Lepee from the back and Steve stumbles forward the front part of his wheelbarrow hitting Thomas Motloung on his heel opening a gash. In pain Thomas pushes his wheelbarrow and it hits Jerry Ntsoane's heel, re-opening the wound which was caused by the leg-irons at Leeuwkop Maximum Prison. Piet is beating at random with his stick on all those he comes across. It is now becoming hot and the tongues of the wheelbarrow drivers are coming out, their legs groggy, sweat dripping from their faces and flowing onto their coarse khaki shirts.

Look at those down in the donga scooping the lime with shovels. There is Matthew Mokoena, the former Radio Announcer. He it was on the morning of 21 March 1960, who, together with Stanley Nkosi and another, broadcast revolutionary songs encouraging the African people to support the Anti-Pass Campaign of the Pan Africanist Congress. Look at how he scoops the lime non-stop. You would not recognise him if you had known him. The sweat and the lime-dust have formed a crust on his face. There's an 11-year sentence before him. Next to him is Chirwa, a Malawian with a 10-year stretch for assisting ANC guerrillas. Here too, they are singing of parole and pitying those still coming. As they throw the lime into heaps, the wind comes and blows the lime dust back into their faces and clothes. They are now of the same colour as the lime. Only the eyes and the teeth show that they are still human beings and not scarecrows. Fourie comes half-running and screaming towards them bidding them to work faster. The scooping goes on mechanically like machines. Here there is no rest. Neither is there time to urinate or have a bowel movement. Not even time to think. There's only senseless work to be done.

There is Jerry Ntsoane who had worked for the South African

Institute of Race Relations. His legs now wobble and buckle, his tongue out. He almost falls down through exhaustion, as he stumbles along with his load. Piet goes to him almost running, to drive him on and on.

Look at Teeman and Tolepi — how they now dance 'indlamu' facing each other. Listen to the words of the song of how mama tried to give birth and the child turned out to be a rogue — a reject of society. 'It is I who is the rogue — because I was born Black. I'm White society's scourge — condemned to live under harsh prison conditions. And prison is the only place for me where every day in the morning our only consolation is to sing about parole — to yearn for parole — and to wait for the guerrillas to release us from Robben Island Security Prison. At 4 o'clock in the morning, when talking about parole, I pity my mama, for she knows nothing about what is being done to her once sweet innocent baby. And that is what makes it painful. Just that. O mother Africa!!! If only she had known . . . But now it is too late. And that's what makes it painful my Black brothers. Auk!!!'

They have got him. It's another rogue. His mother is not here to cry for him — to bid him " 'tula,tula mntanami', do not cry my baby, papa is coming and he'll bring you sweets and ice-cream and rock you to and fro." It is the third member of the Big Six — the one who since morning has not yet been touched. He lifts up his hands to show unconditional surrender — no resistance.

"You're going to be by wyfie," says Bloed.

"As you wish," says the rogue.

"Get on with your work, you'll sleep at the Old Prison tonight," says Bloed victoriously as he moves to another prisoner.

"It's painful my brothers," Teeman's voice sings, "it's painful at four."

Look, old man Tolepi falls face down, arms outstretched. Froth comes out of his mouth and his breathing is heavy. Teeman sees him but pretends he hasn't. "Listen," his voice rises, "we talk about parole in the morning." He leads the song, his right arm outstretched in the Big Fives salute. Jan comes and asks Teeman what the matter is with Tolepi. "He's resting baas," says Teeman, "he has been working hard and is only a new arrival."

"The old man is going to die man," says Jan, "nobody must die here in the Landbouspan. They must die in their cells. Take him to the shade."

Teeman pulls Tolepi by one leg like a bag full of potatoes and drags him to a shade under a tree a few paces away and then returns. He stands on his mound, looks around and goes to the professionals who are struggling with the squeaking wheelbarrows. The song goes on in his absence. Picks go up, are spun in the air and are swung back with force to sink into the hard earth. The sun is now scorching hot, its rays piercing into the human skull. The wheelbarrow drivers are now groggy, stumbling and wobbling as the wheelbarrows squeak and squeal. There is blood on their ankles and heels. Their mouths are dry with thirst, their eyes red with lime-dust and their tongues hanging out gasping for air.

There is Paul Masha, the guitarist, coming up stumbling with his load. The wheel of his wheelbarrow gives out some creaking and irritating music. The way he's pushing is as though he's remembering old pop melodies. Only one of his lungs is now functioning. The left one got punctured when electric shocks were applied on him on 24 April 1963, when he was tortured. It was on the fourth floor of the Grays Building by Pretrius, Caswell and Magoro of the Special Branch while I was in the room next door waiting my turn. One comrade comes from behind being driven by Piet with a stick and his wheelbarrow comes crushing into Paul's left leg opening a bigger wound. He screams in agony.

Listen to the tenor and alto produced by the young former school students as they sing 'Sikhuluma ngengqauze ekuseni'. One of them is doing natural life imprisonment and two others are doing ordinary life. They're now pathetically tired as they scoop load after load with their shovels. And this is only their first year of their life sentences. Worse days still lay ahead of them.

Richmond is back at work scooping the lime with his spade. He's working mechanically as though he's a machine. Old man Tolepi stands up slowly from under the tree as though still dazed. He wipes his eyes and looks around and his mind remembered. He heard the song once again, saw the picks going up and his face brightened up. He dragged his bow legs along, picked up his pick and began to work.

Lunch time came just when I was about to faint. I had last eaten the previous day at the Quarry at lunch time. Tired and terribly hungry, we all went down the donga to have our food — the same boiled maize and puzamandla dished out to us by the Big Fives.

After eating, I rested, sleeping on my back trying to prepare myself for the after-lunch period. No one among the prisoners spoke, we were all too tired for that. Old man Tolepi slept next to me and I could see that his thoughts were far away, probably back in the farm in Nigel where he had been arrested. I wondered whether he was still sane especially after what I had seen him doing. He reminded me so much of my grandfather far away in a Boer farm in Eeram who was also toiling for nought. He also reminded me of my own parents who were once farmhands and how my father had been sjambokked in 1938 soon after my birth for daring to ride the 'oubaas's favourite horse.

And I thought that if he had not escaped, I would have been a farmhand from a very young age. Tolepi had been sjambokked by his master in front of his wife and children and afterwards the 'oubaas' had taken him to the Nigel police station and charged that he was a member of Poqo — something which he did not know. He had been convicted for membership and furthering the aims of a banned organisation and sentenced to three years imprisonment.

The whistle rang and we all stood up and went to our work places. Jerry Ntsoane, a friend, asked me to change places with him. After having seen what was happening to those pushing wheelbarrows, I reluctantly refused. I wanted to help my friend but at the same time I was afraid of undergoing the hardships experienced by those pushing wheelbarrows.

Teeman was already standing on top of his mound urging us to hurry on and start working. Then the song began slowly and gathered momentum until we had all caught up with it.

"Step," cried Teeman. We fell into step, left feet forward. "Up," he screamed again. Holding the pick axe by the forefinger, spinning it first several times in the air, before lifting up, we hopped and then brought them down to sink into the earth.

They were at them again in two groups. The victims were the same two members of the Big Six who had been assaulted in the morning. The assailants were the Big Fives. Right hooks, left crosses, uppercuts and straight rights found their targets at will. Their hands went up in surrender. The battle was over. They were now going to be wyfies of the Big Fives in the Old Prison and tonight all three of them were going to sleep there and have a taste of domination which would make them submissive and dependent and never again to dare fight against the Boer warders and the Big Fives. From now on they would be infused with feminine ideas and play the role of women in prison society. They will be taught to walk like women, smile like women and to sit like women. They will be taught how to prepare food for their soldier-husbands, how to wash and press their clothes and also how to hug them and blow them kisses when they return back from work in the Quarry- and Landbouspans.

There is Jan Kleynhans driving Tyobeka like an ox-wagon driver whipping draught oxen going uphill with a heavy load. Tyobeka, a former bus driver from Cape Town, has lost a lot of weight since he arrived in Robben Island in November to do a three-year sentence. When he arrived he was stoutly built with a rotund figure, as round as a barrel. He had had fat cheeks and a double chin. When he arrived at the Reception Office with other prisoners from Cape Town the warders could not believe their eyes. It was Jan Kleynhans and his brother Piet who set the ball rolling. While Tyobeka and the other prisoners were standing waiting to be called for registration, the warders approached Tybobeka. They bent down and kneeled before him while he stood in surprise and bewilderment. One of the warders was moving around in a circle as though dazed, not far away from them.

"Great Dingaan, Great King of the Zulus," cried Jan in a loud clear voice meant for other prisoners to hear; "we are voortrekkers, Great One. We have come with our young and old, women and children, from far away in the Cape Colony where we have run away from the oppressive laws of the British. We have braved different types of climate, rivers, mountains, wild animals and fierce tribes and have now come, Great One, to beg you for a piece of land; for us and our children, so that we may, at last, have rest, peace and plenty in your rich and fertile lands."

Tyobeka stood still like a statue, torrents of sweat pouring down his face, only his chest heaving up and down. Jan went nearer on all fours and kissed his feet and crept back again. Piet, his elder brother, who was kneeling next to him, also crawled forward on all fours and kissed the feet of Tyobeka.

When they simultaneously rose from the kneeling positions, Tyobeka was in trouble. The first blow that struck him landed on his mouth. It was a baton blow from Jan and three of his teeth came flying out, followed by blood. The other warders were on him landing blows at random on any part of his body. Amid screams and yelling from the warders who kept on shouting "Kill the wizard!", Tyobeka fled as fast as his bulky frame could manage to the nearest cell of the Old Prison which was about 30 yards from the Reception Office. Seeing him going into the cell, wherein he immediately collapsed, the warders turned back thanking God for his kindness in having brought back to them Dingane alive. Since then Jan Kleynhans had been overworking him at the Landbouspan. Though he was no long bulky, he continued to call him 'fatty'.

Working next to me is comrade Johnson, one of the comrades who, since their arrival at the Landbouspan in June 1963, had been daily tortured by Jan Kleynhans and the other warders. He is one of the comrades whom Jan had assaulted, buried alive and pissed into their mouths with the remark that he was making them drink the White man's wine. Next to Johnson also working with a pick is Albert Shweni, the tallest man in Robben Island, over six feet tall. Two of his middle fingers' phalanges were fractured after beatings by Jan and the Big Fives; refused treatment at the prison hospital by sergeant Nel, he had given the fingers some wooden supports tied with an old cloth.

There is Jan Kleynhans now hurrying towards us.

"Collin Abrahams," he shouts, calling the man who's loading sand onto wheelbarrows just in front of us. The man continues working, scooping the sand onto a wheelbarrow with his shovel.

"Hey, you bloody Collin Abrahams," he screams again. The man continues scooping the sand, torrents of sweat dripping down his face. Jan reaches him and grabs him by the collar and shakes him violently. "Can't you hear I'm calling you?" he growls at him; "are you deaf?"

"I'm not Collin Abrahams baas," replies the man.

"Aha, so today you're no longer Collin Abrahams. Then who are you?"

"I'm Abraham Collins," says the man.

"Bloody Indian, you're trying to make a fool of me?" he shakes the man violently.

"I'm not an Indian baas," says the man.

"Are you a kaffir?"

"No."

"Are you Coloured?"

"No."

"And you're not Chinese or are you?"

"No."

"There's only one 'nasie' remaining now and that is European," says Jan, "and you can't bloody tell me you're White! If you're not Bantu, Coloured, Indian or Chinese, then what 'nasie' are you?"

"I'm Malay baas," says the man.

"Bloody Indian, you're playing a fool with me," barks Jan and throws the man to the ground and beats him.

"I'm not an Indian, I'm not Indian!" the man screams while Jan has placed his boot on his chest and continues to beat him. Later on he urges him to stand up. "What 'nasi' are you?" he asks the man poking him with his stick on the forehead.

"I'm coloured of Malay descent baas."

"And why don't you overload these wheelbarrows? Are you also a Poqo?"

"Ek is 'n krimineel baas," (I'm a criminal master).

"Why don't you overload them?"

"The Poqos are now tired baas."

Jan grabs him by the scruff and shakes him violently. "Is that your business when they are tired?"

"Mercy my baas."

"Is that your business?"

"Mercy my baas, 'my groot koning' " (my great king).

"Get back to your work. Let me see you playing with these Poqos again."

"Dankie makhosi," (thank you my king), he bows humbly, half-kneeling. He rushes to take his shovel and begins loading onto the first waiting wheelbarrow. Jan stands watching him.

"There's no mercy this time," says Abraham Collins as he scoops the sand, "I have bloody suffered for you bloody communists." Torrents of sweat pour down his face as he scoops load after load in quick succession. "And you had wanted to topple the government," he continues, "so as to implement your communism here in South Africa. You'll do that over our dead bodies." He continues scooping and loading until the wheelbarrow is filled to the brim and some of the overloaded sand begins to fall on the sides. And then he pats the sand which has now become a mound.

"Right," says Jan, "its now okay."

"C'mon" shouts Abraham Collins to the wheelbarrow driver, "off with your load."

The man spits on his hands and struggles with the wheelbarrow.

"Hey you," shouts Abraham Collins to Steve, the next man coming with his wheelbarrow, "you come walking as though you're a school principal. You must bloody run with that wheelbarrow."

Abraham begins scooping the sand. "They can take the whole of Africa but not Robben Island," he tells Jan; "is that not so baas?"

"Ja," says Jan, "and also not Paarl, my home town." He quickly moves away.

"These Boers are bloody stupid," says Abraham to Steve, "they have no fucking brains; for how long do they think they'll go on oppressing us?" He blows his nose, wipes his nostrils and then begins scooping the sand again. "You should not worry when I overload," he says, "one day these Boers will pay for what they're doing."

(For the next three working days Abraham Collins joined the Big Fives and the warders in overworking political prisoners and seemed to enjoy it. A few weeks afterwards he became sick and joined the Loose span which was composed mostly of patients and engaged mostly in clearing the prison surroundings of rubbish and unnecessary stones. This span consisted mostly of political prisoners temporarily declared unfit to work in the other spans. To his dismay, Abraham Collins collided with some of the prisoners he had ill-treated at the Landbouspan. His appeals for forgiveness went unheeded as the other prisoners avenged and overworked him while the two warders in charge of that span just became indifferent to his appeals to them for protection).

Throughout the whole workplace there is screaming and beatings; warders running this way and the Big Fives running the other way; sometimes coming together whenever there was resistance from a comrade. Time and again a small whirlwind rises and our hair, faces and clothes are bespattered with lime dust and particles of sand. Dust goes into our eyes and blinds them but we work on, all the same, as though we are robots, sometimes we work with eyes closed while waiting for the liquid in the eyes to clear the dust. The eye has its own healing mechanisms.

"In the morning, in the morning men, we talk about parole in the morning, listen, we pity those still coming." The song goes on without end. Froth is now coming out of our dry mouths and our dehydrated voices are now hoarse. The dry sweat has formed white crystals on our faces, our heads filled with sand dust and our coarse convict canvas short pants and khaki shirts littered with lime. We are now singing it low and flat as though it is a requiem for all those who died in the struggle for freedom in South Africa. The tired sun moves slowly towards the west indicating that it would soon be time for our rest too.

Our weary legs slowly move forward as though semi-paralysed and our now flagging arms move heavily up with the picks. Those pushing wheelbarrows are straining themselves to get them moving as though they are going uphill with their loads.

A cold breeze blows and the waves splash over the seashore. The tide is rising and five kilometres away, two passenger liners ply slowly towards Cape Town harbour. They carry many tourists from the Western countries who are going to tour 'sunny South Africa' that southern part of the continent of Africa where a certain section of people of European descent want to be treated like a special category of human beings. These tourists will return back to their countries, some with disgust but others with pleasant memories.

There are the fiends down in the donga next to a cluster of shrubs cracking jokes. William is giving coffee to Jan Kleynhans and the other warders. Teeman, Bloed and other members of the Big Fives are polishing their shoes and waiting with rusty jam tins for coffee and sandwich remnants — their rewards for the day. There are many other days which are going to be like this and there are many political prisoners who are going to be their victims — some are still on trial and others are on their way to Robben Island.

The whistle rings. It is time to go back to prison. After the work tools had been put away, we were led to the sea which was about 300 metres away, to go and wash ourselves. And those of us who had had bowel movements, to rinse their trousers. And then the journey back to prison began. We trudged back on the small narrow winding road with sullen faces, knowing quite well that some of our comrades in the Old Prison were going to be engaged in battles that night when defending themselves from being molested by the Big Fives.

When we arrived at the T-junction, we found that the Quarryspan had already gone past, but the prisoners staying in the Old Prison were waiting for us under the supervision of another evil warder called van Rensburg. There were also a few warders and the Big Fives. Those belonging to the New Prison were sorted out from the Landbouspan. The three members of the Big Six were taken to the Old Prison, while we were marched back to the New Prison by van Rensburg. Tired, we entered the gate and went for 'tauza'.

Perdekop was busy calling the names of those to be starved. A group of them were already standing on one side waiting for Chief Warder Theron's judgement. Most of them belonged to the Quarry span. Unlike Oom Dellie and the other warders in charge of spans. Jan Kleynhans and his cohorts did not take prisoners to Theron to be starved. He meted out the punishment at the Landbouspan himself. Hence there were no prisoners from the Landbouspan who were to be starved that day. It was seldom that he took his victims to Theron or any of the senior officials. Even then he did so after he had already meted out the punishment.

After 'tauza' we went to queue for our delicious supper of maize porridge and cowpeas (half-cooked); and we were sure that if we kept quiet after 8 o'clock that night we would have our breakfast the following morning. Among the comrades to be starved, I noticed about 10 who had been in our group which had been punished the previous day. They stood dejectedly, all smothered with quarry stone dust waiting for Theron to come and pass judgement. Of course they knew just as we did, that there was only one verdict which was going to be passed.

6. *Inspection*

Inspection. First Sunday of our arrival. We are standing erect in our ragged clothing, every man behind his folded mats and torn blankets, holding our tickets before our chests. The silence prevailing in the cell is like that in an old deserted cemetery. The cell door is opened. The Head Warder at the door stands at attention and salutes. "Alles reg hier luitenant, (Everything in order here Lieutenant)," he says.

The lieutenant, with his immaculate uniform and glittering buttons enters with a sneer on his face and moves around looking at each man from head to foot. Behind him follows Perdekop holding a Big Book written in big block letters: COMPLAINTS AND REQUESTS in Afrikaans. Teeman, Bloed and Fynkyk are also in the entourage following behind Chief Warder Theron. They also look at us from head to foot.

One comrade steps forward to complain about the food. "What's wrong with the food?" the lieutenant asks Theron. Theron looks at Perdekop.

"These people here think they're special prisoners," says Perdekop, "they want curried rice and chicken baas."

"There's nothing wrong with the food," Theron tells the lieutenant. Teeman, Bloed and Fynkyk nod knowingly. The lieutenant moves on.

Another comrade moves forward to complain about assault at work. "Where were you assaulted?" asks the lieutenant.

"At the Landbouspan," says the comrade.

"But I don't see anything wrong with you," says the lieutenant.

"I was beaten with batons and sticks on the body. They did not assault my face."

The lieutenant looks at Theron. "Did you report your injuries to the hospital orderlies?" asks Theron.

"They drove me away," says the comrade.

"Hy lieg baas (he's lying master)" says Teeman, "hy's 'n wetslaner (he's a troublemaker)."

"If you make any false accusations against any of my warders," says Theron, "you'll be charged." The lieutenant moves on. Another comrade steps forward. He also complains about the food, that it is little and badly cooked.

"There's nothing wrong with the food," says Theron.

"They want spaghetti, chicken and eggs baas," says Bloed. The lieutenant moves forward. Another comrade complains about the beatings at the Landbouspan. He tells him that Jan Kleynhans assaulted, buried alive and urinated into the mouths of two comrades.

"Rubbish," says Theron.

"Hy lieg baas (he's lying master)", say Teeman and Bloed almost simultaneously.

"Did they do that to you?" asks the lieutenant.

"No," says the comrade.

"Here you must complain about what happens to you," says the lieutenant, "you are not allowed to speak for another prisoner. Now, what is your complaint?"

"I'm complaining about the beatings at the Landbouspan," says the comrade.

"Where were you beaten?" asks Theron.

"The comrade shows him two fresh scars on his head. "They also beat me on the ribs and knee joints with batons," he adds.

"Did you go to the hospital orderlies to report your injuries?" Theron asks.

"They drove me away," says the comrade.

"He's lying baas," says Teeman, "he fell onto the wheelbarrow with his head. Like this . . ." He demonstrates to the lieutenant and Theron how the comrade fell on the wheelbarrow by hitting his head against the air, to the great delight of the two officers and the other Big Fives. Afterwards the lieutenant looks at the comrade from head to foot with a scowl, then moves on.

Old man Vakalisa steps forward to complain. "I'm sick sir," he tells the lieutenant, "and they refuse to attend to me at the hospital." The lieutenant looks at Theron. Theron looks at Perdekop.

"There's nothing wrong with him baas," says Perdekop, "it's only old age."

"It's only old age," repeats Theron to the lieutenant who then moves forward.

Sixteen-year-old Samuel applies for permission to study while in prison.

"To study so that you can make better bombs next time?" says Theron. "Why didn't you study while you were outside?"

"His bombs did not explode," says Fynkyk wryly, "now he wants to study how to make big ones which will explode here in Robben Island baas."

The lieutenant moves on slowly looking at us from head to foot. Then he goes out followed by Theron, Perdekop, Teeman, Bloed and

Fynkyk. The inspection is over and so are complaints and requests. Thirty minutes afterwards it was time for church. My first church service in Robben Island.

"Kirk (church)", a warder screamed as he opened the grille. A few comrades went out and I also followed. I needed a change of atomosphere.

7. *Faith of our Fathers Living Still*

Outside we found other comrades from other cells already waiting for us just next to Block A. Members of the Big Six also came and stood behind us. Georgie was there and so were his lieutenants Dladla and Arab. Another group from the Old Prison came to join us. Teeman, Bloed and Fynkyk were also there. The warders, five in number, made us stand in lines of two.

"Two-two," they screamed.

"Two-two, two-two," Teeman, Bloed and Fynkyk also screamed shoving us into two straight lines. We were about 70 in number as we marched down the road to the church followed by the warders with pistols in their holsters. None carried rifles.

The church was situated near the main road almost midway between the dorpie and the New Prison. Hidden by the trees about two hundred metres away from the church was Sobukwe's two-roomed cell. The two guardposts stood out above the trees. We could see the two warders guarding Sobukwe standing at attention on duty and looking around.

When we arrived at the church, we found a black priest already waiting for us. He carried a hand organ with him. The warders entered and took up strategic positions inside the church. Others stood behind us near the door facing the priest. They had their caps on. Before sitting down the Big Fives first observed on which side the Big Six were sitting and seeing them all going to sit on the right, they went to sit on the left. Political prisoners sat behind both gangs. It was a queer assortment.

The priest greeted us in English and told us that we were welcome in the house of the Lord. He told us that he was an Anglican but had come to conduct the service for all Christians. When I looked around, I saw Bloed with a plaster over his forehead. Next to him sat Teeman with a lump on his right cheek. Next to him sat Fynkyk with a swollen lip. There had been a terrible fight the previous night with some of our comrades as they tried to molest them.

"Peace be unto you," said the priest.

Teeman and Bloed nodded knowingly, but never kept their eyes off the faces of the Big Six. Georgie kept looking at them with a little twickering smile indicating that their days were numbered. I hoped that there would be no fighting in the church. Otherwise there was going to be pandemonium. The priest's hand organ, Bible and hymn books would be used as weapons by either of the two gangs in the melee that would follow.

He lifted up his arms and blessed us. Then he asked us to sing a song which most of us knew.

"Oh, for a thousand years to sing, my great redeemer's faith," the wretch, known as Fynkyk, notorious member of the Big Fives, took up the song in a quivering powerful voice. And we all took it up, Big Fives, Big Six and us politicians. The only exceptions were the warders who stood immobile ready for any action.

 My great redeemer's faith,
 The glory of my Lord and King.
 The triumph of His Grace,
 The triumph of His Grace."

The priest took his hand organ, found the key and led the song. I wondered as we sang, with the warders looking coldly at us, what the priest thought of that congregation before him with bandages, plasters, swollen lips and puffed up eyes. As we sang, I remembered way back in 1956 when I had visited my paternal grandfather how he had taken me along to the farm church built of mud and reed. I had been greatly touched to see all the farm labourers, all battered by hard work and terrible working conditions, coming together on Sundays to give praise to their maker. The local priest, also a farmhand, was semi-literate and it was a struggle for him to read through the Bible. What mattered to him and his congregation was not the stammering and stuttering but getting the message from those written pages of the Bible. And that message he got and repeated time and again to his audience: that there is another world far more wonderful than this one where there are no sorrows, no hard labour, no tears — for there they are wiped away. That in that land lay their eternal happiness.

* * *

I had left Johannesburg in low spirits after the sudden death of my cousin Abel in bitter gang warfare between the Terrors and Peter 'the Goatee's gang. I had hoped that the countryside would revive my spirits once again but after that church service and the general misery of the farm labourers I felt that I had to cut my stay short and return to Soweto. I only spent four days in Eeram. The next four days I spent in Harrismith location with relatives and thereafter returned to Soweto.

The day I arrived Nomsa was there to take me for a stroll.

"It is exactly five months since your late cousin brought us all together," she said as we strolled hand in hand that afternoon, "he didn't want me to fall in love with anyone. He was so jealous of me."

"How did you feel then?" I asked.

"At first I used to think he wanted me to be his lover, but when he did not even kiss me, I began to wonder. Later on he started telling me about you and praising you for your good character. When he intimated that he wanted to introduce me to you, it was then that I understood his intentions."

She later suggested that we sit down. We sat just near the Elkah Stadium and talked of the future. We talked of our plans for our wedding, the type of house we would occupy, the colours in the different rooms, the type of furniture and the number of children we would have. Later that evening we walked slowly until we reached her home. I left her outside and went back home in high spirits.

The following day when I went to see her at her home, I found that her mother, for the first time, was interested in my family's background and my personal ambitions. When we were alone I asked Nomsa why her mother had asked me all these questions.

"I told her everything," she said.

"Including what happened last evening?"

"Yes," she said.

"But why?" I asked in amazement.

"What if I get a baby out of wedlock?"

I was stupified and dropped the subject.

When the Junior Certificate results came out in January 1958, they showed that I had passed and my Nomsa had failed her Form I. It was a disastrous blow to her. She blamed me for her bad results. I was her first lover and she had become crazy with me and could no longer concentrate on her studies. Nomsa was from a poor religious family. Her parents had separated and she stayed with her mother who worked as a washer-woman in town. She also had a younger sister. The result of her failure was that she had to leave school and go hunting for a job in order to assist her younger sister who was still at a primary school.

There was also no money for me to proceed with my Matriculation. So I began trudging the streets of the city of Johannesburg for work. At last I found it at the General Hospital as an unskilled labourer. My work consisted of cleaning paint brushes and wet paint stains on the floor. The painter I had been assigned to was European, a Scot. He was very harsh with me and often kicked and slapped me. There were many other Black unskilled assistants with their European masters who were doing the same work I was doing who also suffered from the same indignities. During tea break we Blacks used to give our

European masters their tea. I was befriended by one middle-aged Black worker from Pietersburg district. His hatred of Europeans shocked me and made me realise that there was one subject at school I had not been taught — the most important subject of them all, more important than science and mathematics — Black/White relations. He used to take all the insults and kicks from his White painter master without complaint, but when we were together he used to insult Europeans and called them dogs. When he prepared his master's tea, he puts some drops of his urine into the tea and bade me to do the same for my master. When I refused, he put his urine drops into my master's tea and bade me go and give it to him. It was a galling experience. After a week, I abandoned the job and went back to tramp the streets again looking for another job. I could not stomach being slapped and kicked and neither could I stomach what my friend was doing. At last, after having been on the streets for three weeks, a friend found me work at the Transafrica Correspondence Colleges as a filing clerk.

A few months after this Nomsa also managed to find employment in the city as a factory hand. In the meantime, during 1958, I fell in love with a very beautiful girl who was a Roman Catholic and very religious. She literally swept me off my feet. It was through her that I saw the inside of a Roman Catholic Church for the first time and the mysticisms that go on inside. After having passed through the entrance, Tsidi annointed herself with water, made a sign of the cross, mumbled some prayer and bade me to do the same. Inside the church I felt lost. Everything was new and strange to me. I only stood or sat down when I saw others doing so. And when it was time for the sacrament and the holy wine I also joined the queue until someone who knew me tipped me to go and sit down again. The whole of 1958 I attended the church every Sunday. Tsidi wanted me to become a Catholic and I offered no resistance. She even persuaded me to join the Young Christian Workers, a youth organisation sponsored by the Roman Catholic Church, which I did. She gave me a Bible, the catechism and a hymn book. She taught me a number of Catholic Church hymns and whenever there was a tune I liked, she would sing it repeatedly for me until I knew it by heart. It was in this way that I learnt "Faith of our Fathers living still" in the Sotho tongue. She encouraged me to cultivate friendship ties with other young men who were Catholics and were members of the Young Christian Workers' branch in Molapo. I made many friends who were all devout Catholics. In the YCW meetings which I always attended, we engaged in various topics and were always involved in fierce arguments amongst ourselves. The Roman Catholic priest, Father Kelly, who also attended the meetings was always ready to adjudicate and redirect the discussions whenever we got lost or when the topics in question became political and highly sensitive. It became obvious to me and a few others that the YCW only operated under the existing political system just like the Roman Catholic Church and had no programme for the overthrow of an evil political system like the one prevailing in South Africa. That led to our frustration and made me seek out my former school mates who were Africanists and were busy agitating for the formation of another political organisation. They were angry young men who believed that the ANC had betrayed the struggle. And I flirted with them for some time. At this time I used to visit Nomsa at least once a month and she never complained (unknown to me she too had another boyfriend).

In April 1959 the job which I was doing was classified 'White' and three of us who were registration clerks found ourselves having to work under White girls. We first had to teach them the jobs and afterwards had to work under their instructions. I resigned my job and found myself in the streets again. I found myself frustrated and neglected by Nomsa. Tsidi was now at a boarding school in Natal and I could only meet her during school holidays. When ultimately I paid Nomsa a visit in July 1959, I found her pregnant by another man.

"Nomsa, Nomsa," I cried when I realised what had happened, "but why did you do it?"

"You deserted me Moses," Nomsa said crying, tears spilling down her face, "I thought you had forgotten all about me."

"For my cousin's sake Nomsa, how could I desert you?"

"For three months you hardly came to see me or ask about my welfare," said Nomsa, "and you know how I have always loved you."

"This then is the end of our affair Nomsa," I said tears welling in my eyes. (Even the affair with Tsidi was heading for the rocks).

"This is our end," she said pathetically.

"Does this man who has done this love you?" I asked.

"He's a gangster," said Nomsa, "I just do not know what made me fall for him."

"And now you're going to have a baby out of wedlock."

"There is nothing I can do."

I bent down my head in agony and tears flowed freely down my face.

"But we can still remain being friends," said Nomsa, "just for old time's sake."

"How can I look at you again after what you have done? And with a gangster at that?"

"It's all your fault Moses," said Nomsa crying, "it's all your fault."

Four months after giving birth Nomsa's child died. By that time her gangster boyfriend was in prison and my love with Tsidi had foundered. My friendship with Nomsa continued until a day before my arrest.

*   *   *

When I thought of my arrest and her role in it, my whole body trembled and shook my thoughts and brought them back to the present. The priest had been giving a sermon on love for one's neighbour, but I had heard little of it. When he finished, he asked us to sing another hymn and before anybody could take it up, I came up with 'Faith of our fathers living still' in the Sotho tongue, and the priest caught up with it with his organ. While the others joined with their voices, I was not thinking then, as I sang, of the Holy Virgin Mary or the Kingdom of God, but of my virgin Nomsa that December in 1956 after my return from Eeram, the same Nomsa who was now a wretch a thousand miles from me. The system had made her and the system had destroyed her.

When the hymn ended the priest prayed and blessed us. We sang two more hymns and then the priest uttered the last prayer and the service was over.

We trudged back to prison in silence as though we had been infused with the Holy Ghost. Even the Big Fives and the Big Six were quiet and I wondered what was in their minds. Did they think of some happy moments in their lives when they were still young and some of them had been altar boys? Or were some of them thinking of both happy and painful memories like I did? Or perhaps were some of them thinking of life after death and what their fate would be after such wretched and sinful lives? Christian upbringing, indoctrination and its melancholy hymns and mysticisms still had its influence in their subconscious minds. But then — there was still the battle to be fought for supremacy. It either had to be the Big Fives or the Big Six.

8. Christmas Day

Christmas Day was just like any other day except that we did not go to work and were given an extra cup of black coffee at 12 o'clock midday. For the criminal convicts of the Big Fives, it was a big day. They were not locked up that day and roamed freely between the Old and New Prisons, singing tribal songs and engaged in tribal dances. (Actually criminal convicts are also fed with Bantustan propaganda and are encouraged by prison officials to go and settle in the Bantustans after release — so as to dump all the large numbers of hardened criminals there for the Bantustan leaders to see how they can cope with such characters and clear the so-called 'White South Africa' of these elements).

In the yard between Section A, Section B and the kitchen, they formed a circle and began chanting tribal war songs. They had been provided with tribal attire by the prison authorities for the occasion. Warders also stood around clapping their hands. There was Perdekop with his big head and tiny scrawny legs, prancing about with a stick in his hand, as though he was a tribal induna. There was Teeman and Fynkyk clapping their hands as Bloed danced and stamped his feet in the centre of the circle imitating seasoned Zulu tribal dancers. They danced on for about an hour supposedly entertaining us. The Big Six and us political prisoners peeped through the windows as we were not allowed out for the occasion. We just looked at them and neither clapped our hands nor applauded. Many of us were enraged at such abuse of our culture by Boer warders and their criminal-convict friends. After about an hour of their gimmick, they left for the dorpie to go and entertain the warders and their families and thereafter to be rewarded from house to house with food left-overs.

At lunchtime we were given little packets of sweets which we later learned were from the World Council of Churches. But those little packets of sweets did us a lot of good. Besides their nice taste and their breaking of the monotony of the same kind of daily food, they helped us in giving us some energy for the coming hectic days. Some comrades stored them away.

One comrade late that afternoon played us a mean trick. And he was to do it for the following four Christmases of his five-year sentence. His name was John Mahapa from Orland East. He began by singing: 'Hark now . . .' and a few of us joined — 'hark now hear the angels singing, listen to what they say, that man will live forevermore, because of Christmas Day."

"I knew that some fools would follow me," he would say laughing while we sang. We would all stop singing and look at him angrily. After about 10 minutes he would begin again: "Hark now . . ." ; and absentmindedly we would begin singing: 'hark now hear the angels singing, listen to what they say . . .'

"I knew that some fools would join me," he would say aloud. He had caught us again. We would stop singing and look at him angrily while he laughed. In the end we would also end up laughing and afterwards begin singing with him the Christmas carol chorus to our hearts' content. Of course, many of us did not know how the carol began, we only knew and were interested in the chorus:

>Hark now hear the angels singing,
>Listen to what they say:
>That man will live forevermore,
>Because of Christmas Day.'

9. *The Prison Dispensary*

In subsequent days, after breakfast, I went to stand at the line of those who were ill or injured. I had a pain in the right side of my chest. Old man Vakalisa who found great difficulty in walking and could not bend down was always there in the queue for treatment. There was also something wrong with his back. Old man Tolepi was also always there with boils all over his face. Gantsha Khuboni was always there too with pains in his body. There were always many others with different types of maladies and injuries sustained at work or through assault at work or in fights with criminal convicts at the Old Prison cells.

The hospital orderlies came with a wheeled tray full of medicines. A criminal convict called Lucas who was a member of the Big Fives and was an orderly assistant, called on all those who suffered from headaches and other pains to stand in one line. Those who complained of stomach aches and other internal problems were told to form another line. Those who had chest pains, coughs, bronchitis, colds and flu were told to form a third line. I usually joined this line. Those who had injuries, wounds, cuts, were told to form the fourth line. The fifth line was of those who suffered from fungus infection around their testicles. This was caused by the short pants which were never properly washed by the cripples and other disabled prisoners who belonged to the washing span and had to wash all the convicts' clothes. Thus it was safer to sleep without the short pants on.

On this particular day old man Tolepi did not know to which line he had to go. He was 'assisted' by hospital orderly Head Warder Nel who pushed him roughly to the line of pains. He was given aspirins and told to go back to his workspan immediately. Old man Vakalisa joined the line of stomach pains and other internal pains and as usual, was given 'Mist Alba' which had been strongly diluted with water. He tried to explain his illness and was pushed away with the remark that he was an old loafer. Nel then instructed him to rush back to his workspan. Simon Gantsha Khuboni who was in the line of 'headaches and other pains' was given aspirins and told to go back to work.

There was one ill man who had been carried to the hospital orderlies by other prisoners. "Why do you carry him?" asked Teezar, one of the convict hospital assistants.

"He can't walk," said one of the men who had carried him.

"Why doesn't he die then? Leave him and get away from here," said the convict. They dropped the man down and left to go and queue in the Quarryspan.

"You stand up," said Head Warder Nel. The man struggled to stand but failed. He then crawled on all fours slowly towards Nel.

"I have a pain here," he said pointing at his appendix. He was given some tablets and left lying there. Later on he was removed to the prison hospital on a wheelbarow. My turn came and I was given two aspirins and told to rush back to work. Dispensing with about 100 patients, some very serious, had taken about 10 minutes.

On my way to the Quarryspan, I passed Old man Vakalisa walking with feet astride, pulling his legs along. Old man Tolepi and Gantsha Khuboni were already standing in the lines. When Corporal Delport saw Vakalisa coming along, he waved him away with his hands angrily. "I don't want old disused crocks in my span," he said.

Old man Vakalisa stood still not knowing what to do. He decided to pull his legs towards the Losspan, but was also waved away by the two warders in charge of that span. He just stood there and watched as the workspans left for work. Then he went to Chief Warder Theron. Theron watched him with amazement as he dragged his legs towards him. "They don't want me in all the spans sir," said Vakalisa, "I'm old and sick."

"You wanted to kill Whites," said Theron, patting his trousers with his baton, "and have been busy fiddling with bombs outside and now you don't want to serve your sentence. Your old jackal's tricks won't work this time. Here you are going to work until your sentence is completed. I want you to clear this yard; there should be no dirt lying around here. Every morning you shall start collecting all dirty dishes and cups after breakfast and go and wash them in the kitchen. Now begin with your work."

"And if you don't work fast and efficiently," added Perdekop, "you'll get three meals off."

With that they walked proudly away with Perdekop following and amusing Theron with jokes on the way. His favourite joke was asking Theron in broken English: "How many sides gotta horse baas?"

Theron: "Only two sides stupid."

Perdekop: "Wrong baas."

Theron: "One?"

Perdekop: "Wrong again baas."

Theron: "How many sides then?"

Perdekop: "There's the left-left side, the right-right side, the back-back side, the front-front side and the round about side." And when he mentioned the round about side, he would turn round about. And Theron laughed. They never tired of this joke, even when Theron was in a bad mood — except for one day — which was a disaster for both of them."

In the last week of January another draft of prisoners arrived from Fort Glamorgan Prison in East London. There were a hundred prisoners from the Transkei and the Eastern Cape. About 30 of them were old men aged from 60 to 80 years. After our draft from Leeuwkop had been followed by the draft of the Big Six from Bellville Maximum Prison, another draft of six political prisoners of the YCC led by Dr Neville Alexander had immediately followed from Cape Town.

With the arrival of this draft of old men, the number of sick comrades increased. The queue at the hospital was now longer and the hospital orderlies harsher; and these old men eventually joined the queue of the ill. But the hospital orderlies were clever, when they realised that a prisoner was about to die, they would admit him at the hospital and take him to the doctor who arrived twice a week on Tuesdays and Thursdays. At the prison hospital the patient would be given vitamin tablets, injections and other drugs. Once he became better, he would be driven back to the Quarry- or Landbouspans to be worked to death again. Such comrades always came back from hospital their faces and bodies puffed up as though swollen — the result of injections and drugs.

Old man Vakalisa was still queueing every day. Sometimes he would stand in the line of those suffering from pains and would be given aspirins, sometimes he would go to the line of coughs, bronchitis and chest pains and he would be given a cough mixture strongly diluted with water. Sometimes he would move from line to line and thereafter drag his feet along as he walked, now half-bent, to go and clean the yard and collect dirty dishes.

Old man Tolepi went daily to the line of those who had pains in the body, took his aspirins and went to join the Quarryspan. The boils were still full in his face. They never healed but only changed places.

Simon Gantsha Khuboni still stood in the line of headaches and pains and was being refused permission to see the doctor. He was always pushed away. Representations on his behalf by other comrades, only made matters worse for him. "I'll bloody beat you damn kaffir," Head Warder Nel, the hospital orderly would always tell him. And slowly, Gantsha Khuboni would turn away to go and join the Losspan as he could no longer walk the distance to the Quarryspan.

A week after the arrival of the draft from Fort Glamorgan, I made friends with one of the old men. The old man sat between me and

Harrison Mbambo. His skin was wrinkled and his muscle flabby but he tried to keep pace with us as we hit stone after stone with the 4lb hammers. He claimed that he was in his seventies.

According to his story the old man told me that he was from Engcobo village. Together with other old men, about 30 in number from the same village, they had been arrested and charged for wanting to kill Whites in the vicinity. They had belonged to this-thing-that-is-spoken-of (Poqo) in their village and together with others of his age group, had held meetings and decided to secretly sharpen their spears and wait for the day when the battle would be declared by this-thing-that-is-not-spoken-of. The old man coughed and coughed while he told his story until I thought his chest was going to burst. Somehow or other they were informed that the day had arrived for the overthrow of White domination. They took their spears and other weapons in the evening and went to a neighbouring forest. But two other old men who were too ill, remained in their huts. They waited in the forest the whole night for a contact man with more information. Early the following morning the forest was surrounded by soldiers. They were beseiged and had neither food nor water. Their contact man had not yet reported; and if he came, he would first have to pass through the soldiers. They were doomed. They either had to fight against the army and face their fire power or surrender.

They stayed in the forest and did not move. The soldiers also remained outside the forest and did not move in after them. The old men held a meeting, some said they should surrender, but others opposed that, saying that they could not surrender to children, they preferred to surrender to men who were their equal in age; meanwhile hunger was sapping their strength. The following morning, realising that the soldiers were still sitting fixed at their posts, they held another meeting. As many of the old men had collapsed as a result of hunger and thirst and others no longer had any energy left for argument, this meeting was attended by only a few. There was only one suggestion and that was to surrender. The old man and another volunteered to go and surrender. They tore a white piece of cloth from one who had a white shirt and tied it on a stick and went to surrender on behalf of the group.

The old men were then taken to the police station and from there to prison. That is where they met their contact man who had earlier been arrested. The two old men who had stayed behind in the village because of illness were brought to court to give evidence against them. In passing sentence, the Magistrate said that as old people, they were supposed to be wise and advise young people against fighting the White man; instead they had done a stupid thing and encouraged the youth to rebel against authority despite the fact that they (old men) had been defeated in the last century and knew the fighting power of the White man. If they had succeeded in their aims, said the magistrate, they would have brought great suffering among both White and Black. Because of their stupidity, he was going to sentence them each to 18 months imprisonment. He was well aware of their age which, in ordinary cases would have been considered in their favour, but in this particular case he would have no pity for them. They had declared war against the White man, therefore he would make an example of them to other Blacks to show what happens to those who took up spears against the regime. After telling me this the old man coughed continuously.

Oom Dellie came and stood before him with his stick, grinning. "What is this?" he said to the old man after he had finished coughing, pointing with his stick at the little heap of stone which had been crushed by the old man. The old man looked at him with his wrinkled face and continued crushing the quarry stones. The cough came back and his chest exploded at last. He fell backwards as though his lungs had disintegrated. For the first time I saw pity on Oom Dellie's face. Meintjies was already at his side.

"He does not want to work baas," said Meintjies. Oom Dellie ignored his remark. "Stand up 'ou-man'," said Oom Dellie helping him up. The old man stood up and removed the wire mesh from his eyes.

"Arme skepsel," (poor creature), said Oom Dellie, "go and clean that yard," he pointed at the toolshed where we ate our lunch, "and when you are tired, you can sit down and rest." The old man understood Afrikaans. He tottered slowly towards the yard to do as Oom Dellie had commanded him. It was the first time I saw Oom Dellie showing mercy to a political prisoner. I was to see him again the second time in April 1966 during the second hunger strike campaign.

10. *The Big Six*

There was tension at lunch time one day while we were eating in the toolshed. As usual the Big Six were sitting and facing where the sun rises and the Big Fives were sitting and facing sunset. We political prisoners sat inbetween the two gangs. Between us and the Big Six there was a little space. I saw one young light complexioned member of the Big Six going to stand in that space whereupon he stood at attention. All of us were busy eating. Then Dladla, Chief Justice of the Big Six, approached the man who was standing in the little space. Dladla flexed his muscles and stood in front of the man. And then, wham! He hit him full blast on the face. The man hardly moved either left or right. He still stood at attention. Wham! Another full blast on his left cheek this time.

"What's going on?" I asked one of the comrades.

"Punishment for resigning from the Big Six," was the reply I got.

Wham! On the right cheek again. Another full blast and he staggers. The Chief Justice points a finger at him. He stands at attention again. "That one is not counted," said the man next to me, "once he shifts from his position or staggers, that clap is not counted. All in all he's going to be clapped eight times."

Wham! He maintains his balance but more blood comes out of his mouth. Whack! Blood begins to come out of his nostrils. He doesn't wipe or remove it. Whang! He falls down to the ground, touching the earth with his hands. He quickly jumps up and stands at attention again. Wham! He doesn't move. He maintains balance, looking straight ahead. Whack! More blood flows from mouth and nostrils and he spits out something. Our eyes follow it. It is a tooth. Whang! He closes his eyes. More blood begins to flow from mouth and nostrils. It's as though he's praying and thanking God that at last the ordeal is over. He's no longer a member of the Big Six. He can now remain an independent or go to join the Big Fives. He's no longer going to be assigned missions of stabbing warders or the Big Fives. And if he behaves himself well, that is if he can allow anything to be done to him by any of the gangs and keep quiet or be made a wyfie, then he'll finish his sentence one day and see his family.

As soon as the Chief Justice was through with the punishment, he shook his victim's hand. And the victim went away, while the Big Fives applauded. Another toothless old man came to stand opposite the Chief Justice. He faced up and stood at attention. He too was resigning from the Big Six. This wagon kept on moving but was never arriving at any destination. I could imagine him thinking of the many fierce battles fought against warders and the Big Fives, but there had been no achievement. Instead new Big Fives were being born every other day. If only he had been an independent and not joined any of these damned prison gangs, he would probably have long been released on parole. The Chief Justice prepared himself. He rubbed and flexed his biceps and triceps, breathed in and out and then . . . wham! The old man tumbled down and rolled over, lying face up. He looked at Chief Justice Dladla and saw him flexing his muscles waiting for him to stand up and receive another wallop again. When I looked at Oom Dellie's office, I saw him and three other warders watching the spectacle.

The old man stood up slowly and as soon as he was upright, he reluctantly showed the Victory Sign. A twickering wise smile showed on his lips and then he spat blood. In excitement Chief Justice Dladla gave him the Victory Sign, hugged him and shook his hand. It was all over now. The old man had rescinded his resignation from the Big Six. He wouldn't have withstood the eight claps of resignation. Many prisoners including the warders laughed and the Big Six welcomed him back.

He showed the Victory Sign once again and turned round to face us. "I was a soldier under General Montgomery in North Africa in the Second World War against the Germans," he said with a sombre expression, "up to now I'm still fighting the Germans." One could see by the many scars on his face and limbs that he had been engaged in many battles. His Big Six pals hugged him in excitement. After the hugging and the congratulations, he went back to the very spot where he had been hit. He stood at attention. Face half-wrinkled, sad eyes which had seen much of the darker side of man, light-complexioned, sunburnt, he stood there immobile, arms at his sides. When I looked at where his eyes were cast, I saw a cargo ship gliding slowly towards Cape Town harbour. I guessed that his thoughts were no longer in Robben island. They were far away in North Africa; remembering fellow black soldiers they had buried there during the fight against Fascism. Hadn't they marched from Cape Town to Cairo led by 'Slim' Janie Smuts, destroying Fascism all along the way, holding the Union Jack aloft, capturing the Nazi German and Fascist Italian standards? Hadn't they withstood the North African heat, sandstorms, sand-dunes and the cold and windy Mediterranean winter? Hadn't they been captured by Rommel at Tobruk and everything had looked gloomy for the Empire at the time? And hadn't Montgomery come up to turn the tables and lead them from victory to victory up to Berlin the headquarters of the Big Fives? "BERLIN!!! BERLIN!!! BERLIN!!!" hadn't they cried and shouted as they doubled their march behind the tanks on their way to that Nazi fortress only to find to their dismay, the Red Flag already flying there?

I saw his lips twitching. Did he remember Victory Day and the shouts of "Pula! Pula!" (Rain! Rain!) and "Nala! Nala!" (Prosperity! Prosperity!) on their return back home when they had been heroes who had saved mankind from the inhuman brutalities of Fascism? And hadn't King George the Sixth personally come to South Africa in 1947 to thank them and all those who helped in the struggle against Fascism? And hadn't they sang 'God Save the King' until their voices were hoarse? Or did he remember perhaps that while they had gone up north fighting Fascism and Nazism, it had reared its tentacles down south and in two years' time, the Big Fives would be in power both inside and outside prison and the struggle against them had to begin once again, first with knives and other crude deadly instruments?

He yawned and afterwards shook his head despondently.

Georgie called him. With a sad expression the old man responded to his leader's call and went to sit next to him on his haunches. Georgie then produced an handkerchief-sized red cloth, waved it up for some time and then brought it down again. "There is going to be war again," said the man next to me, "someone is going to be stabbed."

Later on word went around amongst us political prisoners. The message was from the Big Six. It instructed us to be careful on our way back to the prison, during tauza and during supper; some members of the Big Fives had been sentenced to death and they were going to be knifed. The Big Six did not want us to be involved in the fighting.

On the way to prison, we took the road passing near Sobukwe's cell. Once again we saluted him by removing our caps as we passed by. He had been inside his cell and was attracted by the noise from the warders and the Big Fives as they screamed at us as though we were cattle being driven to a dip. He went to stand in the garden, scooped the earth and let it slowly fall back to the ground. He was reminding us that what we were suffering for was the land question. After we had seen him we really felt highly inspired.

As we went into the tauza yard we did not know what was going to happen. Maybe, some of us were going to join the Big Six in attacking the Big Fives. One may never know, especially where the hatred was as deep-seated as it was between us and the Big Fives. We stripped naked and stood in lines ready for the tauza.

Fynkyk, one of the Big Fives, was busy giving one of the warders who was searching him, his clothes. (The Big Fives, for their own safety, always ran to be in front for tauza). Then he sprang up to do the tauza, his right leg kicking sideways in a side-kick. When he came down, I saw a sharp instrument from the man behind him going into his neck, pulled out and thrust into his shoulder blade. Blood shot out and poured over the bewildered warder, while Fynkyk fell groaning to the sand. The assailant disappeared as quickly as he had appeared, leaving the knife (a crude instrument) lying on the sand. But some of the Big Fives had seen him. It was the toothless old man, the Second World War veteran, who had wanted to resign from the Big Six during lunchtime and had rescinded his resignation after failing to withstand the eight claps. The warders were on him with batons. Blow upon blow landed on his head and he lay flat as though dead. The head, and only his head was being hit. Then his legs began to kick and I guessed that he was dying. Then the warders left him. The hospital Big Fives assistants came rushing with a stretcher and removed Fynkyk. After about 30 minutes, the same assistants came with a wheelbarrow, picked up the old man who was still unconscious and threw him into it as though he was a bag of potatoes and went to empty their load in a kulukud.

After tauza we went to take our food and sat on our haunches squatting, eating and looking behind and at the sides for any attacks. Then I heard the rushing of feet followed by 'hosh' the fighting slogan of the Big Six. There was some screaming and the rushing of feet coming from behind where I was squatting. Dishes tumbled as people ran in all directions. I also stood up and somebody who came running collided with me and my dish, half-filled with maize-porridge and a finger-sized piece of half-cooked meat, went to fall two metres away. The warders came in with batons to restore order. But they were too late. Three members of the Big Fives, among them Meintjies, had been stabbed in the deliberate confusion which had been created by the Big Six. And we political prisoners had been taken up by the confusion and scattered in all directions. Three crude weapons lay next to each of the stabbed Big Fives. It was not known who had done the stabbing or how the knives had found their way inside the prison after such thorough searching and such strict security. Still hungry, we went to queue before our cells. We left the warders and the Big Fives bamboozled. The three injured Big Fives were carried away to the prison hospital. Chief Warder Theron was not there that afternoon, he was in the Old Prison. His deputy, Head Warder van Heerden, just did not know how to respond to the stabbing of the Big Fives.

After we had been locked up in our cells, we heard a report from one of the comrades who were working in the Losspan that a warder had committed suicide that morning near where the foundations were being dug for the new hospital. He had first tried to kill one of our comrades for no apparent reason and missed him. Then he turned the FN rifle at his own head and blew his brains out. I know the warder, he was often morose and temperamental. It just shows some of the agonies our enemies are also undergoing in order to maintain White supremacy.

* * *

I wonder whether the priest from the Anglican Church will be coming next weekend. Many prisoners are looking forward to his sermons. Last week the service was conducted by a Boer dominee from the Nederduitse Gereformeerde Kerk. As we are no longer taken to the church along the main road to the dorpie, the service was held in a cell at the Zinktronk. The dominee was preaching in Xhosa and many prisoners left the service fed up. His sermon was on the devil and the type of person that the devil is. The devil, said the dominee, is always going in and out of the hearts of the pople and telling them to steal, kill, commit adultery and other sins; but once a person is in trouble, the devil runs away. The devil will take you to prison, but once there, will leave you in chains and laugh at you. The devil, Lucifer, will make you commit many sins so that when you die, he should go and cast you in the ever-burning fires of hot hell. By then it will be too late for salvation. You must change your hearts now and while there is still time. You must repent for your ignominous sins and the Lord will have mercy and accept you back. You must stop eating, drinking and dreaming sins. For if you don't, Lucifer with his long tail, will be awaiting you when you die in the red-hot fires of hell where there will be gnashing of teeth for those of you who don't repent. Many prisoners, criminal convicts included, are fed up with his sermons. Some have indicated that they will never go to church again. Listening to the sermon of the dominee was a galling experience. Some of the comrades suspect that he's being used by the government. I don't believe this. The Nederduitse Gereformeerde Kerk is the spiritual guide of the government. It preaches that we Blacks are the cursed descendents of Ham destined to be hewers of wood and drawers of water for Europeans.

11. *Old Man Vakalisa*

One night in February almost two months after we were put in chains at the Leeuwkop Maximum Prison, old man Vakalisa called our attention. He has developed a terrible cough. I suspect he has TB. We all sat up in our beddings to listen to him. He looks as though he's no longer of this world. His eyes seem to be looking far away, but in actual fact he's only looking at the wall opposite. He opens his mouth, his lips move, but no voice comes out. There is complete silence in the cell. Old man Tolepi is sitting next to me. We all look pitifully at old man Vakalisa. He's probably going to bid us farewell. The man is dying and they're refusing him admission at the prison hospital. He opens his lips once again and no voice comes out. Someone starts a song. We sing it drearily as though we are in a vigil, over a corpse. Old man Vakalisa's head is tilted to one side as though he can no longer control the muscles of his neck. The song comes to a slow ending. We are quiet again. The old man begins to speak. His lips twitch open. At last a voice comes out. But it is weak and comes out with some effort. He speaks slowly and bids us farewell.

"Boys," he begins, "I have been in this struggle for the last 20 years and I've done my best to see to it that our people get freedom. I left the ANC because it had abandoned the 1949 nation-building Programme of Action. I'm one of the founder members of the PAC with Sobukwe, Leballo and others. This is the second time I'm imprisoned for my beliefs. The first time was in 1960 for the Anti-Pass Campaign when I served 18 months. This time the Boers have given me five years. I've hardly finished a year of those five and my body is now giving in, though the spirit is still willing to continue with the fight. I have called you to give you my farewell and to encourage you to continue with this noble work of liberating our people. In concluding, I'll quote from the dying words of St Paul to his son in the Second Book of Timothy Chapter 4, Verse 6: "Because my health is now failing, my time for departure has now come. I have fought a good fight; I have finished my journey; have kept the faith and have defeated my enemies. Henceforth I shall be provided with a crown, which the Lord, the righteous judge, shall give me at that day; and not only to me, but unto all them also that loved to have their eyes opened. Goodbye boys." His voice fades away. There is complete silence once again and hardly any movement. We are paralysed in visualising our first death in Robben Island from the Leeuwkop group.

Old man Tolepi is the first to move. He stands up and goes to Vakalisa. He first prepares his bedding and then holds him and stretches him on the sisal mat. He takes his three blankets and covers him with them, with only the head exposed. In silence our eyes watch old man Tolepi's every instinctive movement which shows that he's used to such occurrences from the farm in Nigel where most probably there were frequent deaths. When he finishes he moves slowly and silently to his bedding and sits down. Vakalisa's face is pale. His breathing comes out irregularly. He already looks like a corpse. One comrade begins a song:

'Senzeni na e-Afrika,   'What have we done in Africa,
I-Afrika ikhaya lami,   Africa is my home.
Asihambi e-Afrika.'   We won't leave Africa.'

We sing it low and slowly and repeat it several times. Many of us are deeply touched. Old man Vakalisa, a devout Christian of the Methodist Church, was like a father to most of us who were still in our youth. He was in his late 40s but years of constant struggle and imprisonment had ultimately broken him. He was a close comrade of our President Mangaliso Sobukwe. He was a veteran in the liberation struggle for African freedom. And now he was going to leave us. He was very close to me. I'm deeply moved. I had been touched like this before — some years back in other circumstances like those prevailing in Robben Island. It seemed then as if it was only yesterday. How fast time flies. I remember now it was in 1955/56.

* * *

The slum location of Jabavu was situated about 15 miles to the south-west of the city of Johannesburg. It lay between White city, a location of three- and four-roomed identical matchbox houses which had been built by the City Council of Johannesburg, and Moroka, another slum location identical to Jabavu. Moroka and Jabavu were built of mud-bricks, reed, sacks, pieces of corrugated iron, four-gallon tin containers which had been panel beaten and joined together and many other fittings which could be used to make a hovel.

The distance between the adjacent hovels was a mere yard. They were so close to one another that at night you could actually hear the squeaking of the antiquated bed when the man and wife next door were engaged in their conjugal rights.

The streets of Jabavu were very narrow; in fact, they could be called alleys. When you stood at your door you could actually see inside the house opposite. These alleys were always littered with pools of dirty stinking water where toddlers gleefully bathed and splashed the water about when no one was there to take care of them.

Our hovel which had been built of unequal pieces of corrugated iron and old rusty flattened four-gallon paraffin tin containers, had been divided into four closets. Aunt Bellina and her eldest daughter occupied one, her two elder sons occupied another, Abel occupied another (I often shared this room when I was in Jabavu two or three times a week) and the fourth stood for a kitchen (my two sisters slept here).

It was dangerous and unwise to have windows in Jabavu, for any thief passing through the small passages which divided the hovels could easily see and snatch anything inside. As a result only small apertures were made to represent windows, thus making the hovels dark inside even during day time. But despite the sufferings, the people of Jabavu were very clean and so too were the hovels once one entered inside. With the exception of the dirty pools of water which were the result of lack of proper drainage facilities, their surroundings were also clean. They usually carted rubbish to dustbins which were provided for every street.

Inbetween the Sections there were large corrugated iron structures almost 18 yards long and six feet wide with no roofing on top. These were the toilets which the City Council of Johannesburg had benevolently built. Every Section had two such structures: one for men and boys and the other for women and girls. There was absolutely no privacy at all. Inside these structures a number of small holes stood close to one another — 18 in all. When you entered one of these toilets you'd find a long row of squatting people having bowel movements simultaneously and hear all the different sounds that came from above and below. You'd wait until one finished and rush quickly to go and squat.

In the mornings there were always queues which formed as people were anxious to relieve themselves quickly and then rush to the bus-stop to hurry to work. When it rained and you were hard pressed, there was hell to play. The summer rains in Johannesburg always came down hard and violently and sometimes in hailstorms. There is nothing as searing and frustrating as having a bowel movement while the hailstones bashed on your head with rapid frequency. Sometimes a person would rush from the communal toilet through the tearing rain and hailstones back to his hovel, only to find the roof blown off or one of the mud walls having crumbled, his wife and children huddled together in some dark corner anxiously waiting for him to help. The people of Jabavu and Moroka had to bear all that. After all it was part of that nice parcel of Western civilisation and Christianity which our kind masters had brought along from civilised Europe to the black savages of Africa.

To crown it all, the good City Council of Johannesburg (which was predominantly composed of English speaking liberals) arranged for a mobile film unit to show horrow and gangster (Western) films once a week in Jabavu. And the young curious boys and girls with their innocent minds unpolluted and thirsty for education quickly acquired the knowledge of fighting with fists, stabbing and shooting and learning about the survival of the fittest. Month after month and year after year, these horrors and stabbings and shoot-outs were repeatedly drummed into their minds. The teachers were many: Durango Kid, Zorro and Jesse James. And there was Fu Manchu, Dracula and the Frankenstein monster. To show the superiority of Whites over Blacks there was Tarzan and Jane always followed by a bunch of panicky, semi-nude Blacks with tattoos over their faces, carrying big boxes for their master. And there was the big iron pot filled with water where Tarzan was to be cooked and eaten by the black savages; but as always, he miraculously escaped while the savages were beating drums and engaged in wild exotic dances.

There was a small police station built of corrugated iron sheets which was situated in Moroka and was supposed to restore law and order in the locations of Jabavu, Moroka and White City. It was manned by African policemen who were armed with long spears. They were no match for the gangs that ravaged in these locations armed with pistols. As a result 'law and order' was maintained by these marauding gangs which thrived on the law-abiding workers. Under such circumstances there was bound to be anarchy.

At the end of the small street passing near aunt Bellina's hovel in Section JX, there was a communal toilet for men. And next to this toilet there was a big boulder of rock which stood on the street side. For some time now a man clad in a brown lumber jacket with a small goatee, used to stand on top of this boulder every morning and watch the people as they walked hurriedly past on their way to the bus-stop near the Mavis Isaacson Hall. Some people greeted him and others avoided his eyes. For this man was a great terror in Jabavu and his name was Peter 'the goatee'. Being unemployed, he lived on the sweat of other people.

A gang warfare erupted in December 1954 in Jabavu and continued throughout 1955 taking a heavy toll of many African youths. Peter 'the goatee' and Boy Sevenpence and their gang mostly living in Jabavu East were fighting against the Terrors (many of them members of the Moroka Terrors Football Club — a prominent soccer club in Jabavu which was only second to Moroka Swallows Football Club). The first prominent victim of the gang warfare was Fire Nkuna who played forward for the Moroka Terrors Football Club. One afternoon he was ambushed near the de Jenga Fish and Chips restaurant next to the Mavis Isaacson Hall and was shot dead. He was soon followed by other prominent players and supporters of the club. From then on it was a shoot-out between the two gangs. From the beginning my cousin Abel had been involved in the gang war and belonged to the Terrors for which club he played.

One night while I was at my aunt's house, there was a knock at the door. When I asked who it was, the person replied in a familiar voice that he was the owner of the house. I went to open the door and behold! It was my father. After sitting down, he wanted to know where Abel was. I told him that since I had arrived I had not seen him. He went to see my aunt and they talked together in low tones for a long time in her bedroom. Later Abel came and I told him that the old man had come to see him. When my father heard Abel's voice, he came to join us. He told Abel that he was worried about what was happening in Jabavu, in particular about the fighting between the two gangs and Abel's role in it. He further explained that all this fighting between the two gangs was caused by the system which created unemployment and frustrations among the black youths. And he revealed that he had already talked to Peter 'the Goatee' about bringing the fighting to an end.

"The government is responsible for all these senseless killings" said my father in conclusion.

"How is the government responsible?" asked Abel, "Did it send 'the Goatee' to harass people and kill those of our brothers we have already buried?"

"No my nephew," said my father, "the government did not send him to kill anybody. What the government and the City Council did was to create conditions knowing full well what the end results would be. Look at the hovels in which we are staying and compare them with the luxurious houses in which Europeans stay in the suburbs. Just look at the petty sums of money we are getting as wages and compare it with the fat cheques given to idle White workers at the end of every month. Look at our schools and the type of education given to our children and compare all this with the schools and the type of education given to White children. We have been crying for more police protection; and what do we have? A small police station in Moroka with a few Black policemen armed with long spears; and what do you find in the city suburbs where Whites stay? Every street is patrolled hourly by mobile, well-armed Black and White policemen. It is therefore frustration in our youths who cannot get employment and when employed, are underpaid, that has brought about the present mess in Jabavu. Peter 'the Goatee' and all the gangsters here in Jabavu, including yourself, are therefore the products of the present system. That is why you find that there are no gangsters in the White suburbs who are at each other's throats like you, because the environment there is conducive to a better life and better employment opportunities for European youths. My aim therefore in talking to you like this is first, to bring about an end to this senseless self-slaughter of our youths and afterwards to rally you to join uVukayibambe (The ANC Youth League) so that we can fight against the present system on a national scale."

"What was the Goatee's reply to your pleas?" asked Abel.

"He told me that it was one of my old jokes," said my father.

"How can we then bury the hatchet if the Goatee says you are joking? Go and try him again and tell him you are serious about it."

My father looked at Abel for some time and then shook his head sadly. "Are you sleeping here?" he asked, referring to me.

"Yes," I said.

"Well, I'm now going," he said taking his hat.

"You can't walk alone at this time of the night," said Abel, "I'll go with you."

My father stood up and went to bid farewell to aunt Bellina while Abel went to his small bedroom to load his two pistols. As I watched them going out, I thought of the humiliation that my father suffered in 1950 in Kliptown when he had been punched by the Boer policeman Snyman before our eyes. Before then, Abel and I used to view him as our demi-God; but afterwards all our respect for him had disappeared: our demi-God had been punched and punched until my mother had to come to his rescue. Since then we had never taken him seriously in any advice that he gave us.

It was the first time I heard him talking politics that day when he told Abel that the government and the City Council of Johannesburg were responsible for all the anarchy in Jabavu. Ever since aunt Bellina told me way back in 1949 that he was a member of the ANC Youth League, I had never heard him mention the ANC in his discussions.

By this time Abel was a high-ranking leader of the Terrors. He returned late and sometimes did not sleep at my aunt's house and neither did he sleep at home in Moroka. He had a good supply of pistols and usually carried two at a time. On several occasions aunt Bellina and my mother tried to talk him out of gangsterism but to no avail. He had left school in 1954 after passing his standard five examinations saying that he saw no purpose in furthering his education. Since then he had not worked but carried a lot of money.

"Where did you get this money Abel?" my mother asked him one day when she saw him producing a big roll of pound notes.

"It's protection money," Abel said, "many people pay a protection fee for their own safety."

He usually carried with him Willard Motley's *Knock on any Door*. And he read it avidly always thumbing back through the pages he had already read. He was always dressed in black trousers, a balck shirt and a black lumber-jacket. American Westerns were his favourite films. He was quick to draw his guns. And once he had drawn them, he usually fired. Many other gangsters feared Abel and I lived under his umbrella. No one dared touch me in Moroka and Jabavu. By now he was called Jack of the Terrors.

One afternoon while I was sitting with my father outside our hovel in Moroka, I saw a group of gangsters coming up our small street in Section AN. They were about 15 in number. Abel was sleeping inside my small room. When I looked closer I recognised the man walking in front who was clad in a brown lumber-jacket and had a small goatee to be Peter 'the Goatee'. And I froze. They were now too near our house and there was no way in which I could inform Abel. Peter, Boy Sevenpence and four others stopped near my father and the others went to stand at the back of our house. They were all armed with pistols, long knives and axes.

"It's you Peter," said my father.

"Afternoon uncle," said 'the Goatee'. (All the gangsters in Jabavu used to refer to my father as uncle).

"What do you want in my house Peter?" asked my father; "You know I don't want people of your type inside my house."

"You once told me a good story about uVukayibambe," said Peter mockingly. "I have now brought my whole gang to listen to your story uncle. We want to go in, sit down and listen to what you have to say about the government and the City Council."

"Go into my house armed?" asked my father.

"These weapons are for our own protection uncle," was the reply from Peter.

"I told you a year ago that I don't want to see you again in my house Peter," said my father, "if you go in without permission I guess you know the consequences."

"There's a small puppy," said Peter, "a very small brat that keeps on yelping at me wherever I go and when I want to kick it, it always runs away. I understand that it always hides here in your house. It is a nuisance to me. I want to kick it just once, so that never again should it trouble me."

"There is no puppy here in this house," said my father aggressively, "and if I have a puppy which has been yelping at you in the streets, go and look for it in the streets then, but not here in my house."

"Where is your cousin?" Peter asked me aggressively.

"I left him in Jabavu in the morning," I said meekly.

"Tell him," said Peter with a little smile, "that I'm like a tiger which has many stripes."

He looked at my father and smiled wisely at him. "Goodbye uncle," he said to my father, "see you sometime about uVukayibambe."

"Okay Peter," said my father.

"Let's go," he told his henchmen. They all followed him on their hunt for their opponents.

When I went to wake my cousin, I found him sitting on top of the bed holding his two pistols. He had heard everything. My father had saved his life. Not only had he saved his life, but he had once again established himself to Abel and I as a man; once again we idolised him.

Peter 'the Goatee' and Boy Sevenpence struck again. They killed a number of high ranking members of the Terrors, and created panic throughout the gang. Some fled Jabavu and went to hibernate in the East and West Rands. Others went to the countryside. Peter and Boy Sevenpence had scored a surprise victory. It was then that my cousin Abel emerged as the leader of the Terrors and rallied his depleted forces to stage an extermination campaign. He went to Moroka Location to recruit more members and scoured the neighbouring location of White City Jabavu. He cemented the existing alliance with the Spoilers gang of Alexandra Township who were engaged in a bloody war with the Msomi Gang for the domination of the township. This alliance paid him dividends. It provided the Terrors with an inexhaustible supply of pistols. Next he forced many Taxi owners and drivers to supply him with information about the presence of Peter and Boy Sevenpence.

Abel conducted lightning raids in Jabavu East and led raiding parties in the trains and buses travelling between Soweto and the city of Johannesburg. But Peter and Boy Sevenpence were nowhere to be seen. Peter's brother Tsehla, once a close friend of one of my cousins, was uncovered in one such raid. He was stabbed and hacked with axes. They left him for dead and went on with their operation. Tsehla did not die. Friends of the family took him to the Baragwanath Hospital. And Abel, my cousin, heard of this. He then led a party to follow him up there. Tsehla was found in the operation theatre while the doctors were busy with him. When the gangsters, led by Abel, entered the theatre with their big knives, axes and waving pistols, the doctors and nurses fled. Tsehla was chopped with axes and his skull cracked open. There was to be no operation on him this time.

My cousin led another raiding party to Pimville location, Peter's new stronghold. The residents of Pimville panicked as gunshots rang out and blood flowed during daytime. Some of Peter's lieutenants died in this raid but he, Boy Sevenpence and four others were nowhere to be seen. Then information leaked that they had earlier been arrested for some of the murders they had committed in Jabavu. My cousin was now a hero.

When Christmas of 1955 approached there was jubilation in Jabavu. The residents sighed in relief. At last there was going to be peace. Many people had died fighting and other through cross-fire, others through mistaken identity. The exact number of the dead in Jabavu, Moroka, White City and Pimville was never known. My cousin alone killed 11 people during the fighting. His demeanor had now changed. He seldom smiled now. I used to watch with astonishment gangsters and other members of the underworld coming to pay him homage at my aunt's hovel and to give reports. Jack of the Terrors was now boss and his word was law. A little twickering smile on his lips used to spread happiness and security to those in his company. Even girls were no problem. They idolised him and he used to pick and choose according to his whims.

The Christmas Day of 1955 was a festive occasion in Jabavu. You could hear people laughing heartily aloud, something they had not been able to enjoy for some time. Some men dressed in women's skirts, blouses and pinafores carrying one-gallon tins of African beer or some other concoction, and some women and young girls clad in men's trousers, shirts and overalls, their large breasts jutting out of their chests, some waving cakes and bones, moved from Section to Section in merriment celebrating Christmas, the birth of Jesus Christ. There were cries of "Merry Christmas" everywhere and the hearty response of "same to you". Even dogs barked gleefully and twirled their tails jubilantly as they saw the faces of their masters sparkling with life. Others scratched for bones they had hid long before the fighting. Other dogs which had fled Jabavu during the fighting also returned and were welcomed back by those which had stayed behind. The season of mating had come.

The offal dealers between Mavis Isaacson Hall and Section JZ also returned. The residents of Jabavu could now buy their favourite meat again. And the flies which had disappeared with the offal meat also returned to buzz once again at their favourite joints. They buzzed gleefully as though indicating their happiness that there was peace in Jabavu at last.

'Ngiyiphethe' the bearded beef seller, also appeared on his bicycle in the narrow streets of Jabavu with a broad smile on his face chanting his favour advertisement poem:

"We-mama...	Hey mother...
Awuvele...	Come out...
Ubone...	And see...
Inyama...	The meat...
Embomvu...	It's red...
Ngiyiphethe...	I've got it...
Ngiyiphethe-bo...	I've got it, man...
Ngiyiphethe...	I've got it...
Ngiyiphethe-bo...	I've got it man...
Awu, ngiyiphethe!"	Hey! I've got it.

Children scurried about to call their mothers out of their hovels to come out, see and buy Ngiyiphethne's meat. Others followed him from street to street advertising the meat together with Ngiyiphethe. And he never forget to impress upon the meat buyers of Jabavu that his meat never got finished; that it was man's teeth instead that wore out.

The market women returned to sell 'maheu' and boiled maize. Drunkards once again stumbled about on wobbly knees. The 'shebeen' queens were also happy. No more were they now going to tell their customers to drink in silence. And no more were their 'shebeens' going to be raided by the Terrors looking for Peter 'the Goatee' and his men or *vice versa*. Lunatics, with ruffled hair, attired as usual in various dirty rags which only got washed when it rained, also came out gleefully moving from street to street to pick once again at papers, orange and banana peels. And groups of jubilant children clapping their hands for the lunatics were also there to follow and applaud them from one section of Jabavu to another.

Church bells began to toll loudly calling their congregations back to go and praise the Lord. Dladla's travelling amplifier could be seen once again with young boys and girls, including my younger sister Sonto, colourfully attired, jiving, as coins were thrown by onlookers for entertainment.

In the midst of this jubilation, my cousin was not there. My parents and aunt Bellina had persuaded him to visit Harrismith location where we have some relatives and also Eeram, to see my maternal grandparents. When he came back after the Christmas holidays he appeared to have been ruffled by what he had seen there in the Boer farms. "It's terrible down there," he told me after his arrival, "those people there are suffering and living miserable lives. You must go and see it yourself."

"I'm going there next year," I said.

"Are you still attending those ANC meetings?" I nodded.

"Speaking won't help my cousin," he said, "our people have to

fight and we're there if there's to be any fighting."
"The time for that has not yet come," I said.
"Meanwhile our people are dying!" I did not respond.

Early in January 1956 my cousin was arrested. He had shot and injured a policeman. He was locked up at The Fort Prison (No.4) where Peter 'the Goatee' and Boy Sevenpence were also awaiting trial. We were worried in the family; not about his having shot the policeman (we all hated them) but about the confrontation that was going to take place in prison between him and 'the Goatee'. I did not know then, as I do now, that big-shots don't fight each other in prison but only use their cronies to do the fighting for them. Relatives hurried to go and see him at the Fort. I also followed. I found him happy and relaxed.

"I get my food from the other prisoners," he told me.

"Do you have many friends here? I asked.

"My friends the Spoilers are here and we are running this prison," he said.

"Where is the 'Goatee'?" I asked.

"Ah, Peter," he said nonchantly, "he's here but in another Section; we all belong to the Big Fives here." I did not know then what the Big Fives was.

My cousin stayed at the Fort Prison from January to March 1956. The Terrors threatened all the witnesses who were supposed to give evidence against their leader. The charges against him were dropped and he was released. When my cousin came back from prison there was a family reunion. That night we had a family meeting to discuss the future of Abel.

"You must leave this type of life my nephew," my father said to him during the meeting.

"I'm prepared to leave this type of life," said Abel, "I've now fulfilled my life's ambition, I've shot and wounded a policeman in vengeance for your arrest and subsequent conviction in 1950 and I'm now boss of the Terrors. Powerful people bow before me. I'm satisfied with my achievements and can now retire. But after retirement what else can I do?"

"You can go and work Abel," said my mother, "if you don't work, you won't be able to leave gangsterism."

"Or you can go back to school to finish your standard six," said aunt Bellina, "you are still young."

"Here is your uncle," said my mother, "when you were a toddler he was a gangster in Sophiatown — a big-time gangster — so much so that many people who knew him then still respect him; but with your mother we prevailed on him and he retired and joined the ANC Youth League. Why can't you do the same?"

"I shall think it over," said Abel, "give me time to review my whole life."

When the meeting ended we found that some of his friends were already waiting for him outside. They left with him and disappeared into the dark night.

It became difficult for my cousin to part with his gangster friends. And money kept pouring in. It soon became evident that only a change of environment could separate him from his underworld friends. It also became obvious that he could no longer sit in a classroom before a teacher. He already knew too much of the ways of the world and the idolisation that he got from students, especially the girls, would make him a misfit in any school. I discussed this with my parents and aunt Bellina and they agreed with me that only a change of environment could rehabilitate him.

"But where can he go?" asked my mother.

"Back to Harrismith," said aunt Bellina.

"He doesn't want to see that place again," I told them.

"I've got fears for his life," said my mother, "I don't trust some of his friends; they seem treacherous. They are only flattering him now and will stab him in the back as soon as he turns his his back. Remember how your father was betrayed by Chain in Kliptown?"

I nodded.

"If only he could go to Harrismith," said aunt Bellina, "stay for some time there and breathe the cool air from the Drankenberg mountains, otherwise we're going to lose him."

One day as I dropped from the school bus, I met him at the bus-stop near the Mavis Isaacson Hall, waiting for someone. A girl also dropped from the bus and came to where we were standing. I knew the girl, she was doing her Form One, a class below me at Orlando High School.

"Why don't you visit me any longer?" she asked, holding Abel's hand.

"He'll visit you now," said Abel pointing at me.

"Who's he?" enquired the girl.

"He's your future husband," he said, "Moses, the one I've always been telling you about." The girl blushed and looked at me shyly.

"Moses, this is your future wife."

"What do you mean?" she asked jumping back and scrutinising me closely.

"You'll love him as you've loved me," said Abel.

"You should be joking," said the girl, "but you almost look alike." I looked at this beautiful innocent girl and fell in love with her. But funny, I had never thought of it before.

"Cousin, this is Nomsa," said Abel, "I've already told her a lot about you."

"We left Abel at the bus-stop and went down the road acquainting ourselves with each other. "I will take you as far as your home," I told her, "and then I shall come and see you in the evening."

"I'll be busy today," she said, "why can't we meet tomorrow at school?"

"Okay then," I said. I took her as far as her home, bade her goodbye and crossed the few streets to aunt Bellina's house, skirting the little pools of dirty water that always permeated the streets of Jabavu.

That night Abel told me that he had protected Nomsa from being molested by gangsters on numberous occasions. He liked the girl and wished me to have an affair with her. He had already told her so. "She's a good girl," he said, "and well-behaved. I wish you all the luck with her. The first day I saw her, I thought about you and guessed that you'd make a good match."

I told him that from what I had seen of her, I had been impressed. Even at school she was quiet and studious. I had not yet approached her but would do so in due course. "She's yours," said my cousin emphatically.

When I saw Nomsa at school the following day, I did not beat about the bush. We spent the lunch period together and I told her that since Abel had already discussed everything with her, I was only going to confirm what he had already told her. "What a queer way of making a proposal," she objected, "I never thought you'd approach me like this."

"How did you think I was going to approach you?"

"Like it is always done," she said.

"And how is it done?"

"Well, you must tell me that you love me," she said looking down.

"I love you then," I said. She blushed and said it was too sudden; I did not even know her character.

"But my cousin has already told me about your character," I said.

"And how did he say it is?"

"He said it was impeccable."

"He was exaggerating," she said, "I'm a naughty girl."

"I want you to become my girl friend," I told her.

"You'll have to wait," she said, "I'll have to think it over. Give me a week."

"I want to see you tonight," I said.

"I'll have to ask for permission from my mother," she said.

"I'll come and fetch you from your home."

"Come at 7.00pm," she said.

When my mother returned from work at 6.30pm she told me that her fears about Abel were coming back. He should go back to Harrismith and stay there for six months. Aunt Bellina suggested that he should go back again soon. This was supported by my father.

"He's younger than you," said aunt Bellina to me, "you should persuade him to go back immediately. He may even find a nice country girl there and settle down. Johannesburg is not good for people like him. He's too tough and rough. I don't like some of his friends, they appear treacherous."

"If only he were to join uVukayibambe," said my father, "and exhaust all his energies against the system." And then he shook his head despondently and afterwards exclaimed: "AmaBunu!!!" (The Boers!!!).

At 7.00pm I was at Nomsa's home. She introduced me to her mother and younger sister. Afterwards we went to aunt Bellina's house and I introduced her.

"Where did you get her?" asked my aunt, "she's a diamond and will make a good wife."

Nomsa blushed shyly. Abel came in and greeted Nomsa.

"This is your house," he told her, "feel at home." He went into his tiny bedroom and came out with two of his pistols.

"I want to see you," I told him.

"Is it urgent?" he asked.

"Yes," I said, "because it concerns your future."

"You're sure it doesn't concern my going to Harrismith?"

"Well," I said, taken aback, "we'll discuss it."

"I have an appointment at 9 o'clock in Moroka. I'll be back before 11 o'clock. You'll sleep here today?"

"M-m-m," I said.

"See you later then. 'Bye Nomsa," he said and stepped out.

Later Nomsa and I were standing in a passage about a street away from aunt Bellina's house. A strong, cold icy wind was blowing through our bodies. The roofs of some of the corrugated iron houses were shaking and producing constant clanking irritating sounds. It was as though they were going to be blown off as often happened whenever there were strong winds. Some of the hovels were built of mud and reed and little chunks of earth kept falling to the ground. I held Nomsa's hands as the icy winds cut through our ears which had now grown ice cold.

A car suddenly moved slowly past. Another followed close by and yet another. "They are taking your street," said Nomsa, "but why are they moving so slowly? What's happened? Let's see to which house are they going?"

"Hand in hand we followed the cars and saw them stopping in front of our house. Somebody was carried out of the car into the house.

When we saw this Nomsa's hand gripped mine tightly and I became paralysed with fear. A heart-piercing wail rang out in the cold windy winter night of July.

"It's aunt Bellina's voice," I told her with trembling lips.

"No, it cannot be my Jack," said Nomsa running towards the house. I followed.

The house was already full of people and neighbours were coming out of their hovels attracted by aunt Bellina's wailing. When I went inside the house, I saw her wailing on top of him. "It cannot be, it cannot be," she kept on repeating.

Nomsa knelt beside aunt Bellina and began to wail too. I looked around. Seven solemn faces looked forlornly at the crumpled heap before them. With a thumping heart I approached the body which lay covered with a blanket. With tremulous hands, I removed the blanket over the head. And there lay the dead face of Abel with a small bullet wound through his forehead. His face seemed peaceful and at rest. He had fulfilled his mission on earth, as he had said and also joined me to Nomsa Maliwa.

When I stood up, Mbulawa, a close friend of my brother, came to me and whispered, "It is Peter 'the Goatee's' gang. We must hunt them out now." And the gangsters left.

A few minutes later my parents arrived by taxi from Moroka. They had heard the news. My mother came and sat next to aunt Bellina, her head covered with a blanket. Only her chest moved up and down to show that she was crying silently.

"Awu!" exclaimed my father sadly, "if only he had died fighting for our freedom . . ." He could not complete the sentence and tears flowed down his face while he stood looking at the crumpled heap before him.

"How many of them have died like this," he began again, "butchering one another mercilessly for trifles? How shall our people get their freedom with the majority of our youths turned into gangsters?" Once again he shook his head despondently for some time and wept. He was to weep like that for the fate of Black youths for years.

When we woke up the following morning at 4 o'clock, old man Vakalisa was still alive, but he could no longer speak coherently. His heart-beats were irregular. I sat next to him until the warders came to count us and marched us out of the cell. I was reluctant to leave my old man. I was the last man out of the cell and my eyes could not leave his gaunt face. The old fighter was refusing to die.

A certain official clad in civilian clothes has been prowling around the island for some days. Ultimately he decided to get down to business. He called a few comrades to the office and introduced himself to them as Captain Fourie. He had a list of names of people to be called whom he wanted to interview. All the people who have seen him have come back annoyed. Captain Fourie's main duties are to try to convert political prisoners to support the Bantustan concept. He talks so nicely about the Bantustans as though there are no political prisoners who are from those barren areas. He talks of green pastures and lush plains and preserving tribal culture and traditions from being swallowed and ravaged by Western culture and values.

Captain Fourie is in his late 50s, of medium height with extraordinary large ears. He's a chain-smoker and when he talks he tries to smoothen his gruff voice. He talks of freedom for the Black man during our lifetime, in his own land with his own flag and Parliament. When comrades ask him where, he says in the Bantustans. Such impudence!!!

12. Asking for More

When we returned to prison one afternoon there was tension again during tauza. It seemed as though the Big Six were going to strike again. Three of its members had rebelled and joined the Big Fives. They did not resign formally to the Chief Justice of the Big Six. If they had done so they would each have got the eight claps of resignation, and then they would have been forgotten. Now they were going to be the first targets. For their rebellion, their blood had to flow.

Standing naked in lines, our eyes kept on looking behind and to the sides, but nothing happened. The warders were moving up and down among us with their batons ready to pounce upon any attacker. After being searched, we dressed and went to queue at the kitchen. We took our food and went to squat where we usually ate.

When Thomas Motloung got his plate of food, he found that it was too little. But when he approached the cooks, they drove him away. He went to the warder in charge at the kitchen and tried to explain his request, but he was pushed away. Jan Kleynhans and his cronies came and took his food away. They went to lock him up at the Zinktronk. When we had been locked in the cells for the night, Thomas was fetched from the Zinkktronk and taken to the square between Section A and the kitchen. They brought back the plate of food which they had earlier taken away and told him to eat it and he refused. We were all peeping through the windows and could see vividly what was going on. Jan Kleynhans was the first to hit him. Thomas parried the blows with his arms. Jan and four other warders were involved. They attacked him with batons from all sides. And that enraged all the political prisoners in Sections A, B, C and the Zinktronk who were peeping through the windows. Insults, coming simultaneously from all the Sections, were hurled at the warders. The more the insults were hurled, the more Thomas was assaulted until he tried to fight back but was overwhelmed and thrown down to the ground. More insults followed from the cells and more beatings rained on Thomas until he lay flat, immobile, unconscious. Then the insults stopped and the beatings also stopped. Many of us turned away when Thomas was pulled by one leg and dragged to the showers at the Zinktronk. There water was opened full blast from the taps onto his unconscious body.

When he recovered, he was taken back to the square again, water and blood dripping down from his clothes. Once again they gave him the food to eat and he refused. Once again he was assaulted. This time we looked aghast without making any insults. Again he became unconscious. One of the warders came with a wheelbarrow from the kitchen and he was dumped onto it. The wheelbarrow was pushed by Jan Kleynhans who emptied the load into an empty cell in the Zinktronk and locked the cell. There were no blankets or mats inside.

That was the reward for asking for some more food in Robben Island and it taught us never to commit the same mistake again. All along Chief Warder Theron had stood near the kitchen with Perdekop at his side, watching the whole spectacle, baton patting his trousers as usual.

13. *The Boulders Roll On*

There had been a rumour circulating that we were going to be released by the end of January. Many political prisoners believed this rumour, mostly among the illiterate and semi-literate peasants. A few intellectuals were also taken in. It was said that the United Nations had given South Africa up to the end of January to release political prisoners, failing which it was going to send an army. I doubted the truth of this rumour. I decided to investigate. This thing of getting released is disturbing. What is surprising is that nobody has publicly dismissed it so far. I had expected that someone would speak out against it. The month of January ended two weeks ago and thus far we have not been released. Instead there's another rumour that the Prime Minister has asked for a month's extension to the time limit. Today I was able to trace the originator of this rumour. It is Nkohla — the old man who is plagued by nightmares. I will suggest to other comrades that he be stopped from spreading his malicious rumours. They will have a demoralising effect in the long run.

* * *

Old man Tolepi no longer goes to queue for medicine at the hospital. I have been observing him these past days. On the way to and from the Quarry, there is a certain herb along the road that he always plucks and chews. At first I had thought he was chewing grass to augment the little food we are getting, but I later discovered that it was a herb called 'Umhlonyane' in Zulu. I do not know its name in English but I think it would be called one of those long Latin names. He must have learnt of the healing powers of this herb way back in the farms where there are no medical doctors but only herbalists and witch doctors. This herb must be very good because his condition has improved and there is now only one small boil remaining on his face. Yesterday I walked behind him. After he had plucked the herb, I also plucked a piece of it and chewed it. It has a strong smell and tastes bitter. I should know of such herbs so that when in future I fall ill and they refuse to attend to me at the hospital, I can resort to it.

* * *

Last night I had a bad dream. It was so bad that I woke up at night and sat up, wondering about its meaning. It was the dominee again preaching, "Thief repent — repent you rogue — you black devil — before it is too late. For the bells of hell are already ringing and calling for you — and then you shall be damned to be roasted in the everlasting fires of Lucifer. Descendant of cursed Ham, repent your wicked ways."

That is what the dominee of the Neuerduitse Gereformeerde Kerk had said in the dream when he blasted and harangued us at the cell-church. He was the only holy man and we were all rogues. Some of us had robbed and killed, others murdered in cold blood, others raped young and old women. And I was the worst of them all — I had wanted to steal White man's land.

"Repent while there is still time, you vipers — society's scourge — kick the black devil out of your black hearts. Tell the devil that you are now tired of stealing, killing, raping and robbing. Tell him that now you want to be law-abiding. Repent hypocrite — for eternal damnation is awaiting you. Repent and pay for your wicked black soul."

The warders, two standing behind and two before us had wide grins on their mouths, their faces beaming with satisfaction. The dominee was right. I'll have to turn my black heart to the White God. That is the only way in which I and those of my ilk can be saved. And the dominee will help us to repent. Next time I'll go and kneel before him and ask for his White blessings. And when I finish my sentence I shall have to obey the laws of the land — apartheid laws.

* * *

During March, 50 prisoners arrived from Leeuwkop Maximum Prison. I had been cut by a stone on my ankle at the Quarryspan and had joined the Losspan once again. At about 12 o'clock Jan Kleynhans returned with the Landbouspan to the New Prison. There were three prisoners who were walking in front who had been manacled and he kept beating them.

"Where is the Chief Warder?" asked Piet Kleynhans, his brother, to the warder in charge of our span.

"He's at the Zinktronk," said the warder. The Landbouspan was driven towards the Zinktronk. Some of the comrades told us what happened there.

When they arrived at the Zinktronk they were made to stand just next to the gate while one of the warders went to look for Chief Warder Theron. A few moments later Theron came walking proudly with his nose in the air. Jan Kleynhans and the other warders stood at attention and saluted. "What's going on here?" asked Theron disdainfully.

"These three are the ringleaders chief," said Jan excitedly, "they have incited the other bandits not to work. We also discovered that there was a plot to kill us at work."

"After which," added Teeman, "they were going to take the rifles and seize the boat and escape to the mainland."

"And also," added Bloed, "to rape all the White women and kill all the children at the dorpie."

"And also," added Perdekop who had coming running and had only heard the last part, "to bomb the Houses of Parliament after skinning you alive baas."

Theron, standing proudly astride, his baton patting his trousers, looked at Jan from head to foot. For some few seconds there was silence.

"You say what happened?" asked Theron again.

"There was almost a riot at work chief," said Jan now with less confidence, "it was led by these three."

"It was merely a feint," added Teeman, "to disarm the warders and thereafter escape by boat to Mozambique baas."

"And also," added Bloed, "to escape with the White women after lynching the children."

"And also," added Perdekop, "to kidnap you to Ghana baas, where they say Nkrumah want you dead or alive."

Theron's eyes popped out at the mention of his kidnapping to Ghana where Nkrumah wanted him dead or alive. The muscles of his neck expanded and he swallowed saliva hard as though in pain. He looked scared.

Then he looked at Jan again and for the third time he asked him, now worriedly, "You say what happened?"

"They were refusing to work chief," said Jan meekly. The criminal convicts kept quiet, apparently shocked by Jan's confession.

"They were refusing to work?" barked Theron, eyeing Jan as though in disbelief.

"And working slowly, chief," said Jan softly.

"Working slowly?" asked Theron now regaining composure.

"Yes chief."

"How slowly?" asked Theron, now haughtily.

"They were not running like the others chief," said Jan.

"They were dragging their legs along baas," added Teeman and demonstrating by stooping, arms hanging loosely and dragging his legs drearily on the sand.

"And sitting down," added Bloed.

"And sleeping cosily," added Perdekop.

Theron showed an evil little smile and shook his head. He then looked at the three accused who were still handcuffed and bespattered with blood. "Yes you, what happened?" he asked harshly.

China, one of the accused, stepped forward to state their case. "Stand where you are," chipped in Perdekop, charging at him pugnaciously, "stand where you are." China stepped back.

"We did nothing wrong sir," he began, "we were working like the other prisoners, when suddenly we were pounced upon for no reason at all."

"You want to tell me that the baas is lying? One of my best warders here?"

China kept quiet.

"You were busy fiddling with bombs outside," continued Theron, "and you had wanted to kill all Whites, including women and children." Johnson, the second accused's lips twitched open. He was about to say something.

Perdekop pointed a figer threateningly at him. "When the baas speaks, yours is only to listen," he said.

"Whatever a warder tells you to do," began Theron again, "that you must do. A warder is never wrong." He paused and looked at the three accused individually. "This is not a zoo," he resumed again, "where you can watch animals at your leisure and loiter around. This is prison and here you are supposed to work; and work you must, whether you like it or not. That is what you were brought here for. Three meals off. Take them to the kulukuds." And he moved away.

"Because you do not want to work," added Perdekop, "and want to rape White women and kill children, you are not going to get your nice breakfast, good lunch and delicious supper tomorrow." He too quickly moved away following Theron. The handcuffs were removed from the prisoners' hands and with slaps and kicks they were hurriedly driven to one of the empty cells in the Zinktronk where they were locked up in one cell. One of the three later sued the Minister of Justice and the case was settled out of court and he was compensated.

At 2 o'clock, immediately after lunch, the 50 new prisoners were joined to the Landbouspan as they had finished with their registration. They were all political prisoners. There was Mokgoba a history teacher and there was Rikhotso, also a teacher, who had been arrested with their students. Dennis Brutus the poet was also in the draft. I'm sure to Jan's surprise and gratefulness, there were also seven Indians.

One can see the newcomers by the new prison clothes and sandals. The wind blows and there are dust storms. Look at Teeman! See how he runs at an angle — upper body bent forward. He stops near an Indian, points a finger at him and runs back to Jan Kleynhans. Their work consists of carrying stones (which had previously been heaped by the Losspan near the foundations of the new hospital) and carrying them to the cemetery behind the Zinktronk. We in the Losspan are helping to dig the foundations of the hospital. Look! There is Teeman running back to the Indian. Jan Kleynhans hurries after him, almost running. Teeman arrives first. He stops the Indian and shouts at him. He points at the small stones he's carrying and points at a big boulder. Jan catches up with them. He shouts something. I cannot hear what he says. I'm about 40 metres away from them. Because of what is happening, we in the Losspan are no longer working but watching what is happening. Jan points at the boulder. The Indian throws the stone he's carrying and bends down to roll the boulder. Teeman leaves Jan with the Indian and runs to intercept a former student.

Look at Piet and Bloed. They have got Mokgoba the historian. Piet beats him with his baton on the ribs. He points to another boulder. Mokgoba bends down and slowly, slowly, the boulder rolls towards the old cemetery. There is an up and down movement of running Big Fives and half-running warders. The small stones have all been carted and every prisoner is now pushing his boulder of rock, some individually and others in twos. The wind blasts creating dust storms. Dust goes into their eyes. There is not time to remove it. Nature has its cures. They push on in blindness and others in semi-blindness. The boulders slowly roll on. There is no rest.

One tiny Indian is in trouble. His hands are already covered with blisters and trickles of blood. He looks at them and leaves the boulder. He goes to Jan and shows him his hands. Jan bends down to listen to what the Indian says. And then he bursts out laughing. He asks the Indian whom he calls Napoleon to show him his hands again. The Indian is embarassed but shows him. He laughs again. And then he blows some air with his mouth at the blistered hands of the Indian as parents do to children when they are injured. He says something to him and points at the boulder. I guess that he told him that the hands have now healed. The Indian bends down. He struggles with the boulder. It doesn't move. He flexes his muscles and goes down again. He pushes. The boulder doesn't move. Teeman comes running. He sees Jan looking up, giggling. He giggles also. Then Jan makes a frightening scream. Teeman laughs hilariously. The Indian panics and struggles with the boulder. Slowly . . . slowly . . . it rolls.

Look at Piet and Fourie. They're beating at random on all those they come across. The wind swirls. Particles of sand and dust are blown about. Pieces of paper, feathers and tree leaves fly about. Dust is blown onto their faces settling on their sweat.

What had taken the Losspan three months to clear, has been cleared by the Landbouspan in three hours. When the bell rang at 5 o'clock dissapointment showed in Jan's face. He looked at his watch and shook his head. He had not yet enjoyed himself with the new arrivals especially the Indians whom he called 'coolies'. "But tomorrow is another day", he seemed to say to himself as he bade the prisoners to fall in lines. Teeman and Bloed helped him in counting.

The following day was indeed a good day for Jan and his cohorts. Half the new arrivals, including all the Indians, came back with wounds. One could easily identify them with their new uniforms and bandages on their limbs and foreheads. On top of the beatings, what Jan did was to take them to the southern tip of the island to pull out rotten seaweed which was festering with worms where the sea was shallow but full of sharp stones and pointed quarry rocks. Told to remove their sandals, they were driven in barefooted and as expected, came back with cuts and bruises on their feet and legs. Some who were being driven by the Big Fives slipped and fell and sustained terrible cuts on their upper limbs.

*   *   *

The Big Fives are creating havoc. Almost three times a week now they are making 'bombs' for comrades. Every time we return from work before we are counted in our blankets and mats are searched. And every time a crude weapon, or a letter written in Tarzan English addressed to Sobukwe and setting the date for killing warders, is unearthed in one of the comrades' blankets. The result: the comrades are straight away whisked to Theron to be charged and from there it's punishment through starvation. What is disgusting is that the warders know about these 'bombs' and they see these Big Fives sharpening these weapons to be planted in our blankets. I've actually identified one crude self-made knife being used in three such 'bomb' operations; which means that after the knife has been used in 'bombing' a comrade, it finds its way back to the Big Fives again to be used for another operation. It's sickening. Five comrades were 'bombed' yesterday and whisked to the isolation cells.

14. The Fall of the Big Six

There is still tension between the Big Six and the Big Fives. It seems now that things are heading for a climax. In the morning when eating our breakfast the red handkerchief-sized cloth fluttered again. I saw one Big Six convict named Mapetwane being given a knife by the Chief Justice. Word soon spread around that we politicians should be on the look-out. There is going to be war. Where and when, we were not told. But from experience we already knew that it was either during tauza or when eating. We marched on to the Quarry apprehensive of what was going to happen. Nothing happened on the way. At work I was given a 14lb hammer and went to join others who were already hitting at the chisels. They were still singing the same old song of George the rogue stealing other people's cattle and eating the lungs and the bones. I joined the singing and lifted my hammer straight up and brought it crushing with force on the chisel.

Magwa, who was also a member of the Big Fives, was in charge of our group today. He stood there in front of us shouting orders and threatening us. Black as charcoal, three teeth only remaining in his mouth, muscular arms, eyes red, flat-footed with bunions which made him walk as though he was on a moving ship, he stopped the singing and told us to look at how we should hit at the chisels. Then he lifted the hammer straight up and brought it down crushing with such force that sparks began to fly. That was how we should work, he said. Then he began the song of George the rogue with a powerful voice that enchoed far into the sea. To show his creative mind, he composed some new works for the song.

'Libambe,	Hold it,
Libambe linga shoni,	Hold it, it should not set,
Uthi masenze njani?	You say what must we do?
Wadl'amaphaphu enkomo zabantu.	He ate the lungs of people's cattle.
Uthi masenze njani?'	You say what we must do.

Lifting our hammers way up, our voices roared as we sang. Still leading the song, he began to move slowly in front of us from left to right, doing inspection, his hands behind his back. There's no doubt about it, we of the 14lb hammers group, a sub-section of the Quarryspan, led by the three-toothed, bunioned, semi-bald headed Magwa, are now going to hold the sun from moving. We'll hold it to a standstill while George the rogue eats the lungs of people's cattle. We can even hold the dominee's black Lucifer by the tail while our leader Magwa, alone, with his muscular arms, holds him by the horns.

Just then I saw Mapetwane creeping behind him, his 14lb hammer lifted up. When Magwa tried to look behind him, Mapetwane unleashed the hammer flush on his head. There was an agonising scream and then it was all over. Magwa, the sun, George the rogue, the lungs, people's cattle, all finished. The hammer that landed on his skull brought everything to an abrupt end. The body of Magwa lay lifeless before us and blood oozed from the wound on his head.

When Oom Dellie, the Big Fives and other warders came running, Mapetwane stood triumphantly in surrender, the hammer lying on the ground and his hands up in the air. They were on him all the same, the warders and the Big Fives. In no time, he too lay still.

Magwa was lying face down but I saw him breathing. There was still life in him yet. Oom Dellie knelt down to check his pulse and heart-beats. "He's still alive!" he said in surprise, "quick, go and phone the office."

One warder took Oom Dellie's bicycle and pedalled to the nearest house to phone. It was hard to believe that Magwa was still alive. Imagine a person hit with a 14lb hammer on the head with full force and not dying. Unbelievable. When the van came about 10 minutes later, the Big Fives carried him tenderly onto the back of the van. Mapetwane was lifted up like a bag full of maize and thrown head first behind the van and from there to the kulukuds.

When we returned to prison, we went for tauza as usual. One member of the Big Fives was standing naked in front and was about to hand over his clothes to a warder when suddenly someone from nowhere produced a crude instrument and stabbed him on the shoulder. Blood spurted out. There was another thrust and yet another in quick succession. At first there was confusion as prisoners, including warders panicked and scampered about. Later on the warders regrouped and charged at the assailant. Just then another convict produced a knife and plunged it into the neck of another Big Fives member. Screaming, the man went to fall near where the warders were still assaulting the first assailant. The second assailant was also grabbed by the warders and pummelled. The Big Fives recovered from their shock and went to assist the warders in the beating up of the Big Six assailants. Later on the two Big Fives who had been stabbed were carried to hospital and their assailants taken to the kulukuds.

The fall of the Big Six

Later that afternoon we learned that Magwa had been taken by boat to Somerset Hospital on the mainland. We also learned that Mapetwane had made a confession to Theron. In his confession, he said he was tired of belonging to the prison gangs. He had been assigned the task of stabbing Magwa and not to kill him because Magwa had rebelled some years back against the Big Six. He further told Theron that he was tired of always being given assignments of stabbing warders and other convicts as he had been doing this for the last 10 to 15 years. He had once been a member of the Big Fives and did not want to rejoin it because he hated the idea of informing on other prisoners. He could not at the same time stay an independent as the other gangs would ill-treat him and he would be turned into a wyfie. So he decided that the best thing for him was to kill Magwa so that he should be charged for murder and hanged.

Before sleeping that night we heard frightful news. Georgie, President of the Big Six had been kidnapped. After lock-up, two warders, one of them Jan Kleynhans, went to Section A, cell number three, and told him that he was wanted at the office. They then took him to the Zinktronk and locked him up in the cell of the Big Fives where Teeman and Bloed were staying.

The following day at lunchtime Georgie was nowhere to be seen at the Quarry. We learned that he had remained in the prison to do light work. He was now a bride. We learned that after the warders had put him in the same cell with the Big Fives, a fight had started immediately thereafter. Georgie was overpowered. That evening he had been raped repeatedly in turns, while others held him. Ultimately he broke down, surrendered and promised to abandon the Big Six and its Presidency in return for being a wyfie and a soft job inside the yard.

I'm flabbergasted by the endless horrors that happen in this prison. The warders and the Big Fives are jubilant. The leader of the most powerful gang has now become a wyfie of his antagonists. It's mind-boggling. But it has happened.

The Big Six held a meeting at lunchtime. It was chaired by the Chief Justice assisted by the Chief Advocate of the Big Six. I wondered whether another President was going to be sworn in. We later learned that Georgie had been deposed as President and that the Big Six were being dissolved. All the soldiers of the Big Six were to join another gang which was known as the '28'. The '28' had existed all along but the membership was small. The '28', the Big Six and another gang known as 'The Desperadoes' are allies. Their aims are the same and they usually embarked on joint operations. They only differed in one thing — homosexualism. The Big Six did not condone homosexualism in its ranks whereas the '28' allowed it. That was the only difference.

When we returned back to prison there were no incidents on the way and for the first time we did not look around and about at the tauza yard. Even the warders cracked jokes either with each other or with the Big Fives. While sitting down eating, I saw the former Chief Justice, Dladla, going towards the back. My eyes followed him; he was going to Georgie his former President to deliver the verdict. Georgie sat in the last row next to the former member of the Big Six who resigned in January and was given eight claps. This convict was now called by a feminine name and had been turned into a wyfie by the Big Fives. Dladla sat next to Georgie and began talking to him. Georgie kept on nodding time and again. Afterwards Dladla left him and went to sit next to his pals. There is no doubt about it — the Big Fives have scored a major victory. It is going to be some time before the '28' embark on any operations again. Conditions at work are going to be worse for criminal convicts who do not belong to the Big Fives.

After Dladla had left Georgie, the warders began teasing him (Georgie) and cracking some jokes on the incidents of the previous night. As we went to queue before our cell, I watched Georgie walking alone forlornly towards the Zinktronk where the Big Fives sleep. Teeman and Bloed followed triumphantly behind, cracking jokes. The other convict who now has a feminine name, followed behind them smiling at nothing in particular.

15. Gantsha Khuboni

The month of April has arrived and the weather has completely changed. Robben Island has a Mediterranean type of climate. The rains have begun to fall and the winter is setting in. It is now cold at night and the three blankets are not enough. Some of us are sleeping in twos. You cover yourself with a blanket, your partner also does the same and the other four blankets come on top. At least, it is better this way. I think the prison authorities are deliberately denying us the two extra winter blankets.

Section D and the new offices have been completed. Some political prisoners have been transferred from the Zinktronk to occupy this Section. Meanwhile, next to the offices, foundations have been completed for the new hospital and building is about to begin. Other foundations adjoining the offices have been started. There is a rumour originating from warders that 24 kulukuds are going to be built especially for Mandela, Sisulu and other prominent political leaders. The work is being done very hurriedly. More prisoners have been added to the Bouspan. The Losspan has been dissolved and is now part of the Bouspan. The stone at the Quarry is getting finished. The stones we are now producing are no longer of good quality. I wonder what we are going to do once it is finished. We may have to collect stones right round the island and keep on piling them into heaps. And later be instructed to remove the heaps from one part of the island to another. Or they may decide that we dig holes one day and fill them the following day. There is a new proverb I have learned here: 'prison work never gets finished'.

* * *

Two political prisoners, Jiyane Lucas and Mlotshwa Elliot have won their appeal and are being released. Jiyane had been sentenced to 17 years and Mlotshwa to 15 years imprisonment. They were sentenced in July 1963 at the Johannesburg Supreme Court. The other three who were in the same case with them had their sentences confirmed.

The release of the two comrades who won their appeal has shocked everybody here. From having to serve so many years to nothing. It just shows that some of the judges and magistrates were meting out 'justice' under pressure from above. When one old man heard about this, he became desperate. He is in his late 50s and has a hunch back. He is illiterate but claims that he has a son who is a doctor. In the evening while we were asleep he went to the toilets with a blanket. Unfortunately for him, two other comrades later went to the toilets. They came back running and called us to the toilets. We found old Tshawe hanging by his neck. We quickly rescued him and some peasants began assaulting him. They told him that since he wanted to die, he should best be killed by them. The old man cried and asked for mercy promising that he would never try to take his life again.

Later I asked him about his case and he told me that he had been sentenced to 18 years imprisonment for nothing. He said he was on his way to church somewhere in the countryside around the town of Queenstown when an explosion ripped some pylons.

"I carried a Bible and a Hymn Book," he said, "and was singing and praising the Lord when suddenly I heard this explosion. About half-an-hour later a police van approached in my direction. I was arrested and assaulted and accused of being a member of Umkhonto we Sizwe and the ANC. Later on at the police station, I was forced to make a statement that I was responsible for the explosion. I was then charged under the Sabotage Act. In court the police said they had arrested me on the spot immediately after the explosion trying to flee. The Bible and the Hymn Books were produced as exhibits to show how I had disguised when undertaking the operation. I was found guilty and convicted to 18 years for sabotage. I had never been a member of the PAC or the ANC before. And this is the reward for not having joined these movements." And then he cried.

* * *

Gantsha Khuboni's body is now swollen and he's finding some difficulty in urinating. Yesterday Head Warder Nel, the hospital orderly kicked and pushed him away saying he does not want to see him again. He called him a lazy bastard. This morning Gantsha went to hospital walking slowly with difficulty, pain written all over his face. Head Warder Nel kept on looking at him with an evil eye. His turn came and for the umpteenth time he reported his illness to Nel. To my surprise, the Head Warder told him that he was going to be admitted to the prison hospital. Later on I spread the news to the other comrades in the Quarryspan. We are greatly relieved. At last he will see the doctor and possibly be attended to although even when one is admitted, one is made to sleep on the cold cement floor. There are many other comrades who are ill and also suffering like Gantsha. The beds are still being reserved for the Big Fives and the wyfies who only go there when they feel like resting. 'Holiday' they call it.

We had really been touched by the illness of Gantsha Khuboni. He was very popular among us. He was a source of inspiration with his endless jokes about the warders and the police. While we were at Leeuwkop Maximum Prison, he was fond of cracking jokes and would keep us laughing the whole day. We would laugh until tears streamed down our faces. Sometimes we would call him to order and beg him to suspend some of his jokes about the racists because, by then, we would be too tired of laughing, our cheeks aching. He would then stop cracking jokes and resort to pantomime, imitating warders, the Special Branch and other police officers. And we would endlessly roar with laughter until we were threatened by a warder.

I remember another joke he was fond of making and we usually asked him to repeat it. It was at a certain platteland meeting which was addressed by an eminent orator of the opposition United Party just before the elections. The audience consisted mostly of Boer farmers and their wives. The great orator spoke for three hours using all the stunts of great power oratory trying to convince his listeners about how the world community is against the Nationalist Party's policies of apartheid, the condemnation that South Africa is getting from the United Nations Organisation and other international bodies; how South Africa is getting isolated and is now losing the support of its Western allies and how the Bantustan concept would not solve the racial question. And by the time he finished, his listeners were still confused and did not understand what he had been speaking about and how all that he had said was going to affect their daily lives.

When he stepped down exhausted and perspiring, an organiser of the Nationalist Party, stepped on to the platform.

"Where do I stand?" was the first question he posed to the Boer farmers.

"On the platform," came the reply.

"No," he said agitated, "my question is, where do I stand?"

"In South Africa," some replied hesitantly.

"No," he said pacing the platform, "for the last time now; where do I stand?"

There was silence for some time. His audience looked dumfounded.

"Op die kaffer se kop (on the kaffir's head)", came a lone voice from one old farmer.

It was immediately taken up by the whole audience.

"Yes," said the organiser, "I stand on the kaffir's head."

There was a thunderous applause which grew louder and louder like thunder rumbling in the heavens. Hats were thrown into the air. There was whistling and stamping of feet amid shouts of 'hoor, hoor' (hear,

hear). The organiser stood admiring the spectacle before him while the United Party orator sat sulking. After some minutes of jubilation, there was quiet at last.

"South Africa," began the organiser again, in a loud roaring voice, "is the White man's land and will forever remain so. We have nothing to do with the United Nations . . ." He did not finish. There was another thunderous applause and a clapping of hands which continued for about a minute.

"The Black man must know his place . . . Vote Nationalist to keep South Africa White."

There was pandemonium. The meeting was over. The Nationalist Party organiser was a hero. He was carried shoulder high. One farmer called him the best orator in South Africa. Another said he should be made Prime Minister. The organiser's tragi-comedy had only taken about 15 minutes.

Gantsha Khuboni was from the Randfontein location. He was serving six years for membership and furthering the aims of a banned organisation. He had a rich baritone voice. At Leeuwkop Maximum Prison we had formed a vocal group with other comrades which specialised in Afro-American spirituals. You could hear his baritone voice, rich and heavy, surpassing all the other baritones when we sang 'The Sermonette'.

When we returned from work we had chilling news. We were all taken aback. Gantsha Khuboni is dead. He died at the prison hospital. Now I can understand that evil eye on Head Warder Nel's face as he looked at him in the morning. He knew that his time had come. He didn't want him to die in the cell, lest it should be obvious to everyone, even his superiors, that he had died of neglect. He wanted him to die in hospital so as to give the impression that he had done his best to attend to him.

That night we were all paralysed. There was no conversation in the cell. We lay huddled together in twos unable to converse. I was deeply touched. There was the peaceful face of Abel again, now lying in the coffin.

*   *   *

Abel's was one of the biggest funerals ever seen in Jabavu, for the Moroka Terrors Football Club had been a popular club with followers in Jabavu, Moroka and White City Jabavu. His jersey, trunk, socks and football boots were placed on the coffin. The boxers from the Mavis Issacson Boxing Club were there. Before the gang warfare he was an amateur boxer and was in the same stable with Peter Moledi who later became South African Non-European Flyweight champion.

Gangsters with scars and scratches on their faces, moved about among the mourners with daggers and pistols in their pockets looking around for any follower of Peter 'the Goatee' and Boy Sevenpence who may disrupt the funeral procession. There were many young schoolgirls who milled about. They too had come to pay their last respects to Jack of the Terrors, the man who had protected them over the years. There were many taxis and other vehicles which had been offered to carry the mourners. Aunt Bellina had covered herself with a black shawl and sat next to the coffin. Since no one can be buried in Soweto without the services of a priest, my parents, long frustrated by Christianity, had hastily managed to get the services of a quack priest without a congregation to conduct the burial service. As conducting burial services was the main means for the priest of earning a living, he showed no dedication in what he was reading from the Bible, but seemed rather more in a hurry to finish his job and thereafter rush to conduct another burial service nearby where they were waiting for him.

In a solemn voice, speaking slowly, my father appealed to the gangsters to stop their senseless killings. "Look at the results of all your efforts," he said pointing at the coffin of Abel. The gangsters listened to him with heads bowed as though he was pricking them with sharp thorns.

"How wonderful would it have been," he continued, "if he had died in the struggle for our freedom . . ." Once again tears flowed from his eyes and he could not continue. Nomsa's thoughts were on the deceased, her handkerchief wet with tears. She still could not believe that it was her Jack who was dead. That what once was, breathed life, generated so much love, fear and terror, could now be consigned to dust and nothingness. Better that it was so. What future did Abel have in South Africa in any case? None. If he had taken aunt Bellina's advice and settled in the Boer farms, he would have ended up like old man Tolepi. If he had not died and followed his gangster career, he would have ended up in prison and would have been like Teeman and Bloed. If he had taken my parents' advice and joined the ANC Youth League, he wouldn't have been a member for long, for there was too much wrangling in the ANC then between the Africanists and the ANC leadership over the 1949 Programme of Action and the role of Europeans in our struggle. As a man who loved action, he would not have withstood all that. Well, he lived fast, died young and had a good-looking corpse at 17 years of age — he followed in the footsteps of his hero Nick Romano in Willard Motley's 'Knock on any door'.

* * *

Simon Gantsha Khuboni's corpse was wrapped up and flown to Randfontein his home location. The prisons department, plagued by guilt, waived aside the £100 fee which is usually paid by relatives for the purchase of a dead prisoner's corpse. We later got a report about his burial. It was the largest funeral procession ever seen in Randfontein location. Many Blacks from distant towns and cities converged in Randfontein on that day. To them Gantsha was a symbol of African resistance and aspirations; of African suffering and decay; of voices wailing in darkness and death under the sjambok of the heavy hand of apartheid colonialism and oppression; of voices crying in prisons, mines, farms, compounds, and homelands for fair play; of man's struggle from prehistoric times, first against nature and wild animals and later against his fellow men for freedom and democracy, for justice and brotherhood. Those who saw his face said it looked serene and defiant. The Special Branch and its informers — those special instruments of doom, destruction and evil — moved about among the mourners, stretching their ears to eavesdrop any words of condemnation against the regime. But the words of condemnation were written on the solemn faces of the mourners as one by one they moved past the coffin slowly, to have a last glimpse of the defiant face of their hero. And real priests — true believers — were there to commend his soul to his Maker. Gantsha Khuboni had played his noble role in the liberation struggle and paid the supreme sacrifice.

16. *Bitter April*

Two comrades from Soweto had been called to the office today. They are both serving six years imprisonment. At the office Theron told them with glee that their wives are instituting divorce proceedings against them for malicious desertion. They were asked whether they wanted to oppose the proceedings and they both said they did not. They were also given letters of Power of Attorney for the transfer of all their properties to their wives. One signed the Power of Attorney letter and the other refused. These comrades have been married for some time and they both have children. They came back dumfounded. With all the difficulties and hardships we are undergoing here, to be burdened on top of it all with domestic problems emanating a thousand miles away! Last week three other comrades from Port Elizabeth were called for the same thing. One of them is 55 years old and his wife, I understand, is in the late 40s and they already have children of working age. This thing is demoralising to married comrades. And of the 1,086 political prisoners here, they are in the majority.

I suspect there's an evil hand at work behind all these divorces. Ultimately this matter of divorce will affect many married men from the urban areas. It will not affect peasants and migrant labourers because their wives have deep-rooted traditions and customs. And besides, there is no divorce among peasants. Once married, peasants don't divorce. I discussed this matter of divorces with some comrades and we tried to view it objectively but we came to one conclusion: the Special Branch is behind these divorces. They must have coaxed and threatened these women to undertake such steps. We have strong suspicions that even the legal divorce fees are paid from the Special Branch Counter-Insurgency Fund.

The draft which arrived at the end of March from Leeuwkop Maximum Prison brought us some news about the situation outside. The wheels of oppression are turning on at full speed. The 90-day detention clause is in full swing and many comrades are suffering under it.

* * *

Nkohla has done it again. We had warned this man in February to stop this rumour of promising people about being released. His February deadline ended and there is another extension of three months this time. I suspect this man is no longer normal. I understand he was terribly assaulted last November by the Klenhans brothers at the Landbouspan. They broke his false teeth and spectacles during the process. Prior to this he had previously been tortured by the Special Branch at the Rowland Street Prison in Cape Town. What is really disturbing is the crowd of illiterate and semi-literate peasants who follow him. After we had suppressed him, he went underground together with his followers who number about 20. They no longer sit around him during lunch time or in the cell. Instead, only one peasant goes to him to get the 'news' and thereafter it is circulated. It spreads rapidly until it reaches the ears of the criminal convicts and from there to the warders and ultimately the prison psychologist. And most of this news from Nkohla concerns either our release or guerrilla operations against the system. Nkohla and his followers do not want to believe the news we get from smuggled newspapers.

We get newspaper cuttings from criminal convicts working in the dorpie as houseboys in warders' houses. As most of the warders are Afrikaaners, the papers we get are mostly Afrikaans newspapers. We rarely get English language newspapers and when we get them, they have been smuggled from the houses of prison officials, some of whom are bilingual.

* * *

During the same month of April, the Minister of Justice and Prisons, Advocate John Balthaazar Vorster, visited Robben Island. Prior to this visit the whole prison and its surroundings had been cleared and cleaned of all rubbish. On the day of his visit it was meat day and he spent some time in the kitchen looking at the type of food we were being given. The kitchen of course, was also being run by the Big Fives.

* * *

The weather has changed for the worse. It is raining almost daily now and it is terribly windy and cold. Most of us don't have sandals. We go barefooted to and from work. The road is very rough. Certain portions of the road are not tarred. Some lime and small sharp quarry stones were placed on the road surface. These small sharp-pointed stones are tearing up our feet, especially in the morning when going to work.

When walking to work, I look for some spots along the road where there are no sharp small stones. Some comrades cannot stand this cold and the prickly quarry stones on their feet. And I'm one of them. Some have old sandals of different sizes. A size seven on the left and maybe a size 10 on the right. I have seen some comrades with sandals of the same foot. The wind from the Atlantic Ocean is bitingly cold. On our way to work mucus oozes out of our noses and we just leave it to flow as our hands are hidden in our armpits trying to keep them warm. Our heads are covered with rags called caps. The torn canvas short pants and the coarse jackets cannot protect us from the cold, instead, they absorb it and transmit it to our bodies. The type of food and quantity we are getting does not provide us with heat and energy. Instead the reserves which our bodies had, are being drained bit by bit. Some of the old men are trying to harden themselves by saying that before the week is out, one young boy shall have died from the cold; the young boy's reply is that before the week is out, one old man shall have died from the cold.

At night, it rains heavily and the cold winds blow, forcing us to sleep closer together. We sleep with all the cell windows open. The warders don't want us to close them; they say we need fresh air at night. The cold winds do what they like with our bodies as we shrink and shiver and whine. Even sleeping in twos doesn't help. Others are now sleeping in groups of three and four. But still it doesn't help. One comrade, Jacob Lebone, of the ANC, a boyhood chum in Kliptown, has invented a new way of avoiding the cold. He demonstrated to us how to make a sleeping bag out of three blankets. Then he slid in, feet first and wiggled his body slowly like a worm into the blankets-tube. It was warmer, he said, with his head only remaining exposed and no cold air came in through the sleeping bag. Many of us tried his invention. At least it was slightly better.

* * *

Sunday. 10am. Inspection. Complaints and Requests. Bloed is holding the Big Book today. He runs around the corridor shouting 'complaints and requests' and bidding us to be ready for inspection. Major Kruger enters and looks at us disdainfully in our tattered convict clothes as though we are rubbish bins festering with flies. He's followed by Theron, Muisbek, Bloed, and Meintjies. Perdekop, Teeman, Fynkyk are in the kitchen roasting meat for Jan Kleynhans and themselves.

We complain about food. We complain about clothes. We complain about shoes. We ask for more blankets. Almost all of us put forward our complaints and requests. Even old man Tolepi who was now working in a small span in the dorpie, approached the major with a humble smile on his lips to complain about the food and clothes. Our complaints and requests have been sent to the Commissioner of Prisons for approval — that is what we are told.

One comrade raised the question of the Prison Regulations. The cynical reply he got was that the Prison Regulations were not going to help us. They applied only to criminal convicts and since we were criminal convicts of a special category we were being treated at the discretion of the Commissioner of Prisons. The major instructed Theron to give us the regulations. After inspection we were given one copy and true enough, they applied to criminal convicts and since we were not criminal convicts we were held and treated at the discretion of the Commissioner of Prisons.

17. The Man from the Red Cross

It is now during the month of May and the weather is worse than ever before. On the first day of the month, we were given old torn jerseys and nothing else. The Big Fives criminals and their wyfies (called the Fast Elevens) are putting on military coat lumber-jackets and long warm trousers. They've also got long warm socks and boots. Convict criminals of the '28' and the Desperadoes have bought (with money) some shoes and other warm clothing for themselves from the criminal convicts in charge of the stores where clothing is issued. It's terrible. Some of us have torn short pants and torn canvas jackets. The cold is playing havoc with us. Our enemies have stopped beating us but are enjoying seeing us cringing and shivering. One can actually hear comrades' teeth gnashing. We are a pitiable sight and look like a routed army. The wind blasts, howls, cuts and slices through our bodies at will. The cold absorbed by my bare feet is torturing and the small sharp-pointed quarry stones on the road are like sharp thorns. There is no hope that conditions will become better. We shall have to go through the winter like this. And the greatest insult of them all: criminal convicts walk proudly upright in new warm clothing and shoes while the Big Fives keep on barking at us to keep our 'fours'. We walk about crouching, trying to hide behind one another. Even tall comrades bend low, tucking their heads between their shoulder blades, trying to shorten their tall frames. We can no longer keep straight lines and the warders are unable to control us, however much they scream. When the cold winds blow from the right, we crouch towards the left and when it changes direction and blows from the left, we crouch towards the right. Sometimes we move on in a semi-circle, our shoulders raised up to hide our heads.

* * *

When I went to hospital this morning to get a cough mixture, I saw the hospital patients being moved out. Head Warder Nel is not attending to patients but is busy screaming and giving instructions to Big Fives convicts. There are some re-arrangements taking place and some beds are waiting to be fitted inside the hospital cell. There are also some cardboards full of blankets, pillows, pyjamas and bedsheets — all new. There are also new plates, dishes, cups and spoons. Teeman, Bloed, Meintjies and the other members of the Big Fives are busy assisting Head Warder Nel. All the patients were removed with their old blankets and sisal mats to another cell within the Zinktronk almost diagonal with the hospital and not far from the cell which has showers. I suspect that the doctor may have demanded a complete overhaul of the hospital. I'm sure that when the place has been thoroughly cleaned, new beds and blankets will be provided for the sick. The fate of our patients is now going to be better.

On our way to work, I noticed that all the prominent members of the Big Fives were not going out with their workspans. Only the low ranking members were there.

While we were working, we heard a rumour that an important person from the mainland will be visiting the island. It was not stated as to when he would arrive or as to who he was. But we noticed that none of the warders carried a stick or a pick handle. They moved amongst us lazily just looking at what we were doing. There was no shouting of orders and no reprimands. Since Colonel Steytler took over in January, warders have been warned not to carry sticks or pick handles, but they have continued to carry them. They hide or throw them away when the colonel approaches or is about to do inspection during working hours. But they don't hide or throw them away from the other officers.

I had been sitting next to one of the old men from Engcobo village busy crushing stone after stone with the 4lb hammers, turning out ¼ inch, ¾ inch and ½ inch particles when the colonel's car approached the quarry from the southerly direction, indicating that he was from the Landbouspan. The car stopped a little distance from the compressor engine where the drilling of rocks was going on and the 14lb hammers crushing on the chisels. Out emerged the colonel and a tall slender European in a dark-blue suit. The colonel talked to the man in the dark-blue suit and his hand pointed towards the toolshed, to where we were sitting, at the little pond where many comrades had got injured trying to clear it of sharp quarry stones and at the prisoners who were busy chiseling stone slabs. The man in the dark-blue suit walked slowly towards the compressor engine and before reaching it, he stopped and looked at what was going on. He stood on top of a big boulder of quarry rock. Corporal Oom Dellie emerged out of his office and I watched him, through the wire mesh on my eyes, as he hurried towards where the colonel was standing. He stopped opposite the colonel and saluted. The colonel returned his salute. They conversed for some time and then he walked slowly away towards our direction. For the first time since we arrived at the quarry, he did not shout or scream at any prisoner, there were no Big Fives running round, neither was any prisoner manhandled. Prisoners with wheelbarrows went up and down loading and off-loading quarry stones. For the first time they carried light loads with no one to insult or scream at them. We sat there crushing and crushing our stones not knowing who this dignified man in the dark-blue suit was. After about 10 to 15 minutes, the man in the dark-blue suit turned and went to Colonel Steytler who stood a few paces away. They moved to the car and drove away. Then the screaming from Oom Dellie and the other warders began. Sticks and pick handles were unearthed. Those who had not filled their wheelbarrows were turned back. And from nowhere we saw the Big Fives running up and down and around and about. The situation returned to 'normal'. It was only later on, back in our cells, when we heard that the man in the dark-blue suit was from the International Committee of the Red Cross: his name was Dr Hoffman and he had come to study prison conditions in Robben Island Prison.

After we had been locked up for the night, the comrades from the Landbouspan told us of what had happened there during the day. When they arrived at work in the morning, Jan Kleynhans told them to sit down and rest. As Teeman and Bloed were not there, he told one of the low-ranking Big Fives to stand guard and watch for any vehicles coming to the work place. Then he and other warders began playing with a tennis ball they had brought along. They divided themselves into two groups and threw the ball to each other as is done in basketball. Meanwhile the prisoners began chatting and speculating what the meaning of this could be. Nkohla, who was in the Landbouspan then told them that a representative from the United Nations had come to the island to make arrangements for the release of political prisoners. Around 9 o'clock the warders got tired of playing. Jan came to the prisoners and told them that they should now resume work but that they should work casually and not overwork themselves. The Big Fives member who had been standing guard was recalled and told to work with the others. No warder or agter-reier hurried them to work hard. There were no screams or insults; even those who wanted to go and relieve themselves were given permission. The warders walked about lazily as though they did not know what to do.

At about 9.30am the colonel's car approached and a man in a dark-blue suit emerged. He carried a notebook and pen and kept jotting on the pad as he watched the prisoners walking lazily pushing half-filled wheelbarrows. It was only about 30 minutes later after the colonel and the man in the dark-blue suit had gone that things started changing. The reign of terror resumed.

But what really astounded us was a report we got from Nathaniel Ciliwe, a comrade who had been discharged from the prison hospital that afternoon. Immediately after the hospital cell was opened, Head Warder Nel, assisted by the two Big Fives hospital assistants, removed all the patients with their old blankets and mats and they were taken to an empty cell in the Zinktronk. From the windows in that cell they saw Teeman, Bloed and other Big Fives clearing the hospital and fitting it with new beds, blankets, bedsheets and other utensils. When they had finished they saw head Warder Nel issuing them with new pyjamas and sandals. Then they were taken to the hospital to sleep on the new beds. The two Big Fives hospital assistants were dressed in spotless white uniforms. Head Warder Nel then visited their cell and told them that they should sit down on their blankets. No one was allowed to sleep. Anyone who slept, he told them, would be chucked out of the hospital and sent either to the Landbouspan or the Quarry. There was to be no conversation. If they made any noise, they would be given three meals off and denied medical treatment. Later on he came with a warder to watch over them. But there was one political prisoner who had been left behind in the hospital. He had an acute attack of asthma which had left him very weak and gasping for air. Head Warder Nel decided that he should be left at the hospital.

Later on during the day they saw Colonel Steytler accompanied by a tall European in a dark-blue suit entering the hospital. Chief Warder Theron and Head Warder Nel followed behind. They were inside the hospital for some time. When they emerged, the man in the dark-blue suit went around inspecting other cells. When he was about to go in the direction of their cell, the colonel drew his attention to something else. The man looked at his watch and then he turned and together with the colonel they went to inspect the kitchen.

In the afternoon, all the new beds, blankets, etc., were removed and they were returned to the hospital. The asthma patient who had remained was now better and he told them what had happened in their absence. The man in the dark-blue suit asked some of the 'patients' about the treatment they were getting. The 'patients' had said they were satisfied with the treatment they were getting. What is worse these wretched criminal convicts also claimed they were members of the PAC and the ANC.

For their reward the Big Fives were given full plates of meat and each given four ounces of tobacco. For *their* reward Oom Dellie, Nel and Jan got promotions. Oom Dellie became a Head Warder, Nel became a Chief Warder and Jan was made a corporal. It was then that we understood the purpose of J.B. Vorster's visit in April. He had really done his homework.

A few days after Dr Hoffman had gone, the working conditions and the weather became worse. The beatings in the quarry had long abated since January but they continued in the Landbouspan. The cold tore at the flesh and ate through the marrow. The Big Fives had all the world to themselves. And they were justified. After all, hadn't they welcomed a Cabinet Minister in the kitchen and hadn't they talked face-to-face with a representative of the International Committee of the Red Cross? And, of course, there was also a possibility that in future they would talk face-to-face with a representative from the United Nations Organisation and possibly, perhaps, even with an emissary from the Pope.

Ever since the coup of Georgie, the '28' and the Desperadoes had not yet been properly organised. They were like a ship without a captain. Because of the terrible working conditions and the cold weather that sent us quivering, they resorted to the last clause in their constitution, which allowed them under such conditions to resort to self-destruction and escape the harsh treatment they were getting at the hands of the warders and the Big Fives. A light-complexioned convict with curly hair from District Six called Arab, who was a member of the Desperadoes, set the ball rolling. While we were talking at the Quarryspan, crushing stones into half-inch, quarter-inch and dust with 4lb hammers, he suddenly produced a razor blade and cut his left foot tendon muscle. I watched as the blood gushed out and, in a few moments, it had formed a pool. He was rushed to prison and from there carried by boat to Somerset Hospital. A few days later after this other members of the '28' and the Desperadoes did the same. We political prisoners wondered in astonishment. The Big Fives were jubilant. I asked one of the '28' members why they were doing this. He told me that it was what they usually did in any prison when the working conditions were bad and all resistance had failed. It was a sign of protest against the prison authorities. He told me that he too had done it before on two occasions at Bellville maximum Prison and showed me where he had cut the tendon muscles.

"You have got to be brave and forget about the pain," he said. "You lose a lot of blood and become very weak. There is nothing that the warders can do against you. They just have to attend to you and take you to hospital. In the hospital the muscles are joined again and you stay there for six months in comfort before you are allowed to work again. There is also the possibility while there of escaping. We shall continue doing this until prison conditions improve and thereafter we shall re-organise and plan for the extermination of the Big Fives. Even if they defeat us in this prison, we shall get them when we are transferred to another prison."

18. Dum-Dum

Before the end of May another batch of 50 prisoners arrived from Groenpunt Prison in the Orange Free State province. These convicts were criminals who, while serving their sentences, had 'joined' the PAC and ANC in prison. On top of their criminal sentences they were each sentenced to six years for membership and furthering the aims of banned organisations. To separate them from the criminal convicts and politicians, the authorities referred to them as Poqo-criminals. They were a compact group and looked forward to working with us. But as soon as they realised after a few days, that working conditions and treatment were bad for political prisoners, they disintegrated into three groups. One group joined the Big Fives, another joined the '28' and Desperadoes and the last group worked, suffered and identified themselves with political prisoners. This latter group later split into pro-PAC and pro-ANC.

The Big Fives having absorbed a large portion of the Poqo-criminals were now a formidable force. Despite the fact that a number of drafts consisting of political prisoners had arrived since January, one thing remained, we were not a fighting force but a disciplined political force. Every political prisoner who arrived in Robben Island was strictly warned to observe the PAC motto of 'Service, Suffering and Sacrifice'. Fortunately, all the ANC comrades who later came to Robben Island also followed the precedent we had set despite the fact that there had been no consultations on this matter with them.

Some of the Poqo-criminal convicts recruited to the Big Fives were a nuisance to us. There was one especially, known as Dum-dum. He appeared to me to be an imbecile. At school, he had been unable to catch up with other children in the grades and had early become a drop-out. Life as a thief had proved more attractive, since little intelligence was required here. It only meant loitering around the locations of Port Elizabeth and picking the pockets of careless workers. But even here Dum-dum had failed and thus found himself a convict. He had not even mastered the rudiments of speech. He lisped his words and was always incoherent. We did not understand what he said and I doubt whether the warders did. There was only one word he could pronounce properly and that was the most hated word in the island — 'baas'. And like the other Big Fives, he did not see anything wrong in calling the warders baas. His physical shape was repugnant. Take a child suffering from kwashiorkor and turn it into an adult and you have a good picture of Dum-dum. He had tiny legs, a big extended belly, protruding but unequal buttocks; he had a big head with an ugly-shaped forehead, tiny lurking eyes, a small flat nose, with nostrils just big enough to inhale and exhale air. That is the complete outfit of the human phenomenon Dum-dum. As speech was his great failing, he had long learned the art of gesticulating with his arms to express whatever was in his foggy mind.

But being a member of the Big Fives there was, in any case, not much to say; all he had to do was to scream and point out to warders all those his lurking eyes saw as being lazy. He had horse stamina — at least that was one gift mother nature had endowed him with. When I usually think of him, I just cannot imagine him not running; he ran throughout the whole working day. He would run from one group of prisoners to another; from the prisoners to a warder, from one warder to another and from a warder to prisoners throughout the day. Wherever he went nobody could understand whatever he said. Prisoners would jeer at him but that did not seem to bother him. Warders would sometimes insult him for some stupid act he had done and he seemed to care less. He would misinterpret instructions from warders to prisoners and afterwards be rebuked, only for him to produce his ever ready cloth from his back pocket and polish the shoes of the warder haranguing him. All-in-all, he was what is called in the English language, a fiend.

In the first week of June the quarry stones got finished and we were taken to another area on the south-western part of the island where there were more and better quarry stones. The road to the new quarry went past the Old Prison which was being demolished. We proceeded westwards until we were near the sea and then the road turned south in a semi-circle for half a kilometre. A new shed for the tools and two offices (one for Oom Dellie and the other for the warders) had already been built of planks and corrugated iron sheets. Four guardposts, 30 feet high, had already been erected on the four corners of the worksite. There were many new wheelbarrows with rubber wheels which had been purchased, but the old ones were still there. This time there was oil for their axles and they were oiled twice daily; once in the morning and once after lunch. The cocopans were also brought and their rails were laid. The compressor engine and the water engine had been pulled over and when everything was ready, drilling began. The going was tough and the cold sapping, but at least one person tried to keep warm with his antics — Dum-dum. He was running up and down, to and fro, around and about — sometime to nowhere. Sometimes he would run aimlessly and would suddenly come to an abrupt halt just like a springbok, look around confused as though he had been chased by a pack of hounds, and would then run back again from where he had started. Dum-dum never beat any prisoner, but he was often the cause of our being punished. He was the talk of the New Quarry and outshone all the other Big Fives. Head Warder Oom Dellie did not show any liking for him, yet he tolerated him.

19. Bombed

The new hospital and the 24 kulukuds have been completed. Immediately after their completion, foundations were begun for a hall at the tauza yard next to the kitchen. The tauza orgy has now been moved to the square next to Sections A and B where a gate has been fitted. The workspans are now using this gate when going and returning from work. There is a rumour circulating that the hall to be built will show films on Bantustans and the progress made there, so that a large number of political prisoners should opt for the bantustans after finishing their sentences.

Someone working at the docks saw Captain Fourie arrive and the news has given some of us the jitters. The news has come at a wrong time. We are still shocked by a case of sodomy between two political prisoners of peasant origin. They are both from the rural areas. As it is very cold the two had shared the same blankets. They were discovered at night by other comrades who were going to the toilets. In outrage the comrades, also peasants, then beat them up. There were so many assailants that they nearly killed them. The following day they were removed from their cell in Section C, cell number four. As I was now in the cell committee where the incident happened, I was one of those who had to deal with the case. The first thing we did was to arrange that they be put in separate cells.

When we interviewed the first man, the wyfie, he told us that there was nothing wrong in what they had done. He said it was not for the first time they did it. He had been having an affair with his 'husband' for the last five years while working in the mines in Johannesburg. He further said they were not the only ones who had done it in the mines; there were many whom he knew who were now here in the island. And he mentioned names. He later added that they did not do it like the criminal convicts; in the mines it is done in the thighs. I listened aghast. Many mineworkers, he said, including those from the neighbouring countries around South Africa were well familiar with this thing. "I don't know why we were assaulted," he concluded, "this thing is very common in the mines."

When we met the 'husband', the man was more specific. "Some men pay dowry in the mines," he told us, "in order to have their wyfies. The dowry is paid to friends or relatives of the wyfie who are also in the same mine, or sometimes to a mine induna." He told us that he too had paid dowry because he loved his wyfie very much. Whenever he signed a contract to go to the mines, the wyfie also did the same so that they should be in the same mine and work for the same period. He then also mentioned the names of other homosexuals who had been mentioned by his wyfie. And I knew many of them. I listened to all this stupefied. When he had finished, I told him that our organisation was against homosexualism. He interrupted by asking me to quote a clause in our party constitution or disciplinary code where it was written or implied that sodomy was not allowed. There was no such written clause, one cell committee member told him, but it was accepted tradition in our society that men should not cohabitate.

"But in the mines and hostels it has now become tradition," he said, "times have changed." It was useless to argue with him. We left him to tell other cell comrades of our findings. Many comrades felt that they should be ostracised and later we told them of their punishment. Nobody would communicate with them for a period of two months. They would also be required to clean the cells in which they were staying daily for a month. The wyfie took his sentence in silence but the 'husband' pointed out that they had already been assaulted and that that was punishment enough. More so, since their faces had been battered and they had been given black eyes. Also, when Theron and the hospital orderlies asked them about how they got injured they did not disclose the fact that they had been assaulted in our cell. There was nothing we could do, we told them, we had to maintain strict discipline among ourselves. Our Disciplinary Code was a guide and even in prison we had to abide by its tenets.

This case opened my eyes to this system of migrant labour. I shall have to befriend many political prisoners who come from the rural areas and make enquiries about the whole system and its attendant evils. I'm certain that there are many things which we who come from the urban areas do not know about.

Chief Warder Theron's plans with the Big Fives of turning homosexuals among us hasn't made any headway. The comrades' tough resistance and the general abhorrence of homosexualism have played a great role. On the whole I have been impressed by the resistance put up by former students. They are prepared to die rather than be made homosexuals. There are two comrades who were turned into homosexuals by the Big Fives before our group arrived in Robben Island in December. They have been ostracised by all cells. In fact, we found them already ostracised. No one talks to them except the Big Fives and the warders. They have warm clothing, shoes and socks.

Their cheeks are round and gleaming because of the ndalav and mgqemane they are being fed with daily. At work they do very light work and are hardly being supervised by the warders. In fact, all the warders, including Oom Dellie and Jan Kleynhans and other prison officials, know that they are wyfies of the Big Fives.

After some investigations I managed to pick up a little of their background. They are both in their late 20s and have been tsotsis. They had previously been arrested for criminal offences and convicted. I'm certain that is where they came across pederasty. Later after release they resorted to their old ways — pickpocketing. When they heard that there was going to be a general uprising against White domination in 1963, they 'joined' the PAC in February of that year. They had hoped that during the uprising there was going to be countrywide looting and burglaries and they had hoped to join the gang of looters and burglars, or possibly to lead them. Unfortunately for them, they were arrested in April 1963 in the countrywide swoop and convicted for membership of a banned organisation. When they arrived in Robben Island and saw their former pals (the Big Fives) in power they identified themselves with them.

* * *

Captain Fourie has begun calling political prisoners for discussions and 'reorientation' as he calls it. This time the first 20 comrades who were called are those who arrived here first on the island. If he follows that sequence then it would take a week before our group from Leeuwkop Maximum Prison is called.

Some of the comrades who had been called by Captain Fourie have given us a preview of some of his questions. His first question is what was your reason for joining the PAC or ANC. After one had given him the reasons, he would then rant on about how the Nationalist Party government was doing everything in its power to grant freedom and independence to the different tribes in South Africa. Secondly, he wanted to know all the reasons why you did not want the Bantustans. Thirdly, he wanted to know what your intentions were after completion of your sentence. There were also other personal questions about one's ambition, family, religion, school and place of work.

A week after this, our group was called. Interrogations and 'reorientation' were now being conducted in the new offices. The office into which I was ushered was large and spacious and smelled of wet paint. Captain Fourie sat in a swinging chair, his eyes fixed on some papers before him. My file lay nearby on the table with my name and surname written in big block letters. It was already thick and contained particulars about my life; all obtained from different sources — mostly informers, including Nomsa. He raised his eyes and with a warm smile, he beckoned me to sit down. I sat down opposite him.

"Now" said Captain Fourie after I had sat down, "today we are going to talk business. I want you to be pragmatic and to think about your own future. I also want you to be honest, not only to me but to yourself in the questions I'm going to ask you."

"What do you mean by saying that I should be honest to a representative of a vile system?" I interrupted before he could continue.

"What do you mean," he said agitated, "by saying that I represent a vile system? We inherited the present system from the British. We did not invent racial discrimination and the pass laws. All that came with the British. We are doing our very best to give you freedom and independence in your own lands. The Transkei will get its independence, Zululand will get its independence and so too will the other homelands. What more can we do for the Blacks?"

"We do not want your tribal independence," I said, "and we do not want any balkanisation of South Africa. You say you did not invent apartheid but the British; but the time when the British took over from you in 1806, you had already half-exterminated the Khoisan people and those that remained, you had enslaved. And you trekked away from the Cape Colony in 1836 because you wanted to continue with slavery after it had been abolished in 1834 by the British and you are still indirectly practising slavery up to the present time. That's what Piet Retief's Manifesto of the 1830s was all about — the perpetuation of slavery."

"All that you have said," he resumed, "are the accidents of history and should not influence you in your opting for the Bantustans. Ours is a Christian government which has done everything to uplift the lives of the Blacks. But we cannot achieve everything overnight. It takes time. When we took over in 1948, the Blacks were very poor and lived under the Poverty Datum Line. Today the Blacks have the highest standard of living in Africa. Many Blacks in the African states, given the choice, would prefer to come and work and live here, because here we have stability, prosperity and security, something which is lacking in those states. Just look at what is happening in the Belgian Congo just now. There's complete anarchy."

"Who brought about that anarchy?" I asked.

"Let us leave the Congo alone," he said, "there is enough chaos going on there and as to who started it all, it is none of our business. We are concerned about our future here in South Africa. What I want you to tell me is why you personally don't want the Bantustans. I want you to be frank with me and to pour out everything in your mind."

"We do not want Bantustans . . ."

"No, no, no," he interrupted, "I don't want you to tell me about what the PAC or the ANC say about the Bantustans. We know their policies and have piles upon piles of their documents and other publications including those printed abroad. What I want to know are your own views."

"My views are synonymous with those of the PAC," I said.

"Is that all?..

"That's why I was convicted for membership and furthering the aims of a banned organisation."

"You can go out," said Captain Fourie, "call David Ramagole."

As soon as I was outside I told David that it was his turn.

"Anything new?" he whispered.

"It's the same thing — the Bantustans," I whispered back.

One by one the comrades went in. Some came back angry and others shaking their heads. Some refused to answer any of Captain Fourie's questions. They remained mum throughout. Others like Thomas Motloung, lost their temper and the Captain also lost his, resulting in a fierce exchange of words and sometimes insults.

When the Captain finished with the last man in our group, we went to queue for our supper at 5 o'clock and waited for the workspans to return. After supper we went to stand in front of our cells waiting to be counted in. Suddenly, a warder called van der Berg, a crony of Theron, came accompanied by three members of the Big Fives who were Theron's spies. Two of them worked in the yard cleaning cells and the third, Ralph, was Oom Dellie's agterreier in the Quarryspan. Van der Berg told us to go into our cells and every man to stand behind his folded mats and blankets. Another Head Warder called Zeelie came to join van der Berg.

"Waar's hulle?" (where are they), asked Zeelie.

The three Big Fives came and pointed at me and four other comrades. Then our blankets were searched and out came a crude terrible self-made knife from my blankets. It had a very sharp blade though its sides were rusty. I was shocked. But my shock did not last long. I was kicked in the chest by Head Warder Zeelie and hit by van der Berg. Another kick from Zeelie followed on my belly. After this I was told to stand on one side. In three of the comrades' blankets knives were also found and on the fourth there was a letter purportedly written by our President Mangaliso Sobukwe. After we had been assaulted, the five of us were marched out of the cell. and there we were made to strip naked. As I was a bit slow in stripping, I felt another kick on my chest from Zeelie and another blow on my face from van der Berg.

"Quick, strip," screamed Zeelie.

I quickly stripped naked. They slowly went through my convict clothes while I stood naked. They found nothing. And so too with the other comrades.

"Come," said Head Warder Zeelie after we had dressed.

He took us to Chief Warder Theron who was standing near the guardpost which stood between Section A and the kitchen. Van der Berg held the knives and the letter supposed to have been written by our President Sobukwe. The three Big Fives also came along.

"Yes, what's wrong?" asked Theron.

"Chief," said Head Warder Zeelie, "we have just discovered these five dangerous Poqo 'bandiete' about to start an uprising. They have also been communicating with Sobukwe chief." Van der Berg then showed him the knives — all crude and dangerous weapons.

"These weapons were discovered in their blankets chief," said van der Berg. He handed the letter over to Theron.

Theron read the letter and seemingly he discovered the writer's handwriting; it appeared to be a familiar handwriting to him. I saw saw a little smile on his face and he looked at one of the Big Fives. And the culprit's eyes blinked.

"What happened?" asked Theron to Ralph the criminal convict whose eyes had blinked.

"Last night," began Ralph, "there was a big meeting in the cell. The chairman of the meeting was this one" and he pointed at me. "He addressed the cell and told all the others that they had received a letter from Sobukwe secretly and it instructed them to sharpen their weapons and to kill all the warders here in the island and thereafter seize the boat and escape to the mainland."

"They also said Mozambique is now free baas," added another toothless criminal convict of the triumvirate, a product of District Six. "They said it was now time for them to go and join their brothers in Mozambique because the guerillas were now on their way to South Africa."

"They also said you were supposed to be killed baas," added the third member of the triumvirate.

"In what language were they addressing the meeting?" asked Theron.

"In their own language chief," said Head Warder Zeelie, as though he was there.

"You two skollies," said Theron to the two Coloured criminal convicts, "how did you understand what was being said in the meeting?" The two criminal convicts blushed. They could give no reply. Neither of them understood any of the African languages, except Afrikaans.

"And you Ralph, if there was a big meeting in the cell last night why

didn't you tell me of it first thing in the morning?"
"I forgot baas," said Ralph.
"You forgot?" barked Theron.
"Ja baas," said Ralph timidly.
"How could you forget about such an important meeting? What made you remember it?"
There was silence from all. Theron looked at the five accused.
"Take them to five different cells," he instructed van der Berg.
"And these dangerous weapons?" asked Head Warder Zeelie.
"What about them? They were found hidden in their blankets chief."
"Take them to my office," said Theron calmly.
"And the letter from Sobukwe chief?" asked Zeelie again.
"Take it to my office too."
"How many meal stops did you say they must be given chief?" asked Zeelie.
"I said take them to different cells — there are no meal stops," ruled Theron.

After taking our mats and blankets from our cell we were taken to different cells. I found myself in Section C, cell three. Most of the occupants of this cell were Poqo-criminals. There were about four other political prisoners. One of them was Enock Mathibola (nicknamed 'The-horn-of-the-guinea-fowl' because of an inch long lump of flesh in the centre of his head).

We later learned of the circumstances which led to our being 'bombed'. There was a young light-complexioned comrade in the cell from King Williamstown. For some time Ralph had had his eyes on this comrade. Later on he had approached the comrade and had asked to be 'politicised'. It was during the 'politicisation' process that the comrade realised that Ralph was not interested in his being 'politicised' but had set his eyes on pederasty. The comrade abruptly stopped the lessons, reported Ralph's intentions to us and later changed cell. Ralph and his two friends had to look for some scapegoats and thus had 'bombed' us as the ringleaders who had thwarted their intentions.

"Never tread on my path," were Ralp's words to us after we had been bombed, "otherwise you'll be struck by lightning."

The following day I went to the Landbouspan. When we reached our workplace, we were given tools and we began working. I had a pick and began digging. Teeman came and stood on top of his mound and his voice echoed out loud and clear as far as the seashore. It was the same song: 'In the morning, in the morning men, listen, we talk about parole in the morning and pity those who are still coming." His right arm went up in the Big Fives salute and his eyes were cast far away in the southern horizon, far away where the purple waters of the boiling sea were shimmering. Our voices came out loud in unison, following his. The song was faster, with more vigour and harmony. You could hear distinctly the baritone from the peasants and former migrant labourers.

"Dog, step," screamed Teeman. And we fell into step, left feet forward.

"D-o-g-s, u-p," he screamed again.

And we jumped up, left feet first, simultaneously spinning the picks in the air by their axes and brought them down to sink with force into the hard earth. There is no doubt about it, our Boer masters have got us this time; we have been harnessed just like oxen with heavy yokes on our necks. The ox-drivers are the warders and the Big Fives. And the rifles, just like the ox-drivers' whips, are there to keep us in check. All opposition, despite the continuous and steady resistance was being ruthlessly crushed by hook or crook. We were now like machines. The short tiny Teeman stood triumphantly in front of us. With a little twickering smile, showing his two missing front teeth, he kept shaking his head rhythmically with the song. His hands were hanging loose over his sides, his feet moving rhythmically with the song, as though marking time. He was displaying the same antics which are used by triumphant 'maskandas' (song leaders) in Zulu weddings in Soweto when emerging victorious over their rivals. And I wondered as I swung the pick, whether he was displaying victory over us politicians or maybe perhaps, his former arch-rivals the Big Six.

His voice rose in a crescendo and I guessed that something was going to happen. I heard someone crying and when I looked around I saw Jan Kleynhans beating him. The victim was Richmond — the same man he had assaulted when I first came to work in the Landbouspan in December and had been assaulting ever since. He was now sitting on top of him, throttling him for some time, then leaving him and later repeating the same process again. Richmond was crying. Jan was screaming something at him but I could not hear what he was saying. He stood up and beat him to stand up and go back to his work. Richmond, who for the last two months has been coughing blood, stood up to begin work again.

No sooner had Jan finished with Richmond that he was busy on others again. Piet, Fourie and the other warders assisted by the Big Fives were also running up and down beating prisoners at random.

Lunch came and we were given our food. After lunch we were taken to the seashore to collect seaweed, which had dried along the seashore, into heaps. It was the same seaweed which had been pulled out of the sea in the month of March when so many comrades had been beaten and pushed into the sea to remove it. Despite the howling of the warders to make us work faster, no one was assaulted this time. As we had already become machines, we worked very fast moving from place to place creating heaps. We went as far as the lighthouse. When the time for knocking off came, we were counted and marched through the main road passing through the dorpie back to prison.

"Kyk hoe loop hulle" (look at how they walk), said Jan to Boer Warders' wives and children each time we passed the warders' houses while they peeped at us and some of the children hurled insults at us as communists and Poqos. We were bespattered with lime and dragging our feet along, our heads bowed, eyes looking down at where to put our feet without trampling on the man in front.

20. The-Horn-of-the-Guinea-Fowl

Enock Mathibela was an old man of fifty-six. He had been a trade unionist in Pretoria. One day in 1962 he was invited to a meeting of other trade unionists and there, to his surprise as he later claimed, they were shown how bombs were made. The ingredients were also displayed. He smelled a rat, he later told me, and could see that that path led to prison and possibly death.

In 1963 in the country-wide swoop on ANC activists he was arrested under the Sabotage Act. Some of the people with whom he had been at that meeting had turned State witnesses. Evidence was given that he had been there in one of the meetings where they were shown how bombs were made. When he entered the witness box, he told the court that he did not know when he went to the meeting that they were going to be shown how bombs were to be made, otherwise he would not have attended the meeting. He was asked by the prosecutor why after the meeting he didn't report the whole incident to the nearest police station. Mathiebela failed to give a satisfactory reply. He was found guilty together with others. The judge gave him the minimum sentence of five years.

When Mathibela arrived in Robben Island in April 1964, finding the conditions bad, he wrote a letter to the Minister of Justice and Prisons asking for a pardon and re-stating his position that he had never been a member of the ANC. When the news of this reached the ears of political prisoners, Mathibela was in trouble. He was ostracised as an informer who had been planted by the Boers.

The reply from the Minister of Justice came and it informed Mathibela that his letter had been received and its contents duly noted. It advised him to finish his five-year sentence first and after that his request would be considered. The reply broke Mathibela's back. He became irritable and anti all political prisoners. He then resorted to religion — Judaism as he called it — upholding the teachings of the Old Testament and denouncing Christianity.

Physically he was of medium height, brown in complexion, with a small gap in his front teeth. He had an inch-long lump in the centre of his head, making it look as though he had a horn. Some political prisoners took advantage of that physical deformity to taunt him.

They teased him and called him 'The-horn-of-the-guinea-fowl'. He often went to the prison hospital to request that the lump be removed. Chief Warder Nel and Teezar used to jeer at him and drive him away much to the amusement of his taunters. But he wouldn't give up. The following week he would be back again on his knees praying to the orderly to assist him as the other prisoners were mocking him. Nel loved to crack jokes about his lump of flesh on the head and after touching and patting the 'horn' to the amusement of prisoners, he would then drive him away.

Enock Mathibela, lonely, ostracised and a political outcast, was now one of the occupants of cell three which was full of Poqo-criminals. I learned to appreciate his likes and dislikes, his moods and his feeble hopes. I learned and studied how the ostracism and daily criticism were affecting him. To me he no longer became the bad man of the island but a fellow human being whom many political prisoners did not care to understand. I realised that he needed subtle political re-orientation and therefore decided to embark on the task. When I found him, he had been alone with his God and now I stood inbetween, to share his ideas, correct his erroneous conclusions about man and to encourage and inspire him when tongues as sharp as arrows had been mocking and jeering at him throughout the working day. That he had lost faith in man, was beyond doubt. His only faith lay in the God of Israel. And to that God of Israel he now prayed for comfort and solace.

It is cold — terribly cold. An icy wind came through the door and blew past me — and I shivered. Enock Mathibela was sleeping alone — all alone. His mind possibly ruminating over the accusations and insults hurled at him during the day. The same icy wind blew across him. I saw his face as though shrinking. And then he coughed. After coughing he stood up to prepare for his evening prayers. He had only one withered old mat and three torn see-through blankets. I also had the same. A rough cough came out of his chest and he winced painfully. Then he knelt down and lifted up his hands to heaven, his eyes cast at the cell's concrete ceiling above.

"Thou art holy, Thou art holy . . . Lord God Almighty." His stentorian voice boomed out in the cold cell while all of us prisoners lay shivering. After pausing for some seconds he repeated again: "Thou art holy, Thou art holy, Thou art holy . . . Lord God Almighty. All kings and kingdoms bow before Thee." Then he brought his arms before his chest, his palms together, bowed his head three times almost touching the bedding. Then he prayed in low tones, his voice booming out time and again. When he had finished his prayers, he bowed three times again and then stood up. He tied the buttons of his jacket and went under his blankets fully clad. After his prayer he looked triumphant. Then he began cracking a joke or two with me about the fickleness and foibles of human nature and the everlasting power of the Almighty. Man, he was fond of saying, defied God long ago and now through his science, man was trying to discover the existence of God.

I also prepared my blankets and decided to sleep with my clothes on like Mathibela. My spirits were sickeningly low and my mind indulged in self-pity. I was in one of those terrible moods which sometimes attacked me. My close comrade David Ramagole was now terribly ill and when he coughed blood came out. Nel was subjecting him to the same ill-treatment that he had meted out to the late Gantsha Khuboni. David was a former professional boxer and a Black Belt judoist and together we had shadow-boxed and make breakfalls in the evenings after lock-up ever since we had first met when awaiting trial in Number 4 Prison and continued it up to the island. The 'bombing' incident had also affected me and I could not understand how man could cringe so low and be turned into such a monster like the criminal convicts who had 'bombed' us.

I decided not to think about the dark future lying before me but to reminisce about the dim past which was fast fading into oblivion, but which was still a part of me. To think of where it had all started. How did I become embroiled in all this? To find myself in the company of the wretched Big Fives and now to share the same cell with Poqo-criminals — a crude bunch of human beings and to be in the company of Enock Mathibela — the loneliest and most hated man in Robben Island.

* * *

First it was the procession in 1949 to the Kliptown Police Station. Its impressions had become indelible in my mind and had opened new vistas which otherwise would have been closed for some time to a young boy of my age at the time. My father's arrest and subsequent punching had further confirmed my earlier impressions and in this particular incident, I and my whole family had been personally affected. The stories aunt Bellina related to me had made me begin listening to conversations and to read papers about the suffering and oppression of Black people. I also began attending public meetings of the ANC. When the Defiance of Unjust Laws Campaign was launched in 1952, I was a young boy of 14 doing my standard four at Lilydale Community School. I had followed the campaign with interest from the beginning up to the end. I read about it and listened to conversations about it until it fizzled out. I often attended ANC public meetings at the Dadoo Square between Javabu and Moroka. In 1955 I arrived in Kliptown just when the police were disrupting the ANC conference which was deliberating on the Freedom Charter. But black clouds were already looming on the horizon. All was not well within the ANC. Another group calling themselves the Africanists were already vocal in their condemnation of the ANC programme and tactics. They felt that the 1949 nation-building Programme of Action had been abandoned and that the ANC leadership had been 'captured' by White liberals who were posing under the guise of being communists.

At Orlando High School where I was now schooling, we discussed these issues with other students who were also following the political trends. Some students who knew leaders of both factions of the ANC in Orlando East, went to see them to get some clarifications on key issues in the liberation struggle. We debated these reports and decided that the Africanists were right. Somewhere between 1953 and 1955, the ANC leadership, without the mandate of the people, had made major policy changes and steered the struggle on a rightist course. And that ultimately led to the formation of the PAC in April 1959. Many youths, workers, peasants and intellectuals rallied to the new organisation. Against the repeated advice of my mother, I became a fully fledged member of the PAC after the Sharpeville Shootings. I became a committee member of the Zola Branch and when the Jabulani Branch was opened in early 1961, I became its first secretary and Nelboath Ntshuntsha its chairman. I remembered the nightly meetings, the enrolment of new members, the oath-taking ceremonies. And then, immediately after the Sharpeville Shootings when my father realised that I had joined the PAC, he told me that I had joined the wrong organisation; I should have joined the ANC he said. For the first time we held political discussions with my father and argued into the night. He idolised Albert Luthuli, then President of the ANC, and said his policy was correct because it was aimed at dividing the Whites and having some of them support the Black course. I disagreed and told him that that policy would not work because those South African White liberals were only for reforms and not for a government of the Black majority and as such would not support armed struggle. When the ANC's armed wing 'Umkhonto we Sizwe' began planting bombs against pylons, rails and other government installations, I told him that the White liberals must have had a hand in drafting that strategy as they would not like to see armed struggle in South Africa. My father had no reply to this except to ask me where we who were propagating armed struggle were going to get arms from. We are going to attack all police stations through the country I told him, seize all the weapons and then engage in guerilla warfare. After these conversations my father became sympathetic to the PAC though he still idolised Albert Luthuli and the ANC. After this I would come home with fellow PAC members and he would give lectures two or three times a week on the liberation struggle and prominent personalities in the liberation struggle like Anton Muziwakhe Lembede whom he knew personally.

I remembered the return of Leballo from prison in 1962 and the subsequent establishment of the PAC headquarters in December of that year. I remembered my trip to see him in January 1963 and our deliberations on the struggle. All had gone on well then and it appeared at the time that 1963 was going to be our year of freedom. We were going to give the enemy a surprise attack and deal him a mortal blow.

My last trip to see Potlako Leballo was on 26 March 1963 and the journey had been hectic with the forces of darkness racing behind our heels. It had even forced us to swim across the Caledon River near Ficksburg into Basutoland, to escape from the enemy forces' clutches. The comrade with whom I crossed the river nearly drowned but, having been a good swimmer from Kliptown, I managed to save him and carry him across the wide river which was in flood. That night we had been harboured by the local people and the following day after we had dried our wet clothes, we caught a bus around 10am from Ficksburg to Maseru. When we arrived in Maseru, we went to see Leballo that same afternoon. We gave him a full report about how many PAC functionaries had already been arrested by the enemy in pre-dawn swoops throughout Soweto. Leballo, a chain pipe-smoker kept on sucking at his pipe time and again as the man I was accompanying gave him the report while I made additions here and there. We told him that we were both on the run and had escaped and that our homes were under hourly surveillance.

"There's a meeting tonight," he said after we had finished speaking, "I shall see you there." We were escorted by one of his bodyguards to a number of houses where PAC members were staying.

Around 8 o'clock that night we were taken to another house where we met other comrades who had also just arrived across the border. Some of them were from the Cape Province, one from the Orange Free State and only two of us were from Soweto.

Leballo arrived in the meeting dressed in a dark brown Kaunda-like suit whose trousers tapered towards the shoes. He was holding a pistol. He was accompanied by Mfanasekhaya Gqobose the then Poqo Commander. We were about 17 in all excluding Leballo, Gqobose and the two bodyguards. Leballo was in a fighting mood as he gave us a speech about the situation inside South Africa. "This is the position," he kept on concluding after each harangue. Time and again he kept on holding his pistol and lifting it up as though he was going to shoot at the ceiling. He would put it down and begin puffing at his pipe which on many occasions he forgot to light. And then suddenly, he began telling the others about how we had swum across the Caledon river at night while the enemy police were chasing us. He commended me for having saved the life of the other comrade I had crossed with.

After this he reminded us that we were at war and that we had to fight against the Boer police and soldiers. He wanted to know why we had not fought against the policemen who were chasing us. Why did we instead decide to flee? He called us cowards and told us to go back to Soweto to organise for an armed attack against police stations and other strategic installations. He told us that when we arrive in Soweto we should not stay in our houses. It was stupid of us to stay in our homes when we knew quite well that we were going to lead a revolution. All those who had been arrested, he said, had been caught napping in their homes. "When you are a revolutionary you must not sleep in your home. You must carry a spade and at night you just go to a veld dig a hole and sleep there for the night and when the enemy discovers that hole you can go and dig another hole elsewhere. In that way you'll never be discovered. You can even use that spade in armed combat when discovered. And why don't you make use of those many disused mines?" He picked up his pipe again and lit it and began puffing the smoke.

"That is the position," he repeated, "that is the position." He continued puffing again. "Gqobose," he said to the Poqo commander, "just talk to your soldiers. They seem not to be aware that we are at war."

"We are at war men," said Gqobose also smoking a pipe. He was light complexioned and though in his late forties already had grey hair throughout his head. He said those words slowly and emphatically in English with a slight Xhosa accent. "You must learn how to kill the enemy. There is no other way in which we can get our land back. You must go back to your different places, stay underground and wait for us to give you the green light. But before we give you the green light, don't leave the police and their agents — you must kill them. We want that the informers and the Special Branch must fear you and not the other way round. We don't want people to be coming here for nothing. When you come here it should only be to inform us that you have killed so many of the enemy. We don't want people to be crowding here in Basutoland to come and save their skins. The struggle is not here it is right in South Africa. This place here is only for the co-ordination of our country-wide activities."

"They must all go back," said Leballo, "and to show that they are determined they must kill some of the policemen they come across on their way back home.''

My friend then raised the question of an article which had appeared in *The Star* newspaper of the previous day which attributed to Leballo a press statement to the effect that more than 10,000 Poqo militants were poised to start an armed insurrection and were only waiting for his word. Leballo supported by other officials confirmed this and said that is what Castro and Che Guevara had also done by informing the enemy before embarking on the struggle against Batista. This tactic made the enemy panic and in that way the forces of revolution seized the opportunity to strike at the appropriate moment. Though we were not satisfied by their explanation, we did not argue with them.

We stayed in Maseru for two more days while they gave us last briefings on the tactics to be used against the enemy. On the third day the group from the Cape returned to their areas. They were all arrested after crossing the Caledon river into South Africa. The same day, the man from Welkom in the Orange Free State province was also arrested on the South African side after the train he had boarded left Maseru. He was later sentenced to three years imprisonment and afterwards was used in my case and the cases of many others as a State Witness. The two of us who were from Johannesburg left Maseru individually; I swam across the Caledon River and found my way back to Soweto where, after arriving and giving the report to my chairman Ntshuntsha, I continued with my revolutionary activities and waited for Leballo and Gqobose to give us the date.

Meanwhile the enemy was not asleep. Through informers and others who had been arrested, it was able to gather information which became more frightening as the days passed; that there was going to be a mass uprising against White domination. And then, there were the press reports, first in *The Star* newspaper and later taken up by others, that Leballo had about 10,000 Poqo militants already poised to strike. With the assistance of the British authorities in the protectorate of Basutoland, the PAC offices were raided in Maseru and documents seized, photocopies given to the South African Special Branch. Leballo and his assistants went underground. From the names and adresses found in the PAC office the enemy raided all PAC functionaries throughout the country. The majority of them were arrested in their homes much to the chagrin and disappointment of Leballo and Gqobose. The uprising had been thwarted. It was another ignominious defeat in the long string of defeats that our people had had to endure in the last three centuries. It was to lead to the poking of our arses by the enemy and the pissing into the mouths of others; it was to lead to daily beatings in the Landbou- and Quarryspans and the raping of some of our comrades by the Big Fives. It was to lead during the same year to the arrest of many ANC 'Umkhonto we Sizwe' activists culminating in the arrests of the ANC leaders at Rivonia. After so much preparation and so many risky undertakings, we were now to be on the receiving end and endure humiliations untold of in human suffering. The enemy once again had luck on its side, all because of the assistance they were getting from the Western countries and also because of our inexperience and our leaders' inexperience in conducting a revolution.

Immediately after my arrival from Maseru I went underground. As I was already on the hunted listed of the enemy, I no longer slept at home. I never slept in one place but kept changing my places to sleep. I always made sure that no one knew where I was going to sleep. And neither did I know where I was going to sleep. I always decided on the spur of the moment. It was in this manner that I found myself having to spend a night at Nomsa's home in Senaoane on 19 April 1963. Since our separation we had remained friends. I visited her once or twice a month for a chat for old time's sake. She also often visited my family and it was in this way that she learned that I was on the run and that the police were looking for me.

Nomsa's mother was not happy to learn that I was going to spend the night there. Moreso, there were hourly broadcasts by Radio Bantu which spread propaganda that almost all PAC militants had been arrested and that others who had surrendered urged those still on the run to surrender to the nearest police stations. It also urged 'law abiding' people to report to the nearest police stations on any suspicious characters.

That night I slept uneasily. In the morning Nomsa's mother asked me why I did not report to the nearest police station in Moroka. I told her that I could not do that, not only out of principle, but also because of what the enemy was going to do to me. I also told her that I would definitely be given a very heavy prison sentence. And then Nomsa asked me where I was going to sleep that night. I told her the truth: that I was first going to Diepkloof to collect my money from a former school mate now turned musician whom she knew, after which I was not yet certain as to where I was going to sleep. I parted company with Nomsa and her mother but worried about what the old woman had told me, that I should surrender to the nearest police station.

I arrived at Diepkloof location around 7 o'clock in the evening, found that my friend had not yet arrived from work, unaware that I was being followed by the Special Branch. My friend and his wife arrived with another friend, also a musician, around 8 o'clock. They all knew that I was on the run. When I asked them about the money due to me I discovered that they had none. So my trip to Diepkloof had all been in vain. I was just about to leave when suddenly the door was banged open and I found myself looking at three pistols and three familiar faces entered the house. In a few minutes I was a gory mess. I was under arrest and handcuffed and taken together with my two friends to a waiting car about three streets away, after the house had been ransacked and everything turned upside down. I was actually saved from severe assault while handcuffed by the cries of my friend's wife while left-hooks, right crosses and uppercuts landed on my body from all angles while I stood in dignified silence hardly ducking or warding off the blows. From there we were taken to the other musician's house and while his mother asked what had happened the police were busy turning everything upside down and ignoring her. From there we were taken to the Marshall Square police station where I was further assaulted while still maintaining the same dignified silence but looking at their faces; thereafter I was put in an isolation cell alone.

I was later to learn that the person who had informed on me was Nomsa. She knew one of the African Special Branch policemen who was staying in Mapetla. His name was Caswell. After I had left her home, she had hurried to tell this policeman where I was going to that evening. And the whole of that day the Special Branch police had parked their vehicle near the Baragwanath Hospital waiting for me to alight from the bus travelling between Zola location terminus and the Baragwanath Hospital bus stop. When they saw me alighting from the bus they had sent someone to tail me from behind.

The following day my musician friends were released and I was taken to the Grays Building together with Paul Masha who had also been arrested the previous night of the 20th. While I sat in a room on the fourth floor under close guard, Paul Masha was being tortured in the room next door with electric shocks and I could hear his screams. They had put a tape-recorder in front of him and had wanted him to make a confession. Later they took a statement from him where he implicated himself. But that electric shock torture damaged one of his lungs — the left one. And this was only discovered in Robben Island where he subsequently underwent treatment for tuberculosis.

When my turn came, I walked with dignity accompanied by six Special Branch policemen. In charge of them was Warrant Officer Pretorius who was tall and big shouldered. Magoro and Caswell were the only two Black Special Branch policemen. Lieutenant Viseer and another dignified senior officer whom I suspected to be Colonel Spengler came in for a short while to instruct Pretorius not to waste any time with me. "You understand," said Pretorius after they had gone, "I have instructions not to waste my time with you. If you do not want to speak, then we'll get to work."

"I'm not a criminal," I told Pretorius in Afrikaans, his mother tongue, "and I refuse to be treated like a criminal."

"You come from a good family," said Pretorius, "I have seen your parents — they are both good people and they told me of your good background. What made you associate yourself with these Poqos?"

"And he speaks such fluent Afrikaans," said another Boer policeman.

"Are you going to make a statement?" asked Pretorius.

"Sure," I said, "and in Afrikaans." The special Branch police were all taken aback, even Pretorius did not believe his ears. He asked me the same question again and I gave him the same reply. We then sat down while I spoke and he wrote down what I said. And then I told him that I had finished my statement. He gasped, "God jong," (My God, man), he exclaimed, "you said nothing in this statement."

"Do you want me to incriminate myself?" I asked.

"You must tell us about the PAC and your involvement in it and the names of the people you worked with and the instructions you were given about killing Whites. Or do you want us to torture you?"

"Torture me, what for?" I said, "I'm not a criminal. I haven't killed anybody."

"Now we are going to get down to business," said Pretorius, "I hate to do this but have no alternative. He stood up and I noted that he had a pistol tucked in his waist thus making his brown suit jacket a little bulging at the waist. I was sitting on a chair cool, calm and collected waiting for any eventuality but determined that whatever they did to me, I would always bear myself with dignity and not make any confessions. Later they discussed among themselves what tactics to use against me. I heard them saying in Afrikaans within my hearing that they were appalled by my attitude when being assaulted, that I neither grimaced, cried, warded off the blows nor ducked but just looked at them as they did so. One of them suggested electric shocks but Pretorius replied that they already had enough evidence against me from statements which had already been made by other detainees, some of them who were going to be made State witnesses. And with that, without any further exchange of words, I was taken back to Marshall Square with Paul Masha and after a three-day stay there we were transferred to Number 4 Prison. On 4 September 1963, together with three other comrades from the Zola Branch, I stood trial. The fourth accused was discharged for lack of evidence against him. John Mdakane, accused No.1, Ralfas Jele accused No.3 and myself, accused No.2, were all sentenced to six years' imprisonment each for membership and furthering the aims of a banned organisation. The evidence against me was scanty. The man from Welkom who was brought as a State Witness against me, testified that he knew none of us. Three other witnesses also said they did not know me. The fourth said he knew and had seen me once in the company of the other accused and that accused No.3 had rallied him to join the PAC. When he was asked by the defence lawyer Adv. Davis (from the Defence and Aid) what I and the first accused had said to him on that occasion, he said, we had not spoken to him. Later on the prosecutor told the magistrate that three of the witnesses had been assaulted the previous day in the location and that what they said there in court was different from the statements they had made under oath. He told the magistrate the State witnesses were afraid of speaking against us for fear of being killed when they went back to the location. And thus he prayed that we be given the maximum sentences of three years on each count as it was obvious that we were very dangerous PAC activists.

Poor Nomsa. She was later to regret what she had done. The information leaked and even reached the ears of my parents. And then she became ill and began losing weight until she became almost a skeleton. At the Baragwanath Hospital where she later went, they found nothing wrong with her; even the X-rays showed that there was nothing wrong with her lungs. Ultimately she became an invalid. By selling me to the enemy she had sold part of herself to the devil. She could not live with that memory; but she had to. After all, she was a product of Jabavu and those Western films that she often saw where there was always cheating and double-cheating.

*   *   *

It was during this time that a plane landed at the airstrip in Robben Island carrying the Rivonia trial prisoners. Vehicles went to the airstrip to transport them to the newly completed kulukuds. A few days later they were at work in the square encompassed by the kulukuds, wire-mesh over their eyes, 4lb hammers in their hands, hitting at the quarry stones while a warder called 'Kwarini' van Niekerk walked proudly among them inspecting the sizes of the particles produced.

21. We are starving

The month of June is the coldest month in Robben Island. We are still freezing at night and during the day. It is always cloudy and we hardly get the sun's rays. When it rains during working hours, we are not allowed to rush to the tool shed for protection. The order is that we must first wait for a command from Oom Dellie to go there. In most cases the order comes when we are already wet. After the rain has stopped we are led back to our work again. When it rains heavily and there is no sign that it may stop, we are marched back to prison through the tearing rain. There are no raincoats for political prisoners; they are only there for criminal convicts.

We have been informed by some warders that this is the coldest winter ever experienced in South Africa. Even in the mainland, according to the paper cuttings we came across, the lowest temperatures have been reported in many districts throughout the country. We are still starving and many of us have lost a lot of weight. And the number of ill comrades has increased. Richmond du Preez the ANC comrade who has often been a victim of Jan Kleynhans has now been accepted at the prison hospital. It was discovered that he suffered from TB. Paul Masha the PAC comrade whose left lung got punctured when he was tortured by the Special Branch at the Grays Building, has also been admitted as a TB patient.

My friend David Ramagole is now a pitiable sight. He's virtually a bag of bones. Walking the distance from the quarry to prison every morning completely exhausts him and he's still coughing blood. His pupils are now enlarged, his mouth always dry and his finger nails have turned white. He feels tired very easily and most of the time I have to help by supporting him along the way. I always sit near him when eating and have to force him as he always has no appetite. Most of the time now I give him my soup, vegetables and pieces of meat. We also got some 'umhlonyane' for him and old man Tolepi advised me to try and boil it and give him to drink. Together with Johnson Mlambo and other comrades we managed to get the services of Bezyl King, one of the cooks, to boil the herb for him and smuggle it into the cell in the evenings. 'Umhlonyane' is very good, Tolepi told me one day and has sustained the lives of many farm labourers in Boer farms.

After drinking the herb for about a month with a very marked improvement, David's health suddenly became bad again. "I'll bloody kick you damn kaffir," Nel kept telling him as he saw David shuffling his feet towards him slowly.

The atmosphere in Robben Island is humid thus causing many comrades to suffer from pleurisy. Most of the TB patients are in actual fact, suffering from pleurisy. A few of the comrades have been taken to the mainland where the water had been drained out of their lungs.

Because of starvation many comrades are now eating raw oysters near the sea where sand is being heaped. The oysters are stuck on stones and rocks and it is not easy to remove them. Once you touch the shell you can't get it off the rock again. You have to use a sharp instrument like a space to disconnect it quickly. I tasted one and found it to be delicious. We don't even remove the insides of the oysters, we swallow them whole. The taste didn't matter much, what mattered was getting the proteins. I am now collecting a lot of these oysters and giving some of them to David and encouraging him to eat. And he eats them.

There is one comrade of the ANC named Jacob Lebone who has begun eating worms. Jacob is the same comrade who showed us how to make sleeping bags out of blankets. He has announced that any comrade who sees a worm when digging should call him. And he's been eating them as though he's been doing it for years. And I've watched him pick up weight gradually. I saw some peasants envying him.

There is one comrade from the PAC who has begun eating grass. He's from Langa location in Cape Town. He began playfully and some comrades especially from among the peasants also followed playfully. And this playfulness became a habit while more comrades also joined playfully. I observed the peasants closely and saw them picking out a certain type of grass and eating it but spitting out the curd. It is more or less sweetish. We are involved in the struggle for survival so that we live to fight on another day. The warders and the Big Fives see us doing this without comment. I'm sure they report this to the prison psychologist and other prison officials.

22. The Fall of the Big Fives

While working in the quarry in the last week of June some comrades were called back to the office. In the evening we heard that a government Commission of Inquiry had arrived. It has asked the comrades who had earlier been called about certain incidents alleged to have happened at the Landbouspan like the assaulting of political prisoners, being buried alive and urinated in the mouth. They also wanted to know how these incidents which had happened at the Landbouspan had reached Ghana and London. The comrades described some of the incidents and mentioned the names of the warders and the Big Fives who were involved, thus confirming what had been reported in the Ghana and London papers. They also reported the repercussions that befell those who reported the assaults to Chief Warder Theron, Captain Kriel and the then commanding officer, Lieutenant-Colonel Steyn.

Next to be called before the Comission of Inquiry were Jan Kleynhans, his brother Piet and some of the warders of the Landbouspan. They denied all the accusations. Next to be called was Chief Warder Theron — the king of the island. He also denied any of the incidents ever having happened in Robben Island. The last to be called were Teeman and Bloed. These two corroborated everything our comrades had said and even added more horrors they had committed with Jan and Piet Kleynhans.

When the Commission of Inquiry had finished with these last two, it left as secretly as it had come after confirming what had appeared in the papers as true. We later learnt that this government Commission of Inquiry had been appointed after a report had appeared in Ghana newspapers about what was happening in Robben Island Prison. It was alleged in the Ghana newspapers that a former Robben Island prisoner know as Lindiso Galela had made a statement to that effect. The same report was then taken up by British newspapers. From there it found its way to South African papers.

Head Warder Oom Dellie was shocked. He just couldn't understand how the news of what happened in Robben Island could have reached Ghana and London. He wanted to know whether any of us had ever sneaked out of the island to Ghana or London and back.

And he changed. He became very friendly towards us. He was glad that his name had not appeared in any of the papers. Henceforth he would allow no warder to carry a stick or to assault a prisoner in his workspan.

Theron's dreams were shattered. He and Jan Kleynhans had learned of Teeman's and Bloed's shattering evidence against them. The afternoon after the Commission of Inquiry had left, he walked slowly towards where we were sitting on our haunches and eating our lousy supper. Behind him walked Perdekop also looking demoralised. Theron came and stood before us, eyes glaring as though he was seeing us for the first time and wondering who we were. Perdekop stood forlornly a few paces on his left, his hands behind his back. Theron's large jaws hung loosely and he had forgotten to put in his false teeth. He has possibly forgotten them in his office. His cheeks were sunken and his mouth looked too small for a man with such a large chin. We looked at him stealthily as we ate. The rumour has spread fast throughout the whole prison as to what had happened. His big red belt was no longer shining. I guessed that Perdekop in his demoralisation had forgotten to polish it. This time his hand was not patting at his trousers. Instead, the hands were shaking tremulously. And then he yawned: "tra-la-la", I think I heard him say to himself. Then he yawned again: "a-a-a-a-h", his toothless mouth opened for some seconds.

Muisbek and Meintjies appeared from the direction of the kitchen where they had been eating ndalav. They came running towards him to report whisperingly as usual possibly about our intention of killing warders, lynching children and escaping with White women either to Mozambique or Tanganyika. He drove them away without even listening to their yarn as though he was driving pests, cursing and waving his arms at them. They ran away in disgrace with Perdekop chasing them.

Two warders went towards him, marching in step. They stood at attention near him, saluted and mumbled something. They then gave him a number of tickets of prisoners to be starved. He took the tickets absent mindedly or rather instinctively and asked them what they were for. The warders repeated what they had earlier mumbled. "Get away," he shouted at them in Afrikaans, angrily throwing the tickets at them. We roared in laughter as the warders saluted and went away sulking. Perdekop picked up the tickets and threw them at us.

Whether Dum-dum had seen all that had happened or had heard about what had taken place in the morning, I do not know. But there he was, coming out of the kitchen wiping the fat around his mouth, with his big unequal buttocks and hammer-like head, running towards Theron, to give him what lisping incomprehensible report, I do not know. Theron lifted up his baton and hit him on the head and Dumdum in shock jumped back, only to be kicked from behind on the bigger buttock by Perdekop. We just could not control ourselves. We roared again in gusts of laughter as Dum-dum ran way with Perdekop at his heels.

Turning around Theron walked slowly towards the Zinktronk where Teeman and Bloed were hibernating ever since the devastating testimony they had given to the Commission. Perdekop followed dejectedly behind him. There was a score Theron wanted to settle there. And settle it he must and quickly too. Time was running out for him.

"How man sides gotta horse baas?" asked Perdekop as they both walked morosely towards the gate leading to the Zinktronk. Theron suddenly stopped and glared at him.

"Bloody perdekop" (horse's head) shrieked Theron, waving his baton at him. Perdekop retreated two yards back and stood meekly as though shocked, like a dog which had offended its master. "You have forgotten that you are a 'bandiete' — an incorrigible criminal," said Theron, "tomorrow you must go back to the quarry to crush those rocks into powder again. C'mon, go and squat with the other convicts."

Sulkingly Perdekop came to join us. He kept on shaking his big head while former Big Six and the '28' and Desperadoes booed him.

"Hurrah! Hurrah! Hurrah!" cried some of the '28' members. "Perdekop has fallen — fallen!" "Welcome to the quarry!" "Your 14lb hammer is waiting for you." Perdekop look dazed while some of the warders also laughed at him. Theron continued his slow walk, alone now, towards the Zinktronk.

At 6pm we were counted and went into our cells. It had been a good day. We were all excited and wondering how the drama was going to end. It was the same old story again of 'the rise and fall' with the same ending.

They have got them. They are dragging them along. They are the two convicts who tortured many comrades and manoeuvred to have them assaulted by the Boer warders. The same convicts who raped a number of our comrades at the Old Prison. They are already screaming. I've never heard such heart-rending screams before. They scream for mercy, they scream for peace on earth and they scream to the United Nations and God to assist them. Their eyes are already bloodshot. They already look like dead.

We peeped through the windows and watched them. It is the President and the Chief Justice of the Big Fives, Teeman and Bloed. They are being dragged by Jan Kleynhans, his brother Piet and the other Landbouspan warders, with Theron following a few paces behind them. They are actually being dragged like two goats going to be slaughtered, their feet trying to get some grip or object through which they could resist the dragging. They are being brought to Section C3 which is now being occupied by the '28' and the Desperadoes. And we guessed what was going to happen to them the whole night. When I looked at cell number three I saw the '28' and some of the former members of the Big Six jumping about making the famous Churchill Victory Signs. Some few were ululating. I saw the red cloth which had long disappeared waving again. Dladla, the former Chief Justice of the Big Six moved up and down the cell waving it. He gesticulated to us that they were going to be killed.

That night we never slept. I sat on my blankets shivering, listening to the cries that came from cell number three. It was like a nightmare or seeing a horror film. I've never heard such horrible screams coming from the mouth of a human being before. Teeman and Bloed were repeatedly assaulted and raped by their enemies. And I was worried. The Black people were systematically being turned into creatures worse than animals. And the Boers had a hand in all this.

There was another heart-rending howl. I knew the voice well. How many times had I listened to it at the Landbouspan, with that twickering little smile of triumph and those small eyes which looked like a witchhunter's? It was Teeman. Then he was silent again. There came another long protracted piercing wail. I knew the voice as well and could picture the face full of black blotches, feet running up and down, tripping comrades as they strained themselves to heave the wheelbarrows overfilled with sand at the Landbouspan. The same man who had dug the grave to bury Johnson Mlambo. It was Bloed. Then he too became silent. Then their voices came out fearfully as though it was two beasts being slaughtered. My whole body shook as I trembled when I thought about what was happening to them. Other comrades woke up and sat up listening to the terrifying animal sounds that came from cell number three. I was now tired of sitting up and my feet were frozen already. I lay down to sleep. In my mind I was trying to picture what type of upbringing Teeman and Bloed had had. For at one time they were sweet innocent babies in their mothers' arms.

I was awoken by more fearful screams in our cell. I also heard other screams in other cells. It was as though I was in a haunted house. I sat up and looked around in the semi-darkness. They had got them. They had all been covered with blankets and they were being beaten. The victims were the three convicts who were Theron's informers in our cell. The assailants were my own comrades. They could no longer hold their anger at the suffering and humiliation they had undergone from these criminal convicts. The assailants were so many that others moved around in circles looking for an opportunity to hit. Some pulled others away so that they should also get the chance of throwing a punch or a kick.

I saw one criminal convict being dragged towards the toilets while others kept kicking him. Another peasant took a broomstick and unleashed it on the head of one of the criminal convicts. The broomstick, because of the impact, broke into two pieces. Others struggled with the peasant who held a piece of the broomstick trying to dispossess him for fear that he may kill his victim. Later on the comrades disappeared back into their blankets as though nothing had happened. The three criminal convicts howled and asked for mercy and they begged that they be allowed to sleep for the remaining hours. They promised that the following day they would all leave the cell and go back to the Zinktronk. Nobody replied to their pleas. I lay down to sleep again. My mind was tired. Soon I was fast asleep.

In the morning, after we had been counted out, we joined the slow moving queue to the kitchen. We took our soft porridge and coffee and went to squat at the eating yard waiting eagerly for news from other cells. Then we heard the news about Teeman and Bloed. They had been raped throughout the night and when the bell rang, they were stabbed numerous times and left for dead. They were still remaining in the cell, alive. In all the other cells of political prisoners, Theron's informers had been beaten up. Comrades had taken the precautionary measures of first covering them with blankets before beating them. And they had applied the same tactics which the Special Branch and some warders had used: assaulting the whole body and sparing the head and face. After we had been counted out of the cells, all the informers had taken their mats and blankets to the Zinktronk.

Later on we saw Teeman and Bloed coming out of Section C. They walked slowly as though not knowing where to go. They were both half-bent, their hands holding their bellies. Then we heard from the '28' that their stomachs had been ripped open. They moved slowly until they reached hospital and there they expected to be attended to. Then we saw them returning back. Chief Warder Nel had chased them away. There was no doubt about it, they were on the verge of death.

They tottered slowly towards Section B and there lay on the stairs, their hands still covering their stomachs. We went to stand in lines in our workspans. When we went out of the gate we saw Jan Kleynhans coming up the road with bandages covering his whole head and one of his hands in a sling. He was clad in plain clothes. And we wondered what had happened at the barracks. Chief Warder Theron was nowhere to be seen.

Later on at work we got the report about what had happened at the barracks where the unmarried warders stayed. When the news appeared in South African newspapers, both English and Afrikaans, of what happened in Robben Island to political prisoners, the Landbouspan in particular, the warders were in trouble. When they visited Cape Town in the evening they found some groups of liberal Europeans waiting for them. The warders were teased, cursed and spat at. They were accused of having brought shame on South Africa. Back in the barracks, they argued among themselves. Jan and two of his brothers and friends justified their actions. Another group led by a tall young Head Warder called Lambrecht (Lampies) opposed them. Insults were hurled at one another and a fight ensued. The Jan Kleynhans group was defeated and terribly beaten up.

When we returned to prison after work, we learned that Teeman and Bloed were taken by boat to the mainland on the verge of death — unconscious. We never heard of them again. I'm sure they got the parole for which they had so yearned and hankered. We also heard of the fate of Theron. He was being transferred to Pollsmoor Prison in the mainland where he was going to stay for two years without promotion. The other warders who worked with Jan Kleynhans including his brother Piet were also transferred. Only Jan remained. He was banned from working with any prisoners. The prison administration remained without a Chief Warder. Theron's duties were done by a Head Warder called van Heerden (nicknamed Radebe by political prisoners) an old crony of Theron. He seemed not to have understood what had happened and continued for some time with Theron's policies assisted by Head Warder Zeelie and Corporal van den Berg. At the Quarryspan where he was sent, Perdekop staged a *coup d'état* and displaced Dum-dum as Oom Dellie's agterreier.

With the sudden exit of Teeman and Bloed, the Big Fives became leaderless and disintegrated. Ralph, Fynyk, Muisbek and Meintjies were like toothless bulldogs.

Our one time leader in the 14lb hammer group, Magwa, also returned from the mainland hospital. They had put some zinc on his head. He's quiet and looks at us stealthily. His creative mind seems to be ruminating about the meaning of life. I'm sure he'll find the answer. There's a dent on his head where the 14lb hammer landed. He's now toothless. The last three remaining teeth, which were loose in any case, were pulled out at the Somerset Hospital. He has become the joke of the island — the eighth wonder of the world. A man flattened with a 14lb hammer on the head and not dying.

23. Farewell to the Wrecks of Apartheid

On the last day of June, 150 comrades were drafted to the mainland. Two new farm prisons had been built at Worcester and Paarl for political prisoners. All the comrades who were drafted were those serving under three years. It was about this time that I received a letter from my mother. She told me that she was back home and felt better. She was still continuing with her treatment. My mother had got a heart attack immediately after my conviction which was immediately followed by diabetes. She, my father and aunt Bellina were all looking forward to seeing me again. As I was allowed one letter in six months I decided that the next time we are given letters, I would write to her and tell her that I was also okay and very happy and that they should not worry about me. That was all I could say as the letters were being censored. If I were to tell her the true conditions here, even if the letter was allowed to pass through, it would merely cause my relatives unnecessary suffering.

In November all the criminal convicts were recruited to go and fight in Mozambique against Frelimo. All those who were prepared to register were promised to be given parole — the parole they had been yearning for. During the same month of November, another big draft left the island. Among these were my friends, Katane and old man Tolepi. Katane was ill and we hoped that he would be attended to in the mainland prison hospital; perhaps the prison medical orderlies and the doctor were better there. This time the comrades who were drafted were those who had been sentenced to five years and less. I understand that as soon as the draft reached Cape Town harbour, comrades were to be split into two groups. One group of 30 prisoners would go to Victor Verster Security Prison in Paarl and another group would go to a new prison for political prisoners in Groenpunt in the Orange Free State province. There are still many prisoners who have been sentenced to three years and under who have not yet been called. The transfer of these comrades has been necessitated by the shortage of cells. Many cells are full. Drafts keep on arriving at the island and there are many convictions taking place in the mainland. The wheels of apartheid justice are grinding on relentlessly causing many broken homes among the already burdened and long suffering Blacks.

Throughout all the cells farewell concerts were held for the comrades who were to be drafted. We knew that some of us were seeing each other for the last time; suffering had brought us together and suffering had cemented our friendships; and now we were to part.

"I do not know whether we will ever meet again," said Katane bidding me farewell, "but what will forever linger in my thoughts is the struggle we waged here in upholding the principles of the Pan Africanist Congress and the universal brotherhood of man. As Sobukwe said when he was convicted in 1960, "we are the tools of history and when we are gone history will find other tools." Man's struggle against exploitation, oppression and discrimination will never end as long as these evils exist. I gave my everything to this struggle, but since early this year, my health has been failing. I've got a pain at the back, along the spine and it is becoming worse by the day. All my efforts to get medical attention have failed. You have seen me being driven away by the hospital orderlies and ignored by prison officials and you are a witness to all what they did to me on numerous occasions. I'm left with about 17 months before finishing my sentence. I don't want to believe that the hospital orderlies at the prison where I'm going are any better than these here. But as Pope said "hope springs eternal in the human breast, man never is, but always to be blest"; it is my fervent hope that my health will improve for there are many battles still to be fought." And from then he recited to me his favourite poem which he knew I also liked and at times in the past had recited together at Leeuwkop Maximum Prison. It was Tennyson's 'Ulysses'. I listened to him as he recited it line by line but could not hold myself and joined him in the last half of the poem:

> 'There lies the port; the vessel puffs her sail:
> There gloom the dark broad seas. My mariners,
> Souls that have toil'd, and wrought, and thought with me —
> That ever with a frolic welcome took
> The thunder and the sunshine, and opposed
> Free hearts, free foreheads — you and I are old;
> Old age hath yet his honour and his toil;
> Death closes all: but something ere the end,
> Some work of noble note, may yet be done,
> Not unbecoming men that strove with Gods.
> The lights begin to twinkle from the rocks:
> The long day wanes: the slow moon climbs: the deep
> Moans round with many voices. Come, my friends,
> 'Tis not too late to seek a newer world,
> Push off, and sitting well in order smite
> The sounding furrows; for my purpose holds
> To sail beyond the sunset, and the baths

Of all the western stars, until I die.
It may be that the gulfs will wash us down:
It may be we shall touch the Happy Isles,
And see the great Achilles, whom we knew.
Tho' much is taken, much abides; and tho'
We are not now that strength which in old days
moved earth and heaven; that which we are, we are;
One equal temper of heroic hearts,
made weak by time and fate, but strong in will
To strive, to seek, to find, and not to yield.'

The following morning I shook hands with Katane and Tolepi for the last time. Some of the old men from Engcobo village were also in this draft, coughing endlessly. They were drafted to the mainland security prisons. I wondered as I saw them leave, whether we would ever meet again.

* * *

There was an arrogant warder who worked at the kitchen supervising the cooks and the dishing out of food. He was a boxer and often solved any disagreements with prisoners with his fists. Since the assault on Thomas Motloung by Jan and his friends in February for asking for more, we political prisoners always took our food, however little, without complaint. The only people who still dared protest were the criminal convicts and the Poqo criminals. Whenever a prisoner complained about food this warder would challenge him to a fight and when the prisoner declined, he would then dismiss him. Two criminal convicts, on separate occasions, accepted the challenge and were floored. The had had to be satisfied with the food they were given.

One afternoon Billy Maloale, a PAC member who had mobilised most of the Poqo-criminal convicts at Leeuwkop Maximum Prison, approached the warder with his dish and asked for some more. The warder challenged him to a fight and he accepted. For some weeks past they had been eyeing one another stealthily and sizing each other up. The warder had been told by some convicts that Billy was a judoist and boxer and that since there were no longer any gangs in the Zinktronk, he had hospitalised three criminal convicts after fights with them on three occasions. In reply to that information the warder had told his informant that he wanted a fight with Billy and that he would be so fast with his punches that Billy wouldn't know what floored him. He told them that if he (the warder) were beaten, he wouldn't lay any charge against Billy. The informants relayed the warder's challenge to Billy.

While Billy was placing his dish on the ground, the warder removed his tie and folded his sleeves. In no time they were exchanging fast blows. Billy ducked, bobbed, weaved and parried the warder's punches which came with quick rapidity at his face. And before the warder knew what was happening, Billy had him in a vice-grip, which he kept tightening every few seconds. Dum-dum, horrified at seeing a bleeding warder at the mercy of a convict, ran towards the office and came back with a prison official, a Lieutenant van Niekerk. When Billy saw the officer come almost running, he untightened his grip and the dazed and bleeding warder crumbled onto the sandy ground.

"He challenged me to a fight," said Billy to the lieutenant when he was near.

"I challenged him to a fair fight," said the warder to the confused lieutenant, wiping away blood from his mouth, "don't take him to the kulukuds lieutenant, he beat me fair and square, I respect him."

"Stand up," said the lieutenant in anger, "how dare you speak to me sitting down? Have you forgotten that I'm an officer? I want you to write a statement about the whole incident." The warder wobbled up and stood at attention.

"You," said the lieutenant pointing at Billy, "take your food and get away from here."

Billy went to take his food.

"Get on with your work," said the lieutenant. The warder saluted and went on to supervise once again the distribution of the food. Later on he sent one cook to go and give a plate of ndalav to Billy. A few days afterwards he disappeared and we guessed that he had been transferred.

During the same month there was another rumour circulating that all criminal convicts were going to be drafted to Bellville Maximum Prison in the mainland. For unknown reasons their trip to go and fight in Mozambique was scrapped. The convicts began sharpening their knives again. Both the Big Fives and the '28' and Desperadoes resurrected. And so too did the Fast Elevens who were the wyfies of the Big Fives and also organised themselves into a gang. These gangs now had presidents and chief justices and advocates; but their names were kept a secret, lest they should suffer by the fate of Georgie, Teeman and Bloed.

The criminal convicts are opposed to leaving the island because they live far better lives here than they would in any of the mainland prisons. Here in the island they are a privileged class. They get all that they need. They run the kitchen and smuggle most of the food to sell amongst themselves. They run the stores where we're issued with clothes and shoes. As a result they are the best dressed among prisoners. Good prison clothes are sold by the two convicts working at the stores, while we are dressed in tatters. You can easily see political prisoners by their ragged clothing. They run the hospital. Nel's two assistants are criminal convicts. Vitamin tablets, glucose, cough syrup and penicillin injections are sold among the criminal convicts. And for one to be admitted to the prison hospital, a fee has to be paid. When criminal convicts go to hospital, they call it going on holiday while many of our sick and dying comrades are driven away. They used to run the cells by spying, eavesdropping and reporting on any meetings in the cells. They run the workspans. In all the workspans, they assist warders in seeing to it that politicians work hard. In fact, some of these 'agter-reiers' were so influential that they even used to instruct warders what to do. They run the office. Besides Perdekop, there is another criminal convict S'dumo who worked in the office. S'dumo was a former teacher who got himself involved in the Metal Box robbery in Vereeniging in the '50s and sentenced to 15 years. He still held himself with dignity and did not indulge in all the spying and ill-treatment of prisoners. He cleaned the office, ran errands, did sundry office duties like filing and calling names of any prisoners wanted at the office.

Many criminal convicts work in the dorpie where they act as house servants, do washing, cleaning and cooking. Only criminal convicts are allowed to work in the Lighthouse, in the GI Stores, in the Mess Hall, in cleaning the barracks, as carpenters, plumbers and as mechanics. They also moved up and down with the *Blouberg,* a cargo boat plying between Cape Town harbour and Robben Island. All these jobs went with their privileges. Like the rats of Hamelin, they were everywhere. So they had reason to refuse to leave the island.

There was tension once again. The criminal convicts hoped that once the gang warfare began again, the draft would be suspended. It began. The red cloth fluttered once again. Blood flowed freely at the tauza yard and while eating. Then they were all collected into two cells in Section C. All the Big Fives, the Big Six, the '28', the Desperadoes, and the Fast Elevens (wyfies) and others who were independents were put into the two cells. The warders all carried pick handles — it was official this time. And then Colonel Steytler issued the order for a carry-on. The carry-on continued for almost three hours. The howling, screaming, crying and shrieking that came from those two cells filled the whole prison and beyond. It was frightening.

As many of them were injured during the carry-on, they were taken to hospital and attended to. The day of their leaving the island was postponed. The prison authorities waited for their wounds to heal and another date was set for their final departure. When the date got nearer, the gang warfare began again, this time on a far larger scale nearing anarchy and there were many who sustained stab wounds. The draft was suspended again while the injured were treated.

This time another rumour circulated among the criminal convicts that another date had been set for their departure and that this date, in January 1965, was the last date; whether there were dead or injured, they would all be drafted to Bellville. The stabbings stopped. Then we were surprised by the sudden friendly attitude they adopted towards us. They even requested us not to call them criminal convicts but economic saboteurs. We rejected that. Some of them, in fact many of them, were murderers, and others rapists. One peasant suggested that they be called 'abento zabo' (that is, those who have been convicted for their own things). The criminal convicts heard this and became excited. They like to be be called 'abento zabo'. Even Dum-dum was happy. They had really been hurt by our calling them 'criminals'. They now wished to join the PAC and the ANC rather than leave the island and the privileges. At work, during breakfast, lunch and supper, they lifted up their arms shouting 'Izwe lethu', the slogan of the PAC or 'Amandla' the new slogan of the ANC. They openly told the warders that they were now members of Poqo and the Communist Party and were going to attack the small dorpie, kill all the children and kidnap the women. We were not impressed, neither were the warders and prison officials.

There was Ralph, with his big buttocks, coming to me one day. "I'm now uVukayibambe" (ANC Youth League), he said.

"The ANC no longer has a Youth League," I told him.

"Who killed it?" he snarled, as though he had been a founder member of that once militant organisation.

"All its members formed the PAC," I told him, "it was not killed. It just fizzled out."

"Aha," he exclaimed, "now I see. The child merely changed the name that its mother gave it like some of these youth do by calling themselves Lefty, Teezar or Teeman. So it is still the same thing except that the mother fights with bombs and the child with pangas. I'll join the panga group. I'm now PAC. When do we kill Whites?" I almost burst out with laughter but quickly suppressed it. The swine had probably forgotten about how he had bombed me one day.

Musibek ran to another warder and told him: "I'm a dangerous communist baas, arrest me and sentence me otherwise I'm going to kill all the children at the dorpie." The warder eyed him wryly and did not comment. And there was Georgie wiggling his buttocks before one warder and shouting "Death to the Boers!" The warder chuckled to himself and shook his head.

When they realised that they were being ignored and the date of their departure was getting nearer, the gang warfare began again. While they were at each other's throats, a draft of short-term criminal convicts arrived. It was obvious that they had come to replace them.

Whether injured or not they were all called and drafted to the mainland. They left as they had come, with bandages over their heads and limbs. The wyfies, unscathed, were also there. We later got a report from some of the warders who had escorted them to Bellville Maximum Prison, that even in the boat from Robben Island to Cape Town harbour, the fighting flared up again. Perdekop, long sentenced to death by the Big Six and the '28' fought for his dear life. They fought ferociously with chains and leg-irons on their hands and legs. Knives were produced from their 'suitcases' and some stabbed. Others fought with their teeth — biting at their enemies. Meintjies and Muisbek were stabbed inside the boat. Meintjies died on arrival at Bellville Maximum Prison.

During the fighting in the boat, Perdekop rebelled and joined the '28'. He turned against his former pals and participated in their beatings. Georgie and other wyfies were not touched as they were regarded as non-combatants. Instead, they got new boyfriends from among the '28'.

Robben Island was rid once and for all of those wretches — dregs of humanity who had been crushed by the system and had been brought by our political opponents to come and demoralise us, turn us into homosexuals and make us opt for the Bantustans. They were the toughies from District Six in Cape Town, the 'clevers' from Soweto, Alexandra township and Sophiatown, the ruffians from Claremont and the other locations around Durban and the hoodlums of the locations around Port Elizabeth. All of them were hand-picked by the enemy from the most notorious maximum prisons of South Africa to come and demoralise and humiliate us with the assistance of uncouth, uncivilised, raw Boer warders so that we would never again dare to challenge the system of apartheid colonialism.

But the hoodlums were still our problem — they were a national problem — in fact, they were a national tragedy. Many comrades, myself included, had had patience and forbearance in politicising many of them since the first politicians arrived in Robben Island. The result: only a few especially among the independents opted for either the PAC or the ANC. The majority belonged to gangs, had their own constitutions, aims and objects. They had been hardened by years of imprisonment and many of them had become psychos and urgently in need of psycho-therapy.

After this we held a number of discussions, symposiums and debates on how to rehabilitate such a large number of hardened criminals in our society (the highest figure in the world per population) after getting our freedom and independence. We would need the assistance of some of the world's best psychiatrists and special rehabilitation camps would have to be created to try and cure our fellow brothers who have been victims of a vicious system.

And with them went my cousin, Abel Jacob Dlamini. Their presence had always made me think a lot about him and on many occasions I had dreamed about him. I was never to be totally free of him. He would not be a thing of the past which would no longer gnaw at my thoughts. And with him too went Nomsa Maliwa. After all, what she had done to me was criminal. She too had to follow the criminal convicts back to the mainland. I had to rub her completely out of my thoughts. The wretched woman — she was a member of the Big Fives *(sic)* outside prison.

Part Two

Moral Victory

24. Cultural Renaissance

Colonel Steytler was transferred from Robben Island. Ever since Major Kruger had accompanied the draft to Groenpunt Prison in the Orange Free State province, he had never returned and we guessed that he too had been transferred. The new Commanding Officer was a Major Kellerman. His assistant became van Niekerk, now promoted to captain. Lieutenant Bosch took over the duties of Theron. All Theron's cronies were either sent to the Quarryspan or transferred to other prisons. The prison psychologist was made a major.

My bosom friend David Ramagole who could no longer sleep except sitting upright, has at last been admitted to the prison hospital. It was discovered that he suffered from pleurisy. It was a great relief to me personally. But I'm also ill. There's a terrible pain in my back. I have seen the doctor three times and he discovered nothing wrong with me. And now my friend David is helping me with some of his TB and vitamin tablets. He doesn't swallow all the tablets he's given but reserves some for me which I collect in the morning at the prison hospital. We both know that this is wrong medically but there is no alternative.

*   *   *

After the human dregs had gone there was a blossoming of cultural activities throughout all the cells in the island. The atmosphere became conducive to the emergence of music groups. There were four vocal groups: The Islanders, The Robbenairs, The Summit Tones and the Flames. There was also a 'Choir of a Hundred Voices' conducted by an ex-teacher, Origen M. Ngxwana, which specialised in classical music especially Handel's 'Messiah'. The peasant and migrant labourers had also formed their own choirs in their cells. They held weekly competitions against each other. The workers from Port Elizabeth (mostly ANC) had also formed choirs.

The request for football facilities which had been made to Colonel Steytler way back in February was at last granted. Four teams were formed and matches took place on Sundays. Permission to study by correspondence was at long last granted to a large number of comrades, but applicants could only choose from four colleges. Previous to this only a handful of comrades had had permission to study and two of them wrote their examinations in December 1963 and passed their Junior Certificates. These two were former students who had been arrested in classrooms in Pretoria. Cells No. 1 and 2 in Section C were set aside for those who were studying. In the Zinktronk one cell was converted into a library and books were brought in by the prison psychologist. Anyone was allowed to borrow a book for two weeks. Most of the books had been heavily censored. There were a few political books, but these were English biographies. There were many classical novels (including those by Dickens). We were promised long trousers, sock and shoes. When the winter started in April, we were provided with five new blankets each. There would be no sleeping-bags made of blankets this time. The food remained bad and very little despite the fact that a few political prisoners were now cooks.

In the month of April 1965, 16 comrades of the PAC and two of the ANC initiated a hunger strike. It failed to get the support of either the PAC or ANC leadership. After three days they abandoned it. The two ANC comrades had abandoned it on the first day. But since the names of the hunger strikers had been taken, they were punished by being made to pull a big road roller about six feet high. It was very heavy and the 16 comrades were made to pull it around the yard, between Sections A, B, C and D for three days. The hunger strike failed because the 18 comrades, who were all youths and former students, had been impatient and had not held consultations with the PAC leadership which would then have consulted the ANC leadership. But at least these 18 comrades initiated heated discussions on the urgent need for a hunger strike.

* * *

Sunday. Lunch time. All the cells have been opened. Time for lunch. The tablets I'm getting from David are helping me a lot and my health is improving greatly. I went for my boiled maize at the kitchen and from there I went to Section D, cell 2. There was going to be a competition there of choral music. In Section A, cell 2, there was a concert. Two groups, the Islanders and the Flames were to perform. The Robbenairs were performing at the Zinktronk. In Section C, cell 1, the 'Choir of a Hundred Voices' was going to sing classical music. I was invited to Section D after having heard a lot about the peasant choirs. There has been much talk about this competition the whole week among the semi-literate and illiterate prisoners. A friend of mine, Roto, staying in Section D, promised me fireworks and much entertainment. Moreso, because one choir was of PAC members and the other of ANC.

When I arrived in the cell I found that it was already full of people from cells 1, 3 and 4 of the same Section. There were also a few faces from the other Sections. We sat down cramped next to one another and had our fill of the maize. When the warder came, he only closed the main grille leading to the cells and left all the cell doors opened. There was already tension in the cell as both groups were already there. Members of the audience were already passing some remarks like: "We shall see which is the bull today", "We shall see dreams shattered". My friend told me the names of the two choirs competing. The first was the Leopards Choir consisting of ANC members — they were the workers from the Port Elizabeth area. The other group was known as 'The Morning Star' and consisted of PAC members — peasants and the 'amagoduka' (migrant workers) from the Transkei and some few migrant workers from Paarl.

After we had finished eating, there was a clapping of hands and the MC stood up to announce that two bulls were going to meet and that we were all eager to see which was the real bull. He then gave a short history of the two choirs and their victories over other choirs in the island. They both had a proud record and they both had many fans. He then said for good judgement each choir would give one song and then retire. That procedure would continue until the time for supper at 4.00pm. Both choirs were allowed, as usual, to sing a short chorus before each song, but it should not be too long, in order to get into the real mood. He then called upon the Leopards Choir to come to the stage to give their performance. There was a loud clapping of hands as the members of the choir rose up and went to the stage. Actually there was no stage at all, it was merely the southern width corner of the cell which had been cleared of blankets and mats.

As soon as the members of the Leopards Choir were on their way to the stage, they began singing a chorus and harmoniously gesticulating with their hands. When they reached the stage, they continued singing and stood in a semi-circle, the male soprano and alto in front, followed by the tenor and the baritone at the back. There was no conductor. I asked my friends about him. "Wait, you shall see," he said, so I waited. Meanwhile the members of the choir were singing and moving their bodies from left to right and back again rhythmically. Their feet were stationary and their hands behind their backs. And then two of their singers, one from the left and the other from the right moved to the front and simultaneously a short brown-complexioned man stood up next to where we were sitting and moved to join them. When they met, he signalled with his hands and the singing stopped. I noticed that he was a little bow-legged. There was a

loud applause from the audience. The other two singers returned back to their positions.
Then the conductor moved from left to right sounding the chord and giving them the song. Suddenly he swung his hands up. The song began. It was about human progress and technology. Then he gave his back to the choir and faced the audience. His hands continued giving the beat. Down he went. He was now kneeling. The audience was held in suspence. And then he went backwards and lay flat on his back, his face turned upwards, his hands still waving. There was clapping of hands and a long roar of applause and laughter. I also clapped my hands. I was fascinated. This was really interesting. The same two singers emerged from the back and moved rhythmically singing. They came to the conductor and lifted him up. One held his lower limbs and the other his head. The conductor's hands were still keeping the beat. The audience made another thunderous applause. They dropped the conductor down before the choir and, singing, returned back to their former positions. The conductor brought the song to a stop. The applause and the clapping of hands was prolonged. It had been a spectacular performance. When the choir went back to sit down, the MC jumped up to announce the next choir on the stage, 'The Morning Star'. There was another clapping of hands as the members of the choir stood up to take the stage. They were mostly the peasants and the amagodula. Their conductor was Albert Mgweba from Paarl, tall and lanky. They began with a chorus about young boys who were looking after cattle and had got lost. The front row which consisted of the soprano and the alto were kneeling in front with their left arms over their foreheads, as though they were looking for cattle which were grazing far away. Mgweba, with his hands behind his back, walked up and down for some time before the choir as though he was a 'mnumzane' who had lost all his cattle and did not know what to do. Right at the back, with their jackets held high over their heads, their bodies moving rhythmically, were the baritone singers, their voices booming and almost drowning all the other parts. Then suddenly Mgweba jerked his hands up. The front row stood up. The hands holding the jackets went down and the song slowly came to a stop. There was a loud applause. This was it, fireworks, real entertainment. The peasants and the amagoguka were prepared. They were not even stage shy. They already looked like winners. There was excitement from the audience: "Give them the fireworks Morning Stars", one of their admirers shouted.
"If you don't win against the Leopards, you won't sleep in our cell today," said yet another.
Meanwhile Mgweba's face looked solemn. He sounded a tune. There was harmonious chord. It was followed by another clapping of

hands. Mgweba's hands went up and the song began, with the soprano leading the other voices. There was complete silence from the audience. The cell was packed to capacity. When I looked behind I could see that others were packed near the door vying with one another for a better sight of the singers. The two front windows were also full of peering faces.

I looked at Mgweba again. I looked at his face. It was now beaming. And there was a perpetual smile of jollity. I looked at his hands high up in the air — waving and waving, from left to right as though it was a President waving to his people after an election victory. I looked at the whole choir. All their hands were also waving victoriously. I looked at the baritone singers at the back and saw them with their jackets lifted up like amagoduka returning home in a train from the mines when waving to their wives and children waiting for them at a country siding. The audience roared. Some were standing up to get a better sight. Others at the back urged those in front to sit down. The song continued. It was about the coming of the spring season: when the trees begin to bloom, when flowers blossom, when the bees move merrily from flower to flower, sucking nectar; when calves jump about and the foals gallop in the green grass; when the seedlings sprout and give hope to the harvest that is to be. A time when all nature is coming to life after the cold and biting weather of winter.

I looked at the front row. They were now moving anti-clockwise. The whole choir was now following. They were moving right round Mgweba. All their hands up in the air. Mgweba was standing the circle. He was no longer smiling now. His face was solemn. He was still conducting and his hands gesticulating in all directions, his head loomed high above all the others around him. I was dumfounded. I did not know that the peasants and amagoduka could give such an entertainment.

When I looked again they were now standing still. The audience went wild with excitement. There was a standing ovation. Others ululating. "The Morning Star has won," said others, "it is the bull of the island."

The song came to a stop and Mgweba bowed before the audience triumphantly. Many people ran to the stage. The singers were congratulated and Mgweba was carried shoulder high. I also went to the stage to shake his hand. There was noise throughout the cell and the MC felt powerless. He tried to restore order but nobody listened to him any longer. He called for order again. At last the noise lessened but there was still some rumbling here and there. Finally there was utter silence.

"The concert is not over yet," announced the MC "and nor is the competition. This has only been the beginning. I promise you now that we are going to have more fireworks."

He then called on the Leopards Choir back to the stage. The Leopards went to the stage — sang a chorus and began another song. Their conductor tried his antics again; now doing a frog jump and now imitating a monkey, now lying on his back and conducting with his right leg. All this was to no avail. It only brought laughter and some half-hearted clapping of hands from the audience. And that seemed to break his back, for when the song ended his face showed utter defeat.

Before the MC went to the stage to announce the Morning Star as the next group, its singers were already moving towards the stage singing a chorus: "never mind what you say, we are number one", a mixture of English and Xhosa. When they reached the stage, they stood in a semi-circle, with Mgweba in front of them. There was a loud applause and clapping of hands when they finished the chorus. The next song had a religious message. It was about Saint John in the island of Patmos where he had a revelation and saw an angel who had messages for him. The choristers sang the song so solemnly, with such dignity, power and melody that we were all enthralled. There was hardly a single discordant voice. And Mgweba conducted it with such beauty and expert hands that one would have thought he had read staff notation.

The singers were standing still, their feet together, their hands behind their backs, their faces all looking at Mgwela; only their chests moved simultaneously up and down when breathing in and out. It was as though the choristers had a vivid picture of Saint John on his knees after the sight of the angel. Since the song began there had been complete silence from the audience and hardly a single clap of the hands. When the song ended — there was complete pandemonium.

The MC rushed to the stage to call for order. Nobody heeded him. People were busy congratulating the Morning Star singers as though they had already won. Meanwhile we were attracted by another noise — this time coming from the Leopards Choir and its supporters. They were angry with their conductor. When they went to the stage there was no longer any confidence of victory. The MC announced that they had staged a *coup d'état*. They had appointed another one from one of their choristers. The audience roared in laughter. The first conductor sat on his blankets sulking. The competition was over. The Morning Star had won. The songs which followed from both groups were merely a confirmation of the one-sided affair. Before our Section was allowed to go and have supper, peasants and amagoduka rushed to the stage to go and celebrate the Morning Star's victory. They danced 'umxhetso' and 'umteyo' — popular peasant dances in the rural areas and Boer farms. My friend also took me to the stage and we joined the peasants in the dances. It was a very long time since I had had such entertainment. I was so taken up with the performances, that I even forgot that I was in prison. The day had been well spent. It showed the latent talent that lay among the Blacks. And there was no political rivalry in the singing as PACs and ANCs supported either of the two choirs.

* * *

The hall has at last been finished and there is a rumour circulating that a projector and some films have arrived. There has been a lot of speculation on the type of films to be shown. The majority view is that they are going to be films on the Bantustans and its leaders. A few optimists believe that there may also be shown Cowboy films. But I have no doubt about it, we are only going to be shown Bantustan films. They wil be aimed at our minds to supplement Captain Fourie's wonderful work. I even suspect that he and the prison psychologist are going to choose the type of films to be shown. They are going to be drummed repeatedly into our heads until we think, speak and dream only about Bantustans. Since mid-1964, they have been busy feeding us with the monthly government propaganda organs like *Bantu* printed in English which is really for the Bantustans. Versons of it appear simultaneously in Zulu, Xhosa, Sotho, Tswana, Pedi, Shangaan and Venda. Before the opening of the library at the Zinktronk, they were the only type of literature which we had, with the exception of the Holy Bible.

Many peasants from the Transkei talk of horrifying experiences there. They speak of unemployment, of starvation, of landlessness, of harsh chiefs aligning themselves with the system against their own subjects. They speak of migrant labour being the only way of getting employment. They speak of soil erosion affecting many parts. They talk of many broken families and missing fathers who disappeared in the cities. Kisana, one of the baritone singers of the Morning Star, told me of how Chief Matanzima crushed his opposition; of how his own kraal was set on fire and when he escaped with his wife and children from the burning huts, Matanzima's tribesmen had caught him and driven him, together with his cattle, pigs and goats to the Great Place of the chief; of how he was handcuffed, legs tied and thereafter flogged; of how his cattle had daily been slaughtered at the Great Place to feed the hungry, loyal tribesmen. He spoke of how later he was handed over to the Special Branch of the South African Police. Now he did not know of the whereabouts of his wife and children.

25. *The Forbidden Fruit*

In the early months of 1966, Robben Island was rocked by a scandal. It was very embarrassing to the prison officials. The Immorality Act, one of the pillars of the Nationalist Party's policies, had been violated. The people who dared eat of the forbidden fruit were a Black convict who worked in the dorpie as a houseboy for a certain warder called van Niekerk (whom we nicknamed "Mhlonyane", after Tolepi's herb) and the warder's wife, a young beautiful women who worked at the nursery school in the dorpie. The Boer warders were stupefied. They could not understand why such a beautiful White woman could commit adultery with a Black kaffir while there were so many handsome Boer warders around.

When the news leaked and reached the ears of political prisoners, it spread like wild fire causing amusement to intellectuals and peasants alike. The Black convict had been locked up in the kulukuds and a charge had been laid against him of breaking the Immorality Act. About two days passed before he appeared in court. The presiding magistrate was Kellerman and the prosecutor was Captain van Niekerk. There was only one State Witness. It was a Head Warder nicknamed Lampies but real name Lambrecht (the same man who had assaulted Jan Kleynhans). It was he who had 'seen' the two in the actual act. The woman had been given two alternatives — either to turn State witness against the convict and the charge against her dropped (in which case the convict would be charged with rape) or stand as co-accused with the convict.

We speculated endlessly on what was going to happen. We were interested in the proceedings and were getting the "news" from a warder who supervised us and was at loggerheads with "Mhlonyane". The warder told us that the case could not be taken to the mainland as it would cause an uproar throughout the country. The English language newspapers would use it in order to topple the Nationalist Party government. The whole thing was to be kept a secret and the proceedings would be held "in camera".

The day after the proceedings, he told us of the verdict. The convict had been found not guilty and discharged because of insufficient evidence. The woman had refused to testify. In fact, she refused to attend the proceedings and defied the court. After the verdict "Mhlonyane" had told the CO that he would shoot the Black convict on sight, if he ever saw him at the dorpie again. For another house servant, he picked a young handsome "Coloured" convict with curly hair, to the amusement of warders and prisoners alike.

A few days after this, the Black convict was released from the kulukuds and told to go and work in the Quarryspan. None of the married warders wanted to see him in the dorpie. When he arrived at the Quarry, he was given a 14lb hammer by Oom Dellie. Thus he came to join our group. Being from Krugersdorp some of the comrades from that area knew him before their arrest. I was eagerly waiting to hear what had really happened. One comrade began the conversation by expressing sympathy for having been falsely accused by the Boers and locked up in the kulukuds. "Imagine a Black man being accused of having slept with a missus," I added, "in prison of all places."

He laughed and said, "No, it was not a false accusation. I've been having an affair with the 'madame' for the last three months and we have been deeply in love. When I think of her I feel like flying back to that house. I'm sure she's also crying wherever she is."

"How were you caught then?" asked another comrade.

"That woman," he said, "had a premonition that we were going to be caught by her husband one day. So she decided that the best thing was to have an affair with Lampies who had been running after her for some time, so that her husband should concentrate on the affair between her and Lampies while we continued unsuspected. It was a feint so to say and the ploy succeeded for some time."

"And then?" I asked.

"On this particular day Lampies had come to see her," he said. "He found the kitchen door open. We usually left it open when engaged in sexual intercourse and only closed the bedroom door. Finding no one in the kitchen, he went past the dining room where the door was also open and then came to the bedroom and opened the door. He saw me on top of the woman with her legs around my waist, while she moaned in ecstacy. He closed the door as quickly as he had opened it. But I had seen him. Our eyes had met when he had opened the door. About five to 10 minutes after, the CO and the captain arrived with Lampies. They found me scrubbing the floor in the kitchen. I was roughly bundled and thrown behind the van. They found the woman resting on the bed reading a novel. I do not know what they said to her. In court Lampies was the only State witness. He described exactly how he had seen us and even said the women had her feet tapping my spine and crying sweetly ('sy het lekker gehuil'). The prosecutor asked him why he had gone to that house and he lied and said as a plumber he had gone to check for any leakages from the taps in the house. He was asked whether there were any taps in the bedroom and he answered that there were none; he had gone into the bedroom to ask the woman whether any of the taps were leaking. He was asked why he didn't knock before entering. He said he forgot to knock because he was in a hurry. The prosecutor was asking these questions because he and the CO knew that Lampies had an affair with the woman. The magistrate then said the evidence from Lampies needed corroboration. He had failed to satisfy the court as to what he had wanted in the bedroom and why he had not knocked. I was then discharged and told never to set my feet in the dorpie again."

"Where was Mhlonyane?" asked one comrade.

"He was there in court. From the beginning of the proceedings up to the end, he could not keep his eyes off me. I thought he was going to faint especially when Lampies was describing how his wife was crying sweetly. I saw him close his eyes as though in prayer, with head bowed down, wringing his hands."

During tauza that afternoon Mhlonyane stood away from the other warders and watched us stripping naked. He kept on looking amongst us and I guess that he was looking for Biza, our convict friend. Then he saw him and his eyes followed his movements. His eyes were popped out and he kept fiddling with his fingers as though he was suffering from nerves. Then Biza, who was unaware of the watchful eyes of Mhlonyane began removing his clothes preparing to do the tauza. Mhlonyane looked at his naked body and then he screamed, "m-e-e-h!" just like a goat. We all burst out laughing and to my surprise the warders also laughed. I had thought that I was the only one who had looked stealthily at Mhlonyane, but I was proved mistaken, both warders and prisoners had been eyeing him steathily wanting to see his reactions when he saw his wife's lover after his first day from the kulukuds.

Mhlonyane went to Section A, stood near the wall with his arms over his head. Once again we roared in laughter. That afternoon, the warder who searched me, did not even ask me to do the tauza, he was also laughing and just waved me to pass. Mhlonyane was just being silly. Imagine a man going to peep at the penis of his wife's lover to check its size!!!

The following day and the subsequent days which followed we did not feel the weight of the 14lb hammers as we listened to our friend's exploits. He was about 26 years of age, dark complexioned, of medium height and well built. He was left with only a few months to finish his sentence. Every day he had a new story to tell. He even told us of three other convicts who were having illicit affairs with "madames" at the dorpie.

I enjoyed listening to the story of ward X's wife, not because it was better than the other stories, but because warder X ill-treated us and called us kaffirs ever since we arrived at the island. Warder X always chose handsome prisoners to go and work as his houseboys. He especially preferred Coloured convicts. His wife was not beautiful, she was a bit plump. In November last his houseboy completed his sentence and was released. So Warder X picked on another convict. The new convict worked only for a week and Mrs X fired him. She told her husband that he was lazy. Warder X picked another convict and he too worked for only a week and was fired for the same reason. Warder X once again picked on another prisoner. After the first day's work, the new convict reported to his friends that the woman was very harsh and he did not believe that he too was going to last for more than a week. "You'll last," said another convict, "I know what that woman wants. She wants to be fucked. As soon as you arrive in the morning tomorrow, greet her nicely and pat her buttocks and you'll see. Do it as though it's accidental." "I'll try," said the newly employed house servant.

The following day when he reported back to his fellow convicts he was excited.

"I did as you told me," he said.

"And what happened?" asked the others.

"She smiled and said 'you clever boy', and led me to the bedroom. When the husband came for lunch she told him that she thought I was okay. I was obedient and hard working."

Back in prison whenever I saw Warder X, I chuckled to myself because I knew something which he did not know and the day he discovers he'll be as hysterical as Mhlonyane.

26. The Hunger Strike

In the second week of April 1966, there was a hunger strike at the island. It began on Friday at the Quarryspan during lunchtime. After the failure of the last hunger strike by PAC comrades in April 1965, we analysed our mistakes and prepared for another one. There had been mass mobilisation since then, preparing all the comrades in all the cells for the need for a hunger strike in order to bring about far-reaching reforms in the whole prison machinery. It was necessary mostly because about half of the political prisoners were doing five years and less and when the long-term prisoners remained, they would have to carry all the burden. We had to help our comrades before being released. And besides, there is no remission or parole for political prisoners in South Africa. If one is sentenced to 15 years or 40 years, one would have to serve it complete with hardly a day less. There were a number of comrades who were serving from 10 to ordinary life imprisonment. There were also three other comrades who were serving natural life imprisonment. The aim of the hunger strike was to improve first, the food situation, then the clothing and shoes, followed by the working conditions, the punishment at work for having failed to satisfy a certain quota, the treatment by warders, tauza and many other grievances which we had often raised with the prison authorities since 1963 to no avail.

When it began, the prison authorities felt so powerful that they thought it was going to peter out after the first day. Moreso, because it began on a Friday, they thought that when Saturday came we would hurry to the kitchen on empty stomachs to collect our food. They were mistaken. Lieutenant Bosch who was in charge of the food administration remarked when he heard that we had not taken our food at the quarry, "I know the Bantus, that's how they behave when their stomachs are full. As soon as they become hungry, they'll outrun each other to collect their porridge." He said this on the Friday afternoon to a group of warders after we had not taken our supper. Many comrades heard him and the remark was spread throughout the cells. We were infuriated. Bosch had to be shown of what stuff we were made. Even those who were sceptical of the success of a hunger strike joined in the condemnation of the lieutenant.

We were about 900 by now at the Quarryspan alone. Since the early months of 1965, the food for our lunch was brought in two wheeled trolleys in half-drums at about 12 o-clock mid-day. The cooks would then start dishing out the maize in readiness for 1 o'clock when we knocked off for lunch. As soon as the bell rang for lunch we would leave our tools to go and queue double-line to get our dishes. But on this particular Friday, when we saw the size of the boiled maize, those of us who were in front refused to take it. And the message was passed along to those behind that they should not take it as it was too little.

Others by-passed the lines to peep at the dishes and, confirming what they had been told, also went past without taking their food. We sat down throughout the lunch period prepared to refuse the food despite Oom Dellie's entreaties. After lunch, we went back to work on hungry stomachs, pretending as though our stomachs were full. After work we returned back to prison, went for tauza and from there went past the kitchen to sit on our haunches or flat on our buttocks waiting to go to our cells and be counted in. The hunger strike was on.

That evening we were still too angry about Lieutenant Bosch's remarks. Even the few who might have warned against the perilous journey we were about to undertake joined in the condemnation. Meanwhile those of us who were behind the hunger strike met in groups to draw up the strategy for the dark days ahead. This group was composed of both ANC and PAC cadres (all youths). There was to be no compromise with the enemy. The hunger strike had to drag on indefinitely until prisoners started to collapse. We would continue going to work every day and do whatever we could manage. The hunger strike would not be championed, guided or directed by either the PAC or the ANC. It had to assume spontaneity. Patients and other ill comrades were to be encouraged to continue taking their food. The same applied to the old-aged and the crippled (there were five of the latter). When the enemy was prepared to negotiate, there would be one representative from the PAC, one from the ANC and one independent to represent smaller organisations like the Unity Movement and the YCC. No organisation or group of individuals would be allowed to conduct negotiations on our behalf. All the above conditions were propagated throughout the cells by our secret group as spontaneous decisions not coming from either the PAC or the ANC. By Saturday they had been accepted throughout the cells. "The whole thing was spontaneous", people said, "and had to remain so." "If the hunger strike fizzled out, it had to do so spontaneously." The leaders of the PAC and the ANC were relieved. Talks had previously been held between them for a hunger strike and they had dragged on without any agreement being reached.

On Saturday, the warders opened the cells hopefully thinking that we would take our food. We left the cells and went to the kitchen, but when the cooks gave us the food, we just looked at them and passed back to our cells again. That was the procedure for the rest of the meals that day. The same thing happened on Sunday. By this time, we were, indeed, very hungry and voices of dissent began to be heard. Another incident occurred which we had not foreseen and which almost jeopardised the whole campaign. The patients, the aged and the disabled refused to follow the spontaneous directive that they should continue taking food. Taking food, they felt (after heated discussions among themselves) while other comrades were suffering and sacrificing on their behalf, was like selling out; and that they were not prepared to do. On Sunday they also joined the hunger strike, but continued taking their medicines. We were flabbergasted. Voices calling for an end to the strike were now vociferous, mostly among a few intellectuals. "All our patients are going to die", they said, "and the Boers will not compromise. "Actually we are playing into their hands", some said, "they would like us all to die through starvation." "Where did you ever hear of a hunger strike being successful in South Africa?" "What will the people outside say when they hear that we have starved ourselves to death? They will consider us morons."

Dissent became so loud that it appeared the whole thing would fizzle out by Monday. A meeting was hurriedly called that same Sunday in Section C, cell 2 where I was now staying in a study cell. PAC and ANC representatives met to find ways and means of bringing the hunger strike to an end. We told our two PAC representatives before the meeting that the hunger strike should not be called off and that their stand should be that since the hunger strike was spontaneous the PAC would not be a party to its being called off. The hunger strike had to continue spontaneously up to the end. Our two representatives agreed to this and that was the stand they maintained in their meeting with the two ANC representatives. The meeting wrangled on and on and when the bell rang at 8 o'clock, no agreement had been reached.

Most of the youths in Robben Island at the time were PAC. The ANC had only a few youths who were from the Eastern Cape and Natal and fewer from the Transvaal. It had a large number of the middle-aged and the aged, mostly from the Eastern Cape. Because most of the time PAC youths ran to be in front so as to dissuade others from taking the food the ANC members now suspected that, though we all maintained that the hunger strike was spontaneous, the PAC was leading it.

On Monday morning, we went to the kitchen and went past it and the enemy realised that we meant business this time. They retaliated by hitting hard at our weakest link — the ill, the aged and disabled. They were removed from the hospital holus bolus. "No food — no medicine", they were simply told by Nel. He asked them whether they had understood him clearly. Getting no response, he repeated again aloud and slowly: "No food — no medicine; if you take your food, you get your medicine and remain in bed comfortably; if you don't take your food you don't get your medicine and you go to work at the Quarryspan." The comrades all decided not to take the food and they did not get their medicine. After they had been searched for any tablets or other medicines they may have concealed, they were taken to the Quarryspan. The all left the hospital. Nobody wanted to be a sell-out.

We were standing at our Quarryspan waiting to be counted out to work when we saw the dreadful sight. There they walked slowly, others crawling on all fours. Old man Tshawe (the one who had wanted to commit suicide) was walking in front, held held high. It was the patients, with Chief Warder Nel driving them from behind and repeating out loud for us to hear too, "No food — no medicine." There were TB, asthma, bronchitis, heart, hypertension, diabetic, ulcers and the injured with bandages. I was flabbergasted as I looked at the ghastly spectable. I saw the eyes of many comrades popped out in shock, as though they were going to bust. There were murmurings in whispers at first and then someone burst out aloud, "Let the damn hunger strike be stopped — can't you see what is already happening? Where are the leaders of ANC and PAC?"

It was as though Nel had heard him and he repeated aloud again slowly in a high pitched voice, "No food — no medicine. If you take your food, you'll get your medicine and go and sleep comfortably."

The most pitiable among the patients were two who suffered from asthma. They were crawling on all fours and kept resting, gasping for air. In his hands Nel had their asthma sprays.

Oom Dellie went to Nel and they spoke in low tones. I could see that he was agitated and kept gesticulating with his hands and pointing at the patients, especially the two asthma cases. Lieutenant Bosch also went to join them. I guessed that Oom Dellie did not want the patients. Later on we saw the patients being divided into two groups. The first group was composed of patients who were not so serious, among them old man Tshawe, and Oom Dellie brought them to join us at the back. The other group consisted of those who were very serious. This group was given soft porridge from the kitchen and forced to eat. Actually no force was used to make them eat, they were merely commanded forcefully to do so by Nel and Bosch. And they ate with great relief and relish. I could see it in their eyes. The two asthma patients were given their sprays and with trembling hands, they hurriedly grabbed them and pressed them into their mouths.

The hunger strike

They had not expected the enemy to react like this when they had earlier refused to follow the spontaneous directive. And now they had just had a taste of the galling experiences as a result of their decision. And what was worse, most of them could not do without either tablets or injections. But at least they had played their part and showed the enemy and us their determination. The spirit was willing, as the saying goes, but the flesh was weak. They were now to be taken back to hospital for "medicine, comfort and rest" as Nel had promised, on the cold and hard cement floor. I watched them going back, most of them mere skeletons.

"We are in a mess," said someone next to me, "and God knows how we're going to get out of it alive."

"Who is the smart revolutionary who rallied those patients and the aged to join the hunger strike?" said a tall man in front of me. He was one of those who had been arrested in a bus strike in Port Elizabeth.

"I was not rallied by anybody," said old man Tshawe, "I've joined this hunger strike on my own and I'm prepared to go as far as you."

"But you won't last three days," said the tall man in front.

"I began on Friday," replied old man Tshawe, "and this is Monday. Count as to whether I've not finished the three days you're talking about. I won't be outlived by young boys in this strike. You young people will start falling first and leave me still walking on my legs."

"Young and old, by next week we'll all be dead," said the tall man, "and of all things to die such a slow, miserable and painful death."

On the way to work we walked slowly at a snail's pace. The patients who followed us walked slower at their own pace some distance from us. Oom Dellie urged the comrades in front to walk faster but to no avail. He removed the first eight in front and they were escorted back to prison to the kulukuds. The next eight were also asked to walk faster and they too refused. We were walking at intervals of half-a-foot between our feet. The eight comrades were also escorted back to the kulukuds. All 16 of them were members of the PAC who were peasants and former migrant workers. Meanwhile many comrades were complaining of the snail's pace at which we were walking. It was strenuous and was sapping the little energy we still had. So the next four comrades were urged to increase the pace to normal walking without hurrying. And that was the pace which was kept throughout the hunger strike.

As we began working that Monday morning with the 14lb hammers going up with great effort, we looked like the legion of the doomed. The patients, still walking slowly, arrived at the quarry at about 10 o'clock. Oom Dellie gave them the work of carrying small stones to go and throw them in the sea. The disabled were also there too balancing on their crutches and collecting the small stones. Meanwhile talks between the PAC and ANC leaders on ways to end the hunger strike continued. And then came the brightest news since the beginning of the hunger strike. Robert Mangaliso Sobukwe, our President, in his two-roomed cell, was also on hunger strike. Mandela, Sisulu and the other comrades staying in the kulukuds had also joined the hunger strike. They had gone to dig lime (at the old Landbou site where we used to work under Jan Kleynhans) without taking their breakfast. And then the bombshell: the warders had also gone on a hunger strike — their food, they felt, was also too little. And they refused to be used by the prison authorities to work us to death. Thus whispered our warder friend while we were crushing stones with the 14lb hammers.

Meanwhile the next item on our unfolding programme had to follow. The news of what happened in the other spans reached us through the cooks who brought our lunch. Five prisoners had collapsed at the docks. Three at the Bouspan, four at the Bamboospan and two at the Houtspan. The Quarryspan had to be next. Twenty comrades collapsed minutes after each other. The van was kept busy that day carrying all these comrades from their workspans to the prison hospital. With a few exceptions, most of those who had collapsed had feigned it. And the enemy was prepared for this. They never reached the hospital. As soon as the van reached prison, they were off-loaded onto waiting wheelbarrows and like bags of maize, emptied into the kulukuds and forced to eat.

The pressure to call off the hunger strike was mounting. So we were forced to unfold the last tactic of our programme — informing the people outside of our plight. But how to do it? That was the big question. There were no African or 'Coloured' warders on the island. All the warders were Boers. And they were all out for the system. There was no money to bribe one even if we wanted to. But there were many semi-literate and friendly warders like the one who supervised us. If we only could probe him skilfully, probably we could use him. One comrade was assigned that task and to our surprise, he succeeded. The warder was told to keep the whole thing a secret even from his friends.

At lunch time we went to queue for our food. The dishes were filled up to the brim and looked appetising. When we were told to take it we just went past silently. Our young comrades, as usual, were in front. Oom Dellie's entreaties were to no avail. We usually saw to it of course that those who stood in front were people who understood what the whole strike was about. We always scrambled to occupy the front positions. The warders also refused to take their food which was usually brought to them by van from the mess.

One old man from Port Elizabeth aged about 72 years, was one of the patients who had been dismissed from hospital that morning. He had been undergoing TB treatment. He looked very tired and weak. Many of us tried to persuade him to take his food and he refused, saying in reply that he was an old ANC fighter and could not take the food while we were not. He said he was going to hold out to the bitterest end. Yes, the old fighters must be examples to the younger ones — they must show the younger ones dedication and self-sacrifice. That is how it should be — and that is how it has always been in the past from time immemorial — it's the young who must learn from the old. It can never be the other way round. Come what may, he wouldn't take his food until the hunger strike was over. In 1952, he said, it had been like this when he took part in the ANC Defiance of Unjust Laws Campaign. Many people had tried to persuade him then, not to support the campaign but he had taken part in it and not died in prison.

Then he tried to sit down but his old muscles could not hold out any longer. He just tumbled down and rolled over and was unable to stand up. I rushed to his assistance together with other comrades, some of the ANC. Oom Dellie who was nearer to him also rushed. Together we helped him to sit up. Oom Dellie then went to fetch soft porridge. The old man seemed dazed and his eyes blurry and he seemed not to know what had happened. Oom Dellie came with the soft porridge and with his spoon, scooped the porridge and tried to feed him. But the old man turned his head away.

"Please 'madala'," said Oom Dellie.

"Is the hunger strike over?" asked the old man in a faint voice.

"Eat 'madala'," Oom Dellie begged him in a soothing voice, scooping the soft porridge, "eat my old man." Then he slowly pushed the spoon into the old man's mouth. and slowly, slowly, the old fighter swallowed the soft porridge. "You and I 'madala'," said Oom Dellie in a soothing voice, scooping the soft porridge again, "we are old. We are very old and weak 'madala' and should not follow what these young men are doing. We are old and ill 'madala'." The old man once again swallowed the soft porridge while his head was still tilted to one side. "Time changes man 'madala'," continued Oom Dellie as he scooped another spoonful to feed him. "Once we were robust and strong but now we are finished and our bones are also tired. Yes, they need rest — for our sun is setting. Many of our friends of youth are already resting and we too shall soon have rest. Meanwhile let us eat, for our bodies more than ever need the food." Oom Dellie's voice choked and he could not continue. Then he stood up with shaking hands and went back to his office. I saw him sitting with head bowed down, his hands holding his head. Another comrade continued to feed the old man.

After lunch Oom Dellie sent a warder to go and call for the van. When it came he told the driver to take all the patients and disabled back to prison. I saw him help some old men into the van and when he came back he was shaking his head. We knocked off as usual at 5 o'clock and began our slow journey back to prison. After tauza, we went past the kitchen again. Back in the cell the debate began again. The hunger strike had to be stopped, many of our comrades had already collapsed and the hospital orderlies were not attending them. Instead, they tried to force them to eat in the kulukuds. The doctor had been called from the mainland and after examining a few, had told the prison authorities that we were left with less than 24 hours to live. The food had already been improved after all, the dishes are being filled to the brim and sparkling with fat, so what was the point of continuing with the strike? This is madness, suicide by the leaders of liberation movements. We think that the people outside will glorify us for this mean and cowardly death which is impending? Can't we see that the prison authorities are not prepared to compromise? There was only one reply to all this. The hunger strike campaign was spontaneous and no one is being forced to take part in it. If a person felt like taking his dish, well, let him do so. But he should not rally others to do the same.

Tuesday was the fifth day of the hunger strike. The end seemed not in sight. In the morning, a few comrades fell by the wayside. They had had enough of suffering and sacrifice. Their lives were too precious to continue with this damned spontaneous thing whose end nobody knew and which was led by no one. They took their soft porridge and coffee and were given many extra dishes to fill their precious stomachs. It seemed obvious now to everybody that the road we were following led to certain death. There was now less talking. Our voices were no longer audible. One had to use some effort in order to be heard. Our eyes had become smaller and our cheek bones were sticking out. When we stood naked for tauza, we were a mere bad of bones. We looked frightful with the ribs sticking out as though to be counted. Our mouths were dry, our throats very painful when swallowing ordinary saliva. Even when we laughed, the laughter was hollow and a faint sound came out painfully from the throat.

On the way to work a few comrades collapsed and they were carried back to prison. When we arrived at the Quarry, we were so weak and exhausted that we only dragged our 14lb hammers with great effort. There was now no doubt about it, we were all going to collapse that day. Our friendly warder told us that he had delivered the letter. He wished the damned thing to come to an end. He had good news to tell us: the Commanding Officer, Major Kellerman, had been engaged in a fierce argument with Lieutenant Bosch. The latter had appealed to the CO to negotiate with us and the CO had refused, telling him that it was not his job, but that he (Bosch) should start negotiations immediately. Lieutenant Bosch then appealed to Captain van Niekerk. And that ex-WW2 soldier told him coldly that he (Bosch) had brought about the whole mess and should better begin negotiations with us immediately. In reply Lieutenant Bosch had said he had never conducted negotiations before with 'Bantus'. "This then is your opportunity to learn," the capitain had replied.

"That Bosch is in shit," said our friend, "I wish he is demoted and fired."

By 10 o'clock about 140 comrades had already collapsed. They lay strewn about throughout the whole workplace. Some near their hammers and others near their wheelbarrows. Others near the boulders of rock they had been pulling like oxen with ropes and chains; and others lay near their picks and spades. Others on the verge of collapse, just sat near their worktools unable to work any longer. The van which carried away those who had collapsed could no longer cope and besides, the kulukuds had long been filled.

Oom Dellie was agitated. He felt like crying. He had never experienced anything like this before. The warders were also sitting down — hungry — unable to do supervision. By 11 o'clock all work had stopped — there was no longer any energy left. Nobody spoke. The voices would not come out. The whole area looked like a battlefield after an engagement. The leaders of the PAC and the ANC sat staring at each other with faint eyes next to where we were sitting with our big 14lb hammers. But no voices came out. It was as though they were saying to each other, "We told you so."

Only one man continued woking as never before — Enock Mathibela — 'The-horn-of-the-guinea-fowl'. From the beginning he had never taken part in the hunger strike. With so many extra dishes remaining from each meal, he had been bolting food until his stomach could carry no more. A few paces away from us, he jerked the 14lb hammer up and brought it down crushing on the chisel with a loud bang. "In the morning, in the morning at 4," his stentorian voice boomed out aloud, "we sing about parole in the morning, listen, we pity those still coming." It seemed so bizarre because even the few who had not taken part in the hunger strike and those who had taken their food the previous day and in the morning had also stopped working. Having been insulted so much over the last two years, he cared the less. After all, hadn't the Minister of Justice told him that he should behave himself well in prison and his case would be considered afterwards?

At 11.30am a van arrived and Lieutenant Bosch stepped out. He was alone. He stood outside the van, baton in hand, his arms akimbo and surveyed the sight before him. Head Warder Oom Dellie who had been sitting in his office the whole morning, his arms holding his head, as though from falling, went to salute him. None of the warders stood up from where they were sitting. Even those at the guard posts were sitting fixed on their seats. They had not even saluted Bosch when he arrived, as they usually did to officers on tours of inspection. Enock Mathibela lifted the 14lb hammer up, sang louder, casting his eyes time and again at Lieutenant Bosch, as though to show him that he was not a party to the whole fiasco. He brought the hammer crushing down with such a loud bang that I saw Lieutenant Bosch start and look in his direction. The stentorian voice came out aloud booming, "my mother failed when giving birth, she gave birth to a rogue." And he jerked the hammer up again.

Oom Dellie went to ring the bell and we were all called towards Lieutenant Bosch who was standing near the toolshed. We moved slowly on weak legs, others couldn't move and they stayed where they were. The warders slowly followed reluctantly behind us. We stood around Bosch, waiting anxiously to hear what he had to say. His face looked haggard, his lips were cracked and his eyes sleepy. His trousers and shirt looked shabby as though he had been sleeping in them for several days.

"Men," he began with a shaky voice, "I've come here to get your grievances so that I should try to improve your food and other living conditions here." There was an uproar. There was still life in us yet. It was as though we had reserved our last energies for the confrontation. Amongst those who had collapsed I saw a few crawling towards us to come and listen.

"This is the fifth day of the hunger strike and you've been sitting on your bloody arse all the time. Why didn't you come on the very first day?" one angry intellectual with a dry mouth, cheek bones sticking out, barked at him. It was Leon Sihlale, President of the Unity Movement. He removed his spectacles to have a better look at Bosch and to give him some more.

"Get away bloody Boer!" said another peasant angrily.

"Go and eat the grievances!" said another intellectual with blurry eyes.

"Why don't you call Verwoerd, your Prime Minister?" said a young former student.

"'Hokai, hokai', noise, noise," many comrades shouted.

"Let there be order, let's not be impossible," said one comrade.

"Let one man speak at a time," I also raised my weak voice.

"We want shoes!"

"We want meat!"

"We want vegetables in our food." It was as though it was a match of shouting at Bosch.

"Hold it comrades. Let there be order. We can't all speak at the same time," said someone. Lieutenant Bosch looked appealingly at the warders for possible protection in case of assault, but the hungry warders looked away from him. They also had a bone to pick with him. Realising that he was in a hopeless situation, he appealed again for silence, putting his rank and dignity aside.

"How can we be silent when you have left us to starve to death?" said someone. It was the tall intellectual who since the beginning of the hunger strike had been urging us to call it off. It was a suicide mission, he had said.

"We want our food improved today," said another. He was one of those who took his breakfast in the morning.

"Order," shouted others, "let there be order."

"Okay," shouted Bosch, "since we can't discuss your grievances being so many, choose three people amongst yourselves to represent you in airing your grievances and requests. I will take them with me to the prison now, so that we can start to improve things immediately."

The PAC members chose two representatives and there was an uproar from the ANC. The ANC members chose two representatives and there was an uproar from the PAC.

So the PAC and the ANC chose one each. Then Leon Sihlale of the Unity Movement said he would represent the other smaller organisations. There was no objection from either the PAC or ANC, and neither was there any objection from the other organisations. It was a good compromise. Otherwise there was going to be another deadlock. They went into the van with Lieutenant Bosch back to prison to represent us.

All of us were to return back to prison. Soft porridge had been especially prepared for us. The hunger strike was over. Even those who could not move came back to life and wobbled into lines. The slow march to prison began. On the way the PAC and ANC leaders congratulated each other and shook hands. The hunger strike had been a success and the enemy had been taught a good lesson and had compromised. No one had died. It showed what the two organisations could achieve with united effort. There should be more meetings between the two organisations in the future to plan common strategies against the enemy. There was no need now to wrangle about the past (especially the 1949 Programme of Action) since both organisations had now embarked on armed struggle.

"Everyone of us is a hero," said the tall intellectual of the suicide mission, "except that lousy sell-out — 'The-horn-of-the-guinea-fowl.'"

That day there was no tauza; we went to the kitchen and collected our soft porridge. We swallowed it with pain. Our gullets had already contracted and our throats were painful. But we ate to our satisfaction.

Back in the cells the three-man delegation came to report. All our requests were going to be met, including of all things, an end to the tauza orgy. From now on we would eat our breakfast and supper inside our cells. Our lunch and supper would be cooked in fat and we would be provided with sufficient vegetables daily. We would be given warm clothing in winter, long trousers, shoes and socks. Each prisoner would be provided with two sisal mats, one other soft mat and five blankets and enough soap to do our own washing on weekends. The kitchen, the stores and the hospital would now be manned by political prisoners. After the good news came the bad news. The 16 PAC comrades who had been locked up in the kulukuds for walking slowly on Monday morning, were going to be charged for incitement. The enemy was not prepared to negotiate on that one.

When Lieutenant Bosch had left the Quarry with our three representatives, he first went via the Mandela group and told them of the developments. From there he touched other spans all over the island, including Robert Sobukwe, also informing them of what was taking place, before going back to his office.

The following day at work, our warder "friend" told us that their hunger strike was also over. Their food rations had also been increased. He further told us that the CO and Captain van Niekerk, besides Bosch, had also been blamed for the mishandling of the hunger strike by the Commissioner of Prisons. They would not get any promotions for two years and the first two would immediately be transferred to other prisons.

"The whole thing about the hunger strike was in the newspapers," he told us, "and nobody knows how those damn English language papers got it." We dared not tell him how he had helped.

A few days after this, while we were taking our breakfast, Johnson Mlambo happened to have scooped his coffee with a leaking plastic cup. When he went back to empty the coffee into a better mug, he was stopped by a certain warder named van Niekerk, who we nicknamed 'Kwarini'. Kwarini manhandled Johnson and the coffee spilled over his uniform. He then took Johnson before Lieutenant Bosch who advised him to lay a charge of assault. After a mock trial Johnson was found guilty and sentenced to six lashes. When we heard of this verdict, we guessed that our enemy was hitting back hard because of the setback during the hunger strike. Moreso, Johnson had been one of the three spokesmen after the hunger strike. He had also given evidence to the government Commission of Inquiry that led to the transfer of Chief Warder Theron. It dawned in our minds that our enemy was going to be more ruthless than ever. The 16 comrades who had been charged for incitement were each sentenced to a further six months imprisonment. Then came more bad news. The Special Branch had arrived on the island. Some comrades were called and told that they were being taken back to the mainland prisons to await trial for a "number of murders". There was Mgweba, the conductor of the Morning Star and four of his singers. There was Hans Fikile, one of the singers of the Flames. He was also a good amateur actor. There were 13 others, good comrades all. They were whisked away by members of the Special Branch. (They were sentenced to death, all of them. We later learned of how they had sung our National Anthem, "Nkosi Sikelel-i-Africa", with their palms up in the PAC salute, after the judge had passed the sentence). After this there were many further charges which affected both the PAC and the ANC members in Robben Island. Many came back with heavier sentences while others got the death sentence.

27. Farewell to Robben Island Prison

On 4 June 1966 our cell door was opened and we were counted as we stepped out of the cell to go and get our breakfast at the kitchen. We joined the long queue as it wound slowly to the kitchen. After taking our porridge and coffee we went back to our cells to eat. Since the hunger strike we were now eating our breakfast and supper in our cells. It was while we were eating that another prisoner who worked at the office, came into our cell and began to read names. Fifty names were called. My name was also there. Most of us who were called had been sentenced to six years imprisonment and had about two-and-a-half years remaining. After finishing our breakfast, we were taken to the office. Those of five years and under who had clothes were given their kits and told to check them. Those who wanted to wash theirs were given soap. We were told that we would soon be drafted to the mainland.

Back in the cells in the evening we told our comrades that we would be leaving them. There was a lot of excitement in all the cells. Some of those who were remaining told us to write to them when we had finished our sentences. Others were very sad and told us that they were going to miss us greatly. And a few cried among both those who were leaving and those who were remaining. We had been close comrades through adversity. Tried and tested and found not to be wanting; now we were to be separated.

On the morning of 5 June, we were taken back to the office again. This time we were taken to go and check our money, that is, for those of us who had any. Late in the afternoon we returned to our cells after we had been told that we were to get ready. We were to leave Robben Island the following day. On the way we met the Rivonia group and some PAC leaders returning from work. They looked tired. Their faces and clothes were covered with lime which they had been digging the whole day at the old Landbouspan site — the site of many tortures in 1963/64. Mandela and Sisulu walked in front, followed by Kathrada and Mbeki. There was also Andrew Masondo, former Mathematics lecturer at the University College of Fort Hare, a veteran of the Landbouspan. One of his arms had been semi-paralysed because of the beatings there in 1963/64. There was Makwethu and

Ganya of the PAC and there was Dr Neville Alexander of the YCC. There were about 20 prisoners in all who were confined to the kulukuds. I noticed that Sisulu's hair was fast greying but Mandela still looked robust and had a proud bearing.

"A-a-a-a-h, R-o-l-i-h-la-h-l-a," said some ANC members among us greeting their leader. We greeted them as they marched past by removing our caps and they responded and smiled at us.

"Stilte," barked Kwarini van Nierkerk, the warder who was escorting them; "you will be sent to the kulukuds," he said pointing his long fingers at us. "You know you are not supposed to talk to these people." Of course we knew we were not supposed to converse with the prisoners who were staying in the kulukuds. Kwarini screamed again bidding John Ganya, who was very defiant, to walk in a straight line. He had wanted to leave the line and greet me.

That evening in the cells we bade farewell to our comrades. Farewell songs were sung for us. There was the 'Choir of a Hundred Voices' which gave us *The Hallellujah Chorus*. There was the 'Robbenairs' which gave us *Summertime* and *In my Solitude*. The 'Choir of a Hundred Voices' closed the concert by singing *Senza mathamsanqa* (We bid you Godspeed). Afterwards the conductor of the choir, Origen Ngxwana, short with grey hair, gave a short farewell speech. "The struggle," he said, "is not like a coat which you can put on when it is cold and remove when it is hot. You must continue with the work outside from where you left off. There is no holiday in the struggle. A revolutionary never rests. And remember our people are being killed — dying day in and day out."

Abel Chiloane another veteran of the Landbouspan with many scars, the result of beatings at the hands of Jan and the Big Fives, also stood up and spoke. "Don't go and sit on your buttocks there outside. Remember that our people must be liberated. Time is running out. There is no time for rest in the struggle."

After the concert and the speeches there were many individual farewells. There was old man Tshawe with the hunchback and his ever-smiling face coming towards me. "My son," he said, holding me with both his hands, "you remember in April 1964, I won't forget that month and year, I tried to commit suicide because of the bad working conditions at the time? I'll never try to take my life again. Thank you very much for all the encouragement you gave me at the time. I can now read and write. I now write to my children and have told them to observe my handwriting — how I cross my t's and dot my i's. By the time I finish the remaining 15 years, I'll be singing in English." There were many other touching farewells. Many comrades wept. It was so touching that I also felt tears welling in my eyes.

Early the following morning on the sixth, our names were called and we stood ready to leave Robben Island. I just managed to rush quickly to the prison hospital to bid farewell to my friend David Ramagole and to get my last share of TB and vitamin tablets. He gripped my hand tightly and told me that he thought he was going to survive the pleurisy. We looked at each other for some time afterwards without a word being said. In my heart during those seconds, I was thanking him for having saved my life and I believe that he too was silently thanking me for my solidarity with him when his life was in danger.

"Moses Dlamini! Moses Dlamini!" my name was being called. I had to leave David reluctantly and rush to rejoin the draft. The draft was waiting for me.

We left Robben Island by the same passenger boat which had brought us in 1963, the *Diaz*. Before boarding the boat I watched the 'amangabangaba' (seagulls) gracefully flying above our heads and later moving in the direction of Cape Town harbour as though leading us. As the boat sailed away I peeped through one of the apertures to have a last farewell look at the island. I could not see the prison, it had been covered by the tall trees around it. But the guardposts loomed above the trees; them I could see. I saw Sobukwe near his two-roomed cell by the sea, alone, tilling his garden. Robert Mangaliso Sobukwe — defier of the undefiable — the man who had opened the eyes of the suffering Black masses and shown them that the power to liberate themselves lay in themselves — the man who had created cracks in the apartheid edifice by launching the Anti-Pass Campaign — the man who had said he would open only one page by launching the Anti-Pass Campaign and thereafter all the other pages would open of themselves until the apartheid regime collapses. The two warders guarding him stood erect in their guardposts, looking around. The *Diaz* sailed on as the engine chugged. The lonely figure of Sobukwe became smaller and smaller until I could not see him. And the island itself appeared to be just a small dot on the large ocean. I turned away with blurry eyes and wiped the tears. Enock Mathibela sat next to me and was paging through the Old Testament he had been given by the dominee. At last he found the passage he had been looking for. He put his monocle on his right eye and began to read aloud, his voice booming, "Ye, though I walk through the valley of death, yet will I fear no evil, for thou art with me." He then removed his monocle, closed the Bible and gave out a thick cough, stealthily looking around as though to see whether we had heard what he had said.

Kisana, whose huts had been burned down in the Transkei by Matanzima's tribesmen and later had been flogged before being handed over to the South African Special Branch police, sat forlornly like an orphan not knowing whether he would find his wife and children and a home when he returned. Tyobeka, now minus three of his front teeth, with many scars on his head and face, and now very lean, sat next to him, eyes looking down on the leg-irons on his ankles.

On reaching Cape Town harbour we found other warders already waiting for us. The leg-irons were removed from our feet and only the hand-cuffs remained. We went into two trucks and our eyes gazed for the last time at the tiny spot on the ocean which appeared very small from where we were, but which had made many of us men, in fact and in deed. We had represented man in his struggle against tyranny, oppression and exploitation just as other men had done since time immemorial; and we left others to continue the struggle until such time that people shall live in brotherhood in South Africa irrespective of their colour, race or religion. But, before that state of affairs, Brigadier Aucamp, in charge of prison security, would be his way to Robben Island from his headquarters in Pretoria to go and "set the record straight" so that when political prisoners left Robbin Island, they should be mental and physical wrecks.

Epilogue

Abisai Katane

Immediately after his release in April 1966, Katane was admitted to the Rustenburg Non-European Hospital. The doctors in Robben Island and Victor Verster Security Prison had failed to attend to him. He still complained of the pain in his spine when he was admitted. The Special Branch visited him at the hospital and gave him his banning orders confining him to Rustenburg for a period of two years. They found him unconscious. They left the banning orders under his pillow and tip-toed out of the ward. Katane died immediately afterwards without having seen the banning order.

Thomas Motloung

After finishing his sentence he was released in July 1969 and restricted to Basotho Qwaqwa Bantustan near Lesotho. Ever since he had been assaulted in 1964 for daring to ask for more, he had become more radical in his opposition to the regime's policies. During interrogations about the Bantustan he sometimes refused to speak; and when he did speak it was to denounce the settler Boer regime as fascist and engaged in a systematic genocide of the Blacks. He stayed for a few days in Basotho Qwaqwa and thereafter returned to his parents in Natalspruit where he had been schooling when he was arrested in 1963. The Special Branch left him for a few months. And then he was stabbed to death by unknown people in 1970. His assailants were never found.

Samuel Mokudubete (the small one)

He finished his five-year sentence on 10 September 1968. He was allowed to return to his parents in Sharpeville and put under surveillance. In 1970 he left Sharpeville to visit other friends in Soweto he had met in Robben Island. He never reached Soweto. He was stabbed to death at Park Station and his assailants disappeared among the commuters. His parents found his corpse after two months at the mortuary.

Johannes (Tolepi) Tsotetsi

Tolepi finished his three-year sentence early in April 1966 and was sent back to where he had come from — to those vast destroyers of the human spirit called Boer farms. I wonder how he is now, if he's still alive. Did he smile innocently at his oubaas when he saw him? Or did he join other farm workers unearthing potatoes in the fields with their bare hands and begin teaching them 'Ekuseni madoda' and begin shuffling backwards and forwards and stamping his feet in a frenzy? Perhaps the oubaas sjambokked him to death this time.

Enock Mathibela (The-horn-of-the-guinea-fowl)

For the entire five-year sentence that he served, he kept his part of the bargain. He never engaged in hunger-strikes at Robben Island and Victor Verster Security Prisons, never complained of food, clothing, insults or working conditions. He called warders 'baas' and never idled and always worked hard; even when there was no work, he created it. He also informed on other political prisoners especially when he was at Victor Verster. Having been convicted in 1964, he was released in November 1969 to the great relief of many political prisoners both in Robben Island and Victor Verster Prisons. To his delight, his 'horn' was removed at Paarl Hospital early in 1969. In January 1979, a night watchman was found dead at the Iscor plant near Pretoria. He had died in a sitting position, a knob-kerrie in his hand. He was later identified as Enock Mathibela, now aged 66. The loneliest man in South Africa had been doing the loneliest job. In his lifetime nobody, including the enemy, understood him and he did not understand why. He had invariably been labelled informer, Poqo, communist, opportunist and spy. And he had invariably wondered why. Thumbing through his Holy Bible, he had tried to find solace in his God of Israel, and yet, even though he walked through the valley of death fearing no evil, his God was not with him.

Nathaniel Ciliwe (One of the patients during Dr Hoffman's visits)

He finished his three-year sentence in July 1966 and was sent back to Emndeni location to join his wife and children. In 1967 he was stabbed to death by unknown people not far away from his house. No one was arrested.

Pascal Vakalisa

The old man spent most of his sentence (five years) at Pollsmoor Prison where he was undergoing treatment for TB of the spine. Chief Warder Theron was one of the officials in this prison. X-rays revealed that one of the bones of his spine had broken and thereafter had rotted. He finished his five-year sentence in August 1969 and was sent back to join his family in Zondi location.

Origen Ngxwana (the conductor of The Choir of a Hundred Voices)

He finished his eight-year imprisonment in 1971. Earlier he had been sentenced to three years imprisonment and while serving it he was taken back to await for a further charge and sentenced to an additional five years. After release he continued with his profession as a teacher at Mdantsane Township. Immediately after the 1976 Uprisings he was visited by the Special Branch and questioned about a certain former Robben Island prisoner who was from the independent African states and had visited him. Realising that he would soon be interned he left the country and arrived in Tanzania towards the end of 1976; but his health was already failing. He suffered from ulcers and diabetes. He died at the Muhimbili Hospital after a short illness and was buried at the Kinondoni Cemetery in July 1977.

Chief Warder Theron

Theron reappeared once again in Robben Island Security Prison in the '70s. He was now a captain. According to information from one former prisoner there, he died later in a car accident.

Oom Dellie (Delport)

Before we left Robben Island in 1966, Delport had already been promoted to a Chief Warder. Seeing political prisoners engaged in studies, he also decided to continue his studies for the Junior Certificate by correspondence. He got the services of one political prisoner to help him in his studies during working hours. And he passed his Junior Certificate. According to information from one political prisoner who was released in 1973, Delport resigned his job and was converted to the Watchtower Bible Society. He went about the country preaching about the coming of Armageddon and trying to convince his fellow Boers to repent. Ultimately he committed suicide. "Time changes man 'mandala'," those were his words to the 72-year-old man from Port Elizabeth during the second hunger strike. Time had also changed Oom Dellie. And in time, it would also change his fellow Boers.

Perdekop (Morolong)

Perdekop came from the Bloomfontein area but because of his complexion which was a little light, he claimed to be Coloured in prison and was classified as such by prison officials and thus qualified for a 'D' diet.

Sometimes during 1968, at Worcester 'C' Prison, a number of convicts who were working in the fields, grabbed the warders guarding them, and after overpowering them seized their rifles. They then took the truck which plied between the fields and the prison and began their escape — to freedom. Unfortunately the road they took led to the arid Karroo — a semi-desert. Somewhere on their way to nowhere, petrol ran out. They abandoned the truck and began scampering to the nearest hillock which was also barren of any vegetation. There was no food, no water and no shelter for them. They stayed there for three days with hunger sapping all their strength until they became very weak. Meanwhile a prison helicopter which had been searching for them spotted them and they began waving at it frantically to show their presence. After some hours a number of prison vehicles appeared. The cry of jubilation they uttered as they saw the trucks could only be compared to the cry of Captain Ahab's wretches when they sighted the Moby Dick. The leader of the group was Perdekop, 'Morolong', as Jerry Ntsoane was fond of calling him. They were later charged under the Sabotage Act after some members of the Big Fives had given evidence of their intentions of killing whites in the town of Worcester. All of them got heavy sentences. Poor Perdekop, he tried to make the best out of a bad situation, in a bad country with a bad leadership.

Peter 'the Goatee' Ntshetshana

He finished his 12-year sentence in the early '60s and went back to prowl in Soweto. He became more of a terror than before. He brutally murdered a distant cousin Jabu Ngubeni and his pregnant wife and continued on a murder spree until ultimately the Boer police caught up with him. In 1969 he was sentenced to death and hanged.

My family

Aunt Bellina died in 1974 after a short illness. My mother followed thereafter in January 1976 and my father in January 1977. On my conviction my mother had suffered from a heart attack and she never completely recovered from it. Ultimately it killed her. As my father died while I was in Tanzania, I have not been able to get information about the manner of his death, although I was made to believe that it was from natural causes.

Robben Island Security Prison

There are now 30-foot walls separating each of the four Sections from each other. When one is in Section A, one can no longer see any of the other Sections. PAC prisoners are now kept separate from ANC prisoners. The Black Consciousness Movement prisoners are also kept separate from PAC and ANC prisoners. They only meet at work. It's total apartheid. There are now alsation police dogs with ranks of lieutenant, sergeant, etc., that accompany the prisoners to and from work every day. Apparently the warders are not enough. Psychological warfare and government propaganda on the Bantustans have been intensified. The aim: to break the political prisoners completely so that when they finish their sentences they should be physical and mental wrecks.

Since the death of Gantsha Khuboni there have been a number of political prisoners, PAC and ANC, who died in both Robben Island and Victor Verster Security Prisons. And of course there are many others like Katane who died immediately after release from prison. The Boers long ago declared total war — not against communism as they claim — but against the Blacks.